AAT

Technician Level 4

Unit 11
Drafting Financial Statements
(Industry and Commerce)

Workbook

1167/A01

British Library Cataloguing-in-Publication Data

A catalogue record for this book is available from the British Library.

Published by Foulks Lynch Ltd
Number 4
The Griffin Centre
Staines Road
Feltham
Middlesex
TW14 0HS

ISBN   0 7483 5116 7

Printed and Bound in Great Britain by Ashford Colour Press, Gosport, Hants.

© Foulks Lynch Ltd, 2001

Acknowledgements

We are grateful to the Association of Accounting Technicians, the Association of Chartered Certified Accountants, the Chartered Institute of Management Accountants and the Institute of Chartered Accountants in England and Wales for permission to reproduce past examination questions. The answers have been prepared by Foulks Lynch Ltd. The copyright to the questions remains with the examining body.

CONTENTS

PREFACE

This is the 2001 edition of the AAT workbook for Unit 11 - Drafting Financial Statements. The workbook includes the AAT central assessment 1999.

The workbook has been produced to complement our Unit 11 textbook and it contains numerous practice questions and tasks designed to reflect and simulate the work place environment. These are arranged to match the chapters of the textbook, so that you can work through the two books together.

The workbook also contains practice central assessments to prepare you completely for the assessment procedures which form part of your course.

Fully comprehensive answers to all questions, tasks and assessments are provided, with the exception of those which are designated as being specifically for classroom work.

You will find that completion of all the elements of this workbook will prepare you admirably for the assessments which you must carry out to pass Unit 11.

Class Activities

A feature of this workbook is the section at the end comprising Activities which are specially designed for classroom use. The answers to these are not included in the workbook but are reproduced in the **College Kit** which is available to college lecturers who adopt our material.

College Kits

In addition to the Textbooks and Workbooks, Foulks Lynch offers colleges adopting our material the highly popular **'College Kits'**.

The College Kits for units with a Central Assessment contain:

- additional Devolved and Central Assessment material in looseleaf form which can be photocopied to provide practice classwork for students (much of this additional Central Assessment material is taken from the AAT's own Central Assessments); and

- the looseleaf answers to the class examples from the Workbooks.

These Kits are supplied at no extra cost and may be photocopied under the limited licence which is granted to adopting colleges.

TECHNICIAN STAGE

NVQ/SVQ LEVEL 4 IN ACCOUNTING

CENTRAL ASSESSMENT (DF) DECEMBER 1999

DRAFTING FINANCIAL STATEMENTS

(ACCOUNTING PRACTICE, INDUSTRY AND COMMERCE)

(UNIT 11)

Note that the Answer booklet reproduced here is not identical to that provided by the AAT, because most students will prefer to write their answers in their own study papers rather than attempt to write memos and letters etc in the workbook itself.

The answers have been written by Foulks Lynch Ltd.

This central assessment is in TWO sections, You are reminded that competence must be achieved in both sections. You should therefore attempt and aim to complete EVERY task in EACH section, using the answer booklet provided.

All workings should be shown in the answer booklet.

A Companies Act 1985 Consolidated Balance Sheet pro-forma (format 1), a pro-forma Cash Flow Statement (FRS 1 Revised), a pro-forma for journal entries and a pro-forma profit and loss account suitable for a sole trader are provided in your answer booklet for your use.

You are advised to spend approximately 55 minutes on section 1, and 125 minutes on section 2.

SECTION 1

You are advised to spend approximately 55 minutes on this section.
This section is in two parts.

PART A

Task 1.1

The Accounting Standards Board's Draft Statement of Principles for Financial Reporting
(issued March 1999) states that:

'The objective of financial statements is to provide information about the reporting entity's financial performance and financial position that is useful to a wide range of users for assessing the stewardship of management and for making economic decisions.'

Illustrate this objective by:

(a)   selecting one external user of financial statements from either profit-making organisations or public sector/not-for-profit organisations and showing how it uses financial statements to assess the stewardship of management; and

(b)   selecting one external user of financial statements from either profit-making organisations or public sector/not-for-profit organisations and showing how it uses financial statements to make economic decisions.

PART B

Data

Jonathan Fisher is intending to invest a substantial sum of money in a company. A colleague has suggested to him that he might want to invest in a private company called Carp Ltd which supplies pond equipment to retail outlets. You have been asked to assist him in interpreting the financial statements of the company which are set out below and on the following page.

Carp Ltd
Summary Profit and Loss Account
for the year ended 30 September 1999

	1999 £'000	1998 £'000
Turnover	3,183	2,756
Cost of sales	1,337	1,020
Gross profit	1,846	1,736
Expenses	1,178	1,047
Net profit before interest and tax	668	689
Interest	225	92
Profit before tax	443	597
Taxation	87	126
Profit after tax	356	471
Dividends	42	50
Retained profit	314	421

Carp Ltd
Summary Balance Sheets as at 30 September 1999

	1999 £'000	1999 £'000	1998 £'000	1998 £'000
Fixed assets		4,214		2,030
Current assets				
Stocks	795		689	
Debtors	531		459	
Cash	15		136	
	1,341		1,284	
Current liabilities				
Trade creditors	709		435	
Proposed dividend	42		50	
Taxation	87		126	
	838		611	

Net current assets	503	673
Long-term loan	(2,500)	(1,000)
	2,217	1,703
Share capital	700	500
Profit and loss account	1,517	1,203
	2,217	1,703

Task 1.2

Prepare notes for Jonathan Fisher covering the following points:

(a)   Explain what a 'balance sheet' is and what a 'profit and loss account' is and identify the elements that appear in each statement.

(b)   Explain the 'accounting equation' and demonstrate that the balance sheet of Carp Ltd as at 30 September 1999 conforms to it.

(c)   Calculate the following ratios for the two years;

    (i)   gearing;
    (ii)   net profit percentage;
    (iii) current ratio;
    (iv)   return on equity.

(d)   Using the ratios calculated, comment on the company's profitability, liquidity and financial position and consider how these have changed over the two years.

(e)   Using only the calculation of the ratios and the analysis of the changes over the two years, state whether the company is a better prospect for investment in 1999 than it was in 1998. Give reasons for your answer.

SECTION 2

You are advised to spend approximately 125 minutes on this section.
This section is in four parts.

PART A

Data

You have been asked to assist in the preparation of the consolidated accounts of the Shopan Group. Set out below are the balance sheets of Shopan Ltd and its subsidiary undertaking Hower Ltd, as at 30 September 1999:

Balance sheets as at 30 September 1999

	Shopan Ltd £'000	Shopan Ltd £'000	Hower Ltd £'000	Hower Ltd £'000
Fixed assets		6,273		1,633
Investment in Hower Ltd		2,100		
Current assets				
Stocks	1,901		865	
Debtors	1,555		547	
Cash	184		104	
	3,640		1,516	
Current liabilities				
Trade creditors	1,516		457	
Taxation	431		188	
	1,947		645	
Net current assets		1,693		871
Long-term loan		(2,870)		(400)
		7,196		2,104
Capital and reserves				
Called up share capital		2,000		500
Share premium		950		120
Profit and loss account		4,246		1,484
		7,196		2,104

Further information:

- the share capital of both Shopan Ltd and Hower Ltd consists of ordinary shares of £1 each;
- Shopan Ltd acquired 375,000 shares in Hower Ltd on 30 September 1999;
- the fair value of the fixed assets of Hower Ltd at 30 September 1999 was £2,033,000.

Answer tasks 2.1—2.7 in the answer booklet provided.

Task 2.1

Using the pro-forma provided in the answer booklet, prepare a consolidated balance sheet for Shopan Ltd and its subsidiary undertaking as at 30 September 1999.

Task 2.2

FRS 2 states that 'a parent undertaking should prepare consolidated financial statements for its group'. Give two of the criteria that, according to FRS 2, determine whether an undertaking is the parent undertaking of another undertaking.

PART B

Data

A colleague has asked you to take over the drafting of a cash flow statement for Diewelt Ltd for the year ended 30 September 1999. Your colleague has already drafted a reconciliation between cash flows from operating activities and operating profit for the period. The financial statements of the company, drafted for internal purposes, along with the reconciliation are set out on pages 54 and 55 along with some further information relating to the reporting year:

Diewelt Ltd
Profit and loss account for the year ended 30 September 1999

	1999 £'000
Turnover	9,804
Cost of sales	5,784
Gross profit	4,020
Profit on sale of fixed asset	57
Depreciation	985
Other expenses	819
Operating profit for the year	2,273
Interest paid	365
Profit before tax	1,908
Taxation on profit	583
Profit after tax	1,325
Ordinary dividend	440
Retained profit	885

Diewelt Ltd
Balance sheet as at 30 September 1999

	1999 £'000	£'000	1998 £'000	£'000
Fixed assets		6,490		5,620
Current assets				
Stocks	3,151		2,106	
Trade debtors	2,314		1,470	
Cash	103		383	
	5,568		3,959	
Current liabilities				
Trade creditors	964		1,034	
Dividends payable	264		192	
Taxation	583		491	
	1,811		1,717	

Net current assets	3,757	2,242
Long-term loan	(3,300)	(2,900)
	6,947	4,962
Capital and reserves		
Called up share capital	2,200	1,600
Share premium	800	300
Profit and loss account	3,947	3,062
	6,947	4,962

Further information:

- a fixed asset which has cost £136,000 and had accumulated depreciation of £85,000 was sold during the year;

- all sales and purchases were on credit. Other expenses were paid for in cash.

Reconciliation of operating profit to net cash infow from operating activities

	£'000
Operating profit	2,273
Depreciation charges	985
Profit on sale of tangible fixed assets	(57)
Increase in stock	(1,045)
Increase in debtors	(844)
Decrease in creditors	(70)
Net cash inflow from operating activities	1,242

Task 2.3

Using the pro-forma provided in the answer booklet, prepare a cash flow statement for Diewelt Ltd for the year ended 30 September 1999 in accordance with the requirements of FRS 1 (Revised).

PART C

Data

Elizabeth Ogier has asked you to assist in the preparation of the year end financial statements of her business. She operates a wholesale perfume business. The trial balance as at 30 September 1999 is set out below:

Elizabeth Ogier
Trial Balance as at 30 September 1999

	Debit £	Credit £
Purchases	113,565	
Rent, rates and insurance	8,291	
Motor expenses	5,813	
Bad debts	1,420	
Drawings	24,000	
Trade debtors	38,410	
Trade creditors		18,928
Capital as at 1 October 1998		83,707
Sales		230,461
Returns outwards		2,911
Carriage inwards	1,256	
Returns inwards	3,053	
Carriage outwards	1,571	
Salesperson's commission	2,561	
Bank charges	710	
Depreciation – office equipment	2,312	
Depreciation – fixtures and fittings	602	
Stock as at 1 October 1998	46,092	
Motor vehicles at cost	36,000	
Office equipment at cost	11,560	
Fixtures and fittings at cost	6,019	
Accumulated depreciation – motor vehicles		8,360
Accumulated depreciation – office equipment		3,825
Accumulated depreciation – fixtures and fittings		1,352
Wages, salaries and National Insurance contribution	47,564	
Lighting and heating	3,056	
Postage and stationery	1,037	
Telephone	3,571	
Cash at bank	2,131	
Cash in hand	102	
Accruals		1,562
Discounts allowed	410	
	361,106	361,106

Further information:

- the stock at the close of business on 30 September 1999 was valued at cost at £49,477. However, included in this balance were some goods which had cost £8,200 but it is estimated that they could now be sold for only £4,800;

- included in the rent, rates and insurance balance is a payment of £1,200 which relates to rent for the period from 1 October 1999 to December 1999;

- the purchases figure includes goods to the value of £2,000 which Elizabeth took from the business for personal use and for gifts to friends;

- although depreciation for office equipment and fixtures and fittings has been calculated and charged for the year, no depreciation has been calculated or charged for motor vehicles. Motor vehicles are depreciated using the reducing balance method at a rate of 30% per annum.

Task 2.4

Make any additional adjustments you feel necessary to the balances in the trial balance as a result of the matters set out in the further information above. Set out your adjustments in the form of journal entries using the pro-forma provided in the answer booklet.

Note: Narratives are not required.

Task 2.5

Using the pro-forma profit and loss account in the answer booklet, draft a profit and loss account for the year ended 30 September 1999.

Task 2.6

Draft a letter to Elizabeth justifying any adjustment you have made to:

- the stock valuation on 30 September 1999;
- the balances in the trial balance as a result of Elizabeth taking goods out of the business for her personal use or for gifts to friends.

Your explanations should make reference, where relevant, to accounting concepts, accounting standards or generally accepted accounting principles.

PART D

Data

Geoffrey Thomas, Victoria Bologna and Albertine Rosario are in partnership together and own a florist shop. The partners have decided that they would each like to set up their own business and are thinking of dissolving the partnership. They wish to know how much profit they are entitled to for the year ended 30 September 1999. They have asked you to assist in the production of an appropriation account for the partnership.

They have given you the following information:

(1)   The profit-sharing ratios of the partnership are:

Geoffrey	6/10	
Victoria		3/10
Albertine	1/10	

(2)   The profit for the year ended 30 September 1999 amounted to £115,960.

(3)   Interest on capital is to be paid at a rate of 8% on the balance at the year end on the capital accounts. No interest is paid on the current accounts.

(4)   The partners are entitled to the following salaries per annum:

Geoffrey	£25,000	
Victoria		£19,000
Albertine	£15,000	

(5)   Cash drawings against these salaries during the year amounted to:

Geoffrey	£22,500	
Victoria		£16,300
Albertine	£13,400	

(6)   The balances onthe capital accounts at the end of the year were as follows:

Geoffrey	£56,000	
Victoria		£23,000
Albertine	£8,000	

Task 2.7

Prepare an appropriation account for the partnership for the year ended 30 September 1999.

DRAFTING FINANCIAL STATEMENTS
(ACCOUNTING PRACTICE, INDUSTRY AND COMMERCE)

ANSWER BOOKLET

SECTION 1

PART A

Task 1.1

(a)

Task 1.1

(b)

PART B

Task 1.2

NOTES

(a)

(b)

(c)   (i)

       (ii)

       (iii)

       (iv)

Task 1.2

(d)

(e)

Section 1 Workings

Task 2.1

Proforma Consolidated Balance Sheet (Format 1)

Fixed assets
   Intangible assets
   Tangible assets
   Investments
                        ———

Current assets
   Stocks
   Debtors
   Investments
   Cash at bank and in hand
                        ———

Creditors: amounts falling due within one year

                        ———

Net current assets (liabilities)
                        ———

Total assets *less* current liabilities

Creditors: amounts falling due after more than one year

Provisions for liabilities and charges

                        ———

                        ———

Capital and reserves

                        ———

Minority interest

                        ———

                        ———

Workings for Task 2.1

Task 2.3

Pro-forma Cash Flow statement
(in accordance with FRS 1 (Revised))

£'000

Net cash inflow from operating activities

Returns on investments and servicing of finance

Taxation

Capital expenditure

_____

Equity dividends paid

_____

Management of liquid resources

Financing

Increase/(decrease) in cash

_____

Workings for Task 2.3

Task 2.4

Pro-forma Journal Entries

Account	Debit £	Credit £

Workings for Task 2.4

Task 2.5

Pro-forma profit and loss account
(suitable for a sole trader)

	£	£
Sales		
		————
Less Cost of sales		
	————	
		————
Gross profit		
Less Expenses		
	————	
		————
Net profit		
		————

Workings for Task 2.5

DRAFTING FINANCIAL STATEMENTS (DF)
(ACCOUNTING PRACTICE, INDUSTRY & COMMERCE)

ANSWERS

SECTION 1

Task 1.1

(a)   Stewardship of management:

Non profit making	*User*	*Example of use*
Charities	Donors	Help them to decide if donations have been used effectively.
Clubs	Members	To see if the officers have run the club efficiently.
NHS Trusts	Trustees	To decide if managers have run the trust effectively.
Public sector	*User*	*Example of use*
Local authorities	Taxpayers	To decide if value for money has been given.
Profit making	*User*	*Example of use*
Companies	Shareholders	To assess profits and calculate investment returns.

(b)   **Economic decisions**

ONE of the following

Organisation	*User*	*Example of use*
Companies	Creditors	To decide if the gearing or liquidity make lending a good choice.
Charities/Trusts	Investors	To help decide if it is worth investing in.
Local Authorities	Bank	To decide whether to grant a loan.

Task 1.2

Notes for Jonathan Fisher

(a)   A balance sheet gives a financial position at a particular point in time. It is a list of the assets and liabilities of a business.

A profit and loss account is a list of all the income and expenditure for a business over a period of time.

(b)   The accounting equation is as follows:

$$\text{Assets} - \text{liabilities} = \text{ownership interest}$$

For example with Carp Ltd at 30/9/99

Assets	=	4,214 + 1,341
	=	5,555
Liabilities	=	838 + 2,500
	=	3,338
∴ Assets – liabilities	=	5,555 – 3,338
	=	2,217
	=	Share cap + P&L = ownership

(c)   (i)   *Gearing*

		1999	*1998*
	$\dfrac{\text{Debt}}{\text{Capital employed}}$	$\dfrac{2,500}{4,717} = 53\%$	$\dfrac{1,000}{2,703} = 37\%$
	or		
	$\dfrac{\text{Debt}}{\text{Equity}}$	$\dfrac{2,500}{2,217} = 113\%$	$\dfrac{1,000}{1,703} = 59\%$
(ii)	Net profit	$\dfrac{668}{3,183} = 21\%$	$\dfrac{689}{2,756} = 25\%$
(iii)	Current ratio	$\dfrac{1,341}{838} = 1.6:1$	$\dfrac{1,284}{611} = 2.1:1$
(iv)	Return on equity	$\dfrac{356}{2,217} = 16\%$	$\dfrac{471}{1,703} = 28\%$

(d)   **Gearing ratio**: The gearing of the business has increased in the year. This means that a greater proportion of the long-term finance of the business is provided by debt than the previous year. This increases the risk that if profits reduce the company may not be able to meet interest payments.

Net profit percentage: The net profit percentage has fallen in the year. This is the result of the fall in the gross profit percentage as the percentage of expenses to sales has fallen by 1% in the year.

Current ratio: The current ratio has decreased during the year. This means that the company has not got as many current assets to meet its current liabilities as it did in 1998. Given the fall in quick assets (debtors and cash) compared to current liabilities the company may have difficulty in meeting creditor payments next year without a further injection of finance.

Return on equity: The return on equity Ms decreased during the year. This means that the company is not generating as much profit from the use of the equity finance as it did in the previous year.

Overall, profitability and liquidity' has fallen and the financial position of the business has deteriorated.

(e)   Due to the decrease in profitability and liquidity and the deterioration of the financial position of the company in 1999 the company is a worse prospect for investment than it was in 1998.

Task 2.1

W1   Holding in Hower Ltd

Shopan Ltd   = 375,000 ÷ 500,000
               = 75%
Minority interest = 125,000 ÷ 500,000
               = 25%

W2   Revaluation Reserve

	Dr £	Cr £
Revaluation reserve		400,000
Fixed assets	400,000	

Fixed assets now £(6,273 + 400)k + £1,633k = £8,306,000

W3   Goodwill

£'000	Total Equity	Shopan Ltd (75%)	Minority Interest (25%)
Share capital	500	375	125
Share premium	120	90	30
Revaluation reserve	400	300	100
P&L	1,484	1,113	371
	2,504	1,878	626
Paid		(2,100)	
Goodwill arising on consolidation		222	

Shopan Ltd

Consolidated balance sheet
As at 30 September 1999

		£'000	£'000
Fixed assets (W2)			8,306
Intangible assets (W3)			222
			8,528
Current assets			
Stocks	(1,901 + 865)	2,766	
Debtors	(1,555 + 547)	2,102	
Cash	(184 + 104)	288	
		5,156	
Creditors due within 1 year			
Trade creditors (1,516 + 457)		1,973	
Tax	(431 + 188)	619	
		2,592	
Net current assets			2,564
Creditors due after 1 year			(3,270)
			7,822
Capital and reserves			
Share capital			2,000
Share premium			950
Profit & loss			4,256
			7,196
Minority interest (W3)			626
			7,822

Task 2.2

A company is a parent undertaking of a subsidiary undertaking if *any* of the following apply (FRS 2):

- It holds a majority of voting rights in the subsidiary undertaking (SU)

- It is a member of the SU and has the right to appoint or remove directors holding a majority of voting rights at meetings of the board on all or nearly all matters

- It has the right to exert dominant influence over the SU.

- It has a participating interest in the SU and

    - it actually exercises dominant influence, or
    - it and the SU are managed on a unified basis

- a parent undertaking is also treated as the parent undertaking of the SU of its subsidiary undertakings.

FOULKS*lynch*

Task 2.3

(W1)   **FA additions**

Opening balance   =   5,620
Closing balance   =   6,490
                         _____
Difference   870

NBV of assets sold =   136,000 − 85,000
                    =   51,000

∴ Additions   =   870 + 51 + 985
                    =   £1,906

(W2)   **Profit on sales of FA**

Profit on sale   =   57
NBV on sale   =   51
                         ___
Cash received   108

(W3)   **Dividends paid**

Dividends owing last year   192
Dividends on P&L   440
Dividends owing at end of this year   (264)
                                       ____

                    368 cash paid in dividends.

Task 2.3

Diewelt Ltd
Cashflow statement for the year ended 30/9/99

	£'000	£'000
Net cash inflow from operating activities		1,242
Returns on investment and servicing of finance		
Interest paid		(365)
Taxation		(491)
Capital expenditure		
Payments for new FA (W1)	(1,906)	
Cash on sale of assets (W2)	108	
		(1,798)
Dividends paid (W3)		(368)
		(1,780)
Financing		
Loan	400	
Issue of ord share capital	1,100	
(2,200 − 1,600) + 800 − 300		
		1,500
Decrease in cash		(280)

Task 2.4

		Dr	Cr
(a)	Stock (P&L)		46,077
	Stock (BS) (49,477 – 3,400)	46,077	
(b)	Rent/Rates/Ins		1,200
	Prepayments	1,200	
(c)	Drawings	2,000	
	Purchases		2,000
(d)	Depreciation MV (P&L)	5,292	
	Dep to date MV (BS)		
	30% (36,000 – 18,360)		5,292

Task 2.5

Elizabeth Ogier
Profit and loss account for the year ended 30 September 1999

	£	£
Sales	230,461	
less Returns inwards	(3,053)	
		227,408
less Cost of sales		
Opening stock	46,092	
Purchases	111,565	
Carriage inwards	1,256	
less Returns outwards	(2,911)	
	156,002	
less Closing stock	(46,077)	109,925
Gross profit		117,483
less Expenses		
Rent, rates and insurance	7,091	
Motor expenses	5,813	
Bad debts	1,420	
Carriage outwards	1,571	
Salesperson's commission	2,561	
Bank charges	710	
Depreciation – Motor vehicles	5,292	
– Off ice equipment	2,312	
– Fixtures and fittings	602	
Wages, salaries and NIC	47,564	
Lighting & heating	3,056	
Postage and stationery	1,037	
Telephone	3,571	
Discounts allowed	410	
		83,010
Net profit		34,473

Task 2.6

AAT Student
The Exam Room
City
AA01 2BB

3 December 1999

Dear Ms Ogier

Final accounts adjustments

I am writing to explain some of the adjustments that I have made to the balances in your accounts for the year ended 30/0/99.

Stock   Stock is valued at the lower of cost and net realisable value. In the stock valuation of £49,477 an item was included at its cost price of £8,200 but they can only be sold for £4,800. Therefore I have reduced stock by £8,200 – £4,800 = £3,400. Therefore the total value of stock should be £46,077.

Purchases I have reduced purchases by £2,000. This is because £2,000 of goods were for personal use and are classed as drawings.

If you have any questions relating to these adjustments do not hesitate to contact me.

Yours sincerely

AAT Student

Task 2.7

Partnership Accounts
For the year ended 30/9/99

			£	£
Net profit				115,960
Less	Partners' salaries			
	Geoffrey	25,000		
	Victoria	19,000		
	Albertine	15,000		
				(59,000)
				56,960
Less	Interest on capital			
	Geoffrey (8% × 56)	4,480		
	Victoria (8% × 23)	1,840		
	Albertine (8% × 8)	640		
				(6,960)
				50,000

Profit share

Geoffrey	$\frac{6}{10} \times$ 50K	30,000
Victoria	$\frac{3}{10} \times$ 50K	15,000
Albertine	$\frac{1}{10} \times$ 50K	5,000
		50,000

QUESTIONS

Chapter 1

FINANCIAL STATEMENTS AND FRAMEWORK

1 Activity

(a) What is the fundamental objective of financial reporting?

(b) To whom should information in financial statements be communicated?

(c) What are the desirable characteristics of information which will satisfy the fundamental objective of financial reporting?

(d) Describe briefly the kind of information needed by **two** of the groups of people that were mentioned as users of financial information in (b).

2 Activity

Briefly explain the role of company law and the accounting profession as regulatory influences on the preparation of financial statements for companies.

3 Activity

Describe the main differences in capital structure between a sole trader, a partnership and a limited company.

Chapter 2

GAAPS AND CONCEPTS

---

1 Activity

It is frequently suggested that accounting information and accounting reports should attempt to be relevant and reliable. These terms could be explained as follows.

'Information has the quality of relevance when it influences the economic decisions of users by helping them evaluate past, present or future events or by confirming, or correcting, their past evaluations.

'Information has the quality of reliability when it is free from material error and bias and can be depended on by users to represent faithfully in terms of valid description that which it either purports to represent or could reasonably be expected to represent.'

Task

(a)   Explain what accountants mean by objectivity.

(b)   Why do shareholders need to read published accounts of companies in which they own shares?

(c)   'From the viewpoint of shareholders, objectivity will tend to lead to accounts being more reliable, but less relevant.' Do you agree?

---

2 Activity

The use of certain concepts is fundamental to the preparation of accounts.

The fundamental concepts are referred to as:

(a)   the going concern concept;
(b)   the accruals concept;
(c)   the consistency concept; and
(d)   the prudence concept.

Task

Explain these four concepts. In each case, use an example to identify the importance of the concept.

Chapter 3

SOLE TRADERS AND THE TRIAL BALANCE

1 Activity

Ledger accounts for Harold's business have been written up for July. (There are no balances brought forward as the business started on 1 July.)

Cash

20X4 Jul	Details	£	20X4 Jul	Details	£
1	Capital	4,000	2	Purchases	1,130
31	Debtors ledger control	190	8	Wages	13
			8	Sundry expenses	2
			22	Fixtures & fittings	350
			25	Wages	38
			26	Drawings	80
			31	Rent	500

Capital

		£	20X4 Jul	Details	£
			1	Cash	4,000
			1	Motor car	1,750

Motor car

20X4 Jul	Details	£			£
1	Capital	1,750			

Purchases

20X4 Jul	Details	£			£
2	Cash account	1,130			
18	Creditors ledger control	85			

Wages

20X4 Jul	Details	£			£
8	Cash	13			
25	Cash	38			

Sundry expenses

20X4 Jul	Details	£			£
8	Cash	2			

Sales

		£	20X4 Jul	Details	£
			9	Debtors ledger control	190
			14	Debtors ledger control	240

Debtors ledger control

20X4 Jul	Details	£	20X4 Jul	Details	£
9	Sales	190	31	Cash	190
14	Sales	240			

Rent

20X4 Jul	Details	£			£
31	Cash	500			

Creditors ledger control

		£	20X4 Jul	Details	£
			18	Purchases	85

Fixtures and fittings

20X4 Jul	Details	£			£
22	Cash	350			

Drawings

20X4 Jul	Details	£			£
26	Cash	80			

Task

Balance each of these ledger accounts at 31 July and extract a trial balance as at 31 July.

2   Activity

The transactions for Samantha Wright's first month of trading are listed below.

(1)   Deposited £10,000 in a business bank account
(2)   Paid one month's rent of £140
(3)   Bought goods for cash of £730
(4)   Bought a van for £4,050 cash
(5)   Sold goods on credit for £2,575
(6)   Bought goods on credit for £1,912
(7)   Paid wages of £370
(8)   Sold goods on credit for £2,316
(9)   Took £700 in drawings
(10)   Sold goods for £380 cash
(11)   Received £2,575 from debtors.

Task 1

Record these transactions in ledger accounts and balance each account.

Task 2

Prepare a trial balance from the ledger accounts.

3   Activity

A trial balance has been produced from the books of Smith and Co and has revealed a difference of £86,000, the credit column being greater than the debit column.

The following errors were discovered.

The proceeds of £4,000 from the disposal of a van has not been posted from the cash receipts book.

The total for sales from the sales day book of £123,000 was correctly posted to the credit side of the sales account but written in as a figure of £213,000.

Task

Produce a suspense account and show the entries to clear it in the suspense account and in journal entry format.

4   Activity

On extracting a trial balance the accountant of ETT discovered a suspense account with a debit balance of £1,075 included; he also found that the debits (including the suspense account) exceeded the credits by £957. He posted this difference to the suspense account and then investigated the situation. He discovered:

(a)   A debit balance of £75 on the postages account had been incorrectly extracted on the trial balance as £750 debit.

(b)   A payment of £500 to a creditor, X, had been correctly entered in the bank account, but no entry had been made in the creditors control account.

(c)   When a motor vehicle had been purchased during the year the bookkeeper did not know what to do with the debit entry so he made the entry Dr Suspense, Cr Bank £1,575.

(d)   A credit balance of £81 in the sundry income account had been incorrectly extracted on the trial balance as a debit balance.

(e)   A receipt of £5 from a debtor had been correctly posted to the debtors control account but had been entered in the cash account as £625.

(f)   The bookkeeper was not able to deal with the receipt of £500 from the proprietor of ETT's own bank account, and he made the entry Dr Bank and Cr Suspense.

(g)   No entry has been made for a cheque of £120 received from a debtor.

(h)   A receipt of £50 from a debtor had been entered into the debtors control account as £5 and into the cash at bank account as £5.

Task

Show how the suspense account balance is cleared by means of a ledger account.

5   Activity

When the trial balance of YTZ Ltd was extracted on 30 June 20X2 it showed the following totals:

	Dr £	Cr £
	103,457	102,113

At the time a suspense account was opened to record the difference but investigation has now followed and the following facts have emerged:

(1)   An invoice for travel expenses of £132 was entered in the travel expenses account as £123, although correctly entered in the creditor's account.

(2)   The returns outwards book was undercast on one page by £100.

(3)   An electricity bill for £154 that had not been recorded or accrued for was discovered.

(4)   Discounts received of £1,870 had not been entered in the purchase ledger control account.

(5)   The bank statement that has recently been received showed an amount of interest on the overdraft of £28 which has not been recorded in the ledgers.

(6)   A small item of machinery costing £1,450 was charged to the repairs account. Depreciation is charged on machinery at the rate of 20% per annum on cost.

(7)   Discounts allowed of £30 were not recorded in the cash received book.

(8)   A settlement by contra entry of £3,200 was only recorded in the purchase ledger control account.

(9)   Bank charges of £23 had been correctly entered in the expense account but not in the cash book.

Task 1

Clear the suspense account balance by correcting each of the errors detailed above.

Task 2

Prepare a statement of adjusted profit showing the original profit of £97,499 and the net profit after correcting the items above.

6   Activity

At the year end of TD, an imbalance in the trial balance was revealed which resulted in the creation of a suspense account with a credit balance of £1,040.

Investigations revealed the following errors:

(i)   A sale of goods on credit for £1,000 had been omitted from the sales account.

(ii)   Delivery and installation costs of £240 on a new item of plant had been recorded as a revenue expense.

(iii)   Cash discount of £150 on paying a creditor, JW, had been taken, even though the payment was made outside the time limit.

(iv)   Stock of stationery at the end of the period of £240 had been ignored.

(v)   A purchase of raw materials of £350 had been recorded in the purchases account as £850.

(vi)   The purchase returns day book included a sales credit note for £230 which had been entered correctly in the account of the debtor concerned, but included with purchase returns in the nominal ledger.

Task 1

Prepare journal entries to correct EACH of the above errors. Narratives are NOT required.

Task 2

Open a suspense account and show the corrections to be made.

Chapter 4

SOLE TRADERS – THE ACCOUNTS

1   Activity

Spanners Ltd has a car it wishes to dispose of. The car cost £12,000 and has accumulated depreciation of £5,000. The car is sold for £4,000.

Task 1

Work out whether there is a profit or a loss on disposal.

Task 2

Show all the entries in the general ledger T-accounts.

2   Activity

Light Engineering Ltd own a number of vehicles, details of which are given below.

*   Director's car, LEL 6 purchased for £17,000 on 1 June 20X3

*   Salesman's car, M843 GLN purchased for £12,500 on 1 August 20X4

*   Van, M601 VFA purchased for £19,400 on 2 February 20X5

On 5 September 20X5 the salesman's car was sold for £7,600 and was not replaced.

The company uses the straight line method of depreciation for its vehicles, making a full year's charge in the year of purchase and no charge in the year of sale. All vehicles have an estimated life of four years and a residual value of 10% of their original cost.

Task

Write up the motor vehicles cost account, motor vehicles provision for depreciation account and a disposals account covering the period 20X3 to 20X5, bringing down balances at each 31 December year end.

3   Activity

Grasmere has been trading for many years, making up his accounts to 31 December.

On 1 July 20X2 he purchased a van for £2,400. He estimates that its useful life is five years, with a £300 residual value. He provides depreciation on a straight line basis on all his fixed assets.

Grasmere sold the van on 1 April 20X4 for proceeds of £1,800.

Task

Enter the above transactions in the relevant ledger accounts and show the effect on the financial statements for each year.

4 Activity

Harry Evans set up in business on 1 January 20X0 as a violin maker. At the end of his first year of trading, 31 December 20X0, the amounts owing to him from customers totalled £6,570. After some consideration Harry decided that of these debts a total of £370 was unlikely ever to be received and should be written off as bad. Of the remaining debtors he decided to be prudent and provide against 4%.

By 31 December 20X1 Harry's debtors had increased to £8,400 and of these £1,500 were considered to be bad. Harry decided that his provision for doubtful debts could be reduced to 2% of the remaining debtors.

At 31 December 20X2 Harry's debtors totalled £6,250. There were no debts that were considered bad but a specific provision was to be made against one debt of £350 and a general provision of 2% was to be continued on the remaining debtors.

Task

Write up the provision for doubtful debts account and the bad debts expense account for the years ended 31 December 20X0, 20X1 and 20X2.

5 Activity

The following list of balances is taken from the books of Alpha for the year ended 31 December:

	£
Sales	39,468
Insurance	580
Plant repairs	110
Rent and rates	1,782
Motor van	980
Plant	2,380
Purchases	27,321
Stock at 1 Jan (opening)	3,655
Wages	3,563
Discount allowed to customers	437
Motor van expenses	1,019
Shop fittings	1,020
General expenses	522
Capital account - balance 1 Jan (opening)	2,463
Sundry debtors	3,324
Sundry creditors	4,370
Cash on hand	212
Personal drawings	2,820

Additional information:

(1)   The difference in the trial balance is the bank balance at 31 December.
(2)   Stock at 31 December amounted to £3,123.
(3)   Adjust for cost of goods taken by Alpha for personal use amounting to £220.

Task

Prepare the trading and profit and loss account for the year ended 31 December and a balance sheet as at that date.

6   Activity

The following is the trial balance extracted from the books of Delta at 31 December 20X9:

	£	£
Capital at 1 Jan 20X9		20,000
Loan account, Omega		2,000
Drawings	1,750	
Freehold premises	8,000	
Furniture and fittings	500	
Plant and machinery	5,500	
Stock at 1 Jan	8,000	
Cash at bank	650	
Provision for doubtful debts		740
Purchases	86,046	
Sales		124,450
Bad debts	256	
Bad debts recovered		45
Trade debtors	20,280	
Trade creditors		10,056
Bank charges	120	
Rent	2,000	
Returns inwards	186	
Returns outwards		135
Salaries	3,500	
Wages	8,250	
Travelling expenses	1,040	
Carriage inwards	156	
Discounts allowed	48	
Discounts received		138
General expenses	2,056	
Gas, electricity and water	2,560	
Carriage outwards	546	
Travellers' salaries and commission	5,480	
Printing and stationery	640	
	157,564	157,564

Task

Draw up the trading, profit and loss account for the year to 31 December 20X9 and the balance sheet at that date, after taking into account the following:

(a)   stock at 31 December 20X9 £7,550;

(b)   interest on the loan at 5% pa had not been paid at 31 December;

(c)   rent includes £250 for premises paid in advance to 31 March next;

(d)   depreciate plant and machinery by 10% pa;
         depreciate furniture and fittings by 5% pa;

(e)   adjust the provision for doubtful debts to 5% of trade debtors;

(f)   show wages as part of cost of sales.

Chapter 5

THE EXTENDED TRIAL BALANCE – SOLE TRADERS

1 Activity

PG Trading has the following draft trial balance.

PG Trading Trial balance as at 31 December 20X6

Account	Dr £	Cr £
Capital account		63,000
Stock (see below)		
Sales		150,000
Purchases	105,000	
Rent and rates	15,000	
Drawings		18,000
Electricity	3,000	
Motor van cost	12,000	
Motor van provision for depreciation		6,000
Bank balance	6,750	
Trade debtors	30,000	
Trade creditors		31,500
Sundry expenses	750	
Wages and salaries	37,500	
	210,000	268,500

The following information is available:

(a) The bookkeeper is not sure what to do with £22,500 of opening stock. From his studies he can vaguely remember that there is a stock figure in the trial balance, but he cannot remember which one, so he has left it out.

(b) The following year end adjustments to the trial balance are required:

(1) a bad debt of £1,500 is to be written off;
(2) depreciation of £750 is to be charged; and
(3) a mis-posting of £300 to rent and rates that should have been wages is to be corrected.

(c) PG Trading requires accruals for wages of £225 and for sundry expenses of £75. In addition, rates are prepaid by £1,200.

(d) Closing stock is £25,500.

Task

Prepare the extended trial balance for PG Trading on the pro-forma given below.

PG Trading Extended Trial Balance at 31 December 20X6

Account	Trial balance Dr £	Cr £	Adjustments Dr £	Cr £	Profit and loss Dr £	Cr £	Balance sheet Dr £	Cr £
Capital account								
Stock								
Sales								
Purchases								
Rent and rates								
Drawings								
Electricity								
Motor van cost								
Motor van provision for depreciation								
Bank balance								
Trade debtors								
Trade creditors								
Sundry expenses								
Wages and salaries								

Chapter 6

BASIC PARTNERSHIP ACCOUNTING

1	Activity

Owen and Steel are in partnership, sharing profits equally after Owen has been allowed a salary of £5,000 per year. No interest is charged on drawings or allowed on current accounts, but interest of 10% pa is allowed on the opening capital account balances for each year. Their bookkeeper has been having trouble balancing the books and has eventually produced the following list of balances as at 31 December

	£
Capital account:	
Owen	9,000
Steel	10,000
10% loan account:	
Steel	5,000
Williams	6,000
Current account balance on 1 January:	
Owen	1,000
Steel	2,000
Drawings:	
Owen	6,500
Steel	5,500
Sales	113,100
Sales returns	3,000
Closing stock	17,000
Cost of goods sold	70,000
Sales ledger control account	30,000
Purchase ledger control account	25,000
Operating expenses	26,100
Fixed assets at cost	37,000
Provision for depreciation	18,000
Bank overdraft	3,000
Suspense account	

You ascertain the following information

(a)   The sales ledger control account does not agree with the list of balances from the ledger. The following errors when corrected will remove the difference

(i)   the sales returns day book has been undercast by £100

(ii)   a contra entry with the creditors ledger for £200 has been omitted from the control accounts

(iii) an invoice for £2,000 was incorrectly entered in the sales day book as £200.

(b)   A fully depreciated fixed asset, original cost £5,000, was sold during the year. The proceeds of £3,000 were entered in the bank account only, and no other entries in connection with the disposal were made.

(c)   It is agreed that hotel bills for £500 paid by Steel from his personal bank account are proper business expenses. Owen has taken goods out of the business for his own use, costing £1,000. No entry has been made for either of these items.

(d)   No interest of any kind has yet been paid or recorded.

(e)   Any remaining balance on the suspense account cannot be traced, and is to be treated in the most suitable manner.

Task 1

Prepare a trial balance and establish the balance on the suspense account.

Task 2

Prepare journals (without narrative) to incorporate the necessary adjustments to this trial balance.

Task 3

Prepare final accounts for presentation to the partners.

Chapter 7

ACCOUNTING FOR PARTNERSHIP CHANGES

1 Activity

The following trial balance as at 30 September 20X7 has been extracted from the books of River, Stream and Pool who are trading in partnership:

	£	£
Freehold land and buildings - net book value	42,000	
Fixtures and fittings - net book value	16,000	
Stock	9,000	
Debtors	6,000	
Balance at bank	2,000	
Creditors		7,000
Capital accounts as at 1 October 20X6:		
River		30,000
Stream		20,000
Pool		15,000
Current accounts as at 1 October 20X6:		
River		1,000
Stream		700
Pool		-
Drawings:		
River	21,000	
Stream	13,000	
Pool	11,000	
Net profit for the year ended 30 September 20X7 per draft accounts		46,300 48300
	120,000	120,000

Pool joined River and Stream in partnership on 1 October 20X6 under an agreement which included the following terms:

(1)   Pool to introduce £15,000 cash to be credited to his capital account.

(2)   The goodwill of the business of River and Stream as at 1 October 20X6 to be valued at £28,000, but a goodwill account is not to be opened.

(3)   The value of the stock of River and Stream as at 1 October 20X6 to be reduced from £9,000 to £7,000.

(4)   £10,000 is to be transferred on 1 October 20X6 from Rivers' capital account to the credit of a loan account; River to be credited with interest at the rate of 10% per annum on his loan account balance.

(5)   Pool to be credited with a partner's salary of £11,000 per annum.

(6)   Interest at the rate of 5% per annum to be credited to partners in respect of their adjusted capital account balances at 1 October 20X6.

◈ FOULKS*lynch*

(7)   The balances of profits and losses to be shared between River, Stream and Pool in the ratio 5:3:2 respectively.

It now transpires that effect has not yet been given to the above terms 2 to 7 inclusive in the partnership books.

Up to 30 September 20X6 River and Stream had no formal partnership agreement.

Task 1

Prepare the partnership profit and loss appropriation account for the year ended 30 September 20X7.

Task 2

Prepare the partners' capital and current accounts for the year ended 30 September 20X7.

2   Activity

Smart and Swift were in partnership as hotel proprietors sharing profits and losses: Smart three-fifths, Swift two-fifths. No interest was charged on drawings or credited on capital.

The following was a summary of their trial balances as at 31 December 20X8:

Debits	£	£	Credits	£	£
Debtors		600	Bank overdraft		4,590
Fittings and fixtures		1,800	Loan - Smart at 6%		3,000
Foodstuffs - stock			Partners' capital accounts:		
at 31 December 20X7		420	Smart	3,000	
Foodstuffs purchased		2,600	Swift	500	
Freehold premises		6,000			3,500
General expenses		810	Sundry creditors		210
Partners' drawings:			Takings		5,100
Smart	520				
Swift	750				
		1,270			
Motor vehicle		700			
Wages		2,200			
		16,400			16,400

For the purpose of accounts as on 31 December 20X8 the stock of foodstuffs was valued at £300, and £200 was to be written off the book value of the motor vehicle and £100 off fittings and fixtures. A provision of £60 was required for accrued general expenses and Smart was to be credited with a year's interest on his loan account.

The partnership was dissolved on 31 December 20X8, it being agreed that:

(a)   Smart should take over the stock of foodstuffs for £250 and part of the fittings and fixtures for £600.

(b)   Swift should take over the motor vehicle for £400.

(c)   Interest on Smart's loan should cease as on 31 December 20X8.

During January 20X9:

(a)   The freehold premises were sold, realising a net amount of £6,800.

(b)   £480 was collected from debtors (the balance proving irrecoverable).

(c)   The net proceeds from an auction of the balance of fittings and fixtures were received amounting to £1,400. It was agreed that the few unsold items should be taken over partly by Smart at a value of £40 and the rest by Swift at a value of £20.

(d)   Creditors were paid in full together with incidental realisation and dissolution expenses of £120.

(e)   All amounts receivable or payable by Smart and Swift were settled.

Task 1

Prepare the profit and loss account for the year ended 31 December 20X8 excluding any profit or loss arising on dissolution.

Task 2

Prepare the realisation account.

Task 3

Prepare the cash account for January 20X9.

Task 4

Prepare partners' capital accounts (in columnar form) showing the final settlement on dissolution.

Chapter 8

LIMITED COMPANIES – INTRODUCTION

1 Activity

You are provided with the following trial balance of Aysgarth Ltd at 31 December 20X6:

	Dr £	Cr £
Ordinary share capital (50p shares)		60,000
5% Preference share capital (£1 shares)		20,000
Sales		80,000
Discount allowed	400	
Discount received		200
Carriage inwards	1,000	
Carriage outwards	800	
Debtors and creditors	10,000	2,000
Stock at 1 January 20X6	10,000	
10% Debentures 20X9		50,000
Debenture interest paid	5,000	
Fixed assets, at cost	230,000	
Fixed assets, aggregate depreciation		100,000
Purchases	49,000	
Administrative expenses	4,000	
Salaries (excluding directors)	4,000	
Preference dividend paid	1,000	
Profit and loss account balance		8,000
Cash at bank	5,000	
	320,200	320,200

Adjustments are required for:

(a) stock at 31 December 20X6, at cost £15,000;

(b) directors' salaries not yet paid £5,000;

(c) corporation tax for the year £5,000;

(d) proposed ordinary dividend 2.5 pence per share;

(e) depreciation charge for the year £4,600;

(f) accrued audit fee £1,000;

(g) creation of a plant replacement reserve of £1,000.

Task

Prepare a balance sheet and profit and loss account in vertical form, suitable for presentation to the directors.

2   Activity

You are presented with the following summarised trial balance of Floyd Ltd in respect of the year ended 31 March 20X5:

	£	£
Ordinary share capital (25p shares)		100,000
Plant and machinery:		
Cost	307,400	
Depreciation (1 Apr 20X4)		84,600
Debtors	52,030	
Creditors		38,274
Stock	61,070	
Profit and loss b/d		45,910
Cash at bank	41,118	
Cash in hand	126	
Share premium account		20,000
Sales		998,600
Interim dividend paid	2,500	
Provision for doubtful debts		1,860
9% debenture stock 20X9		75,000
Cost of sales	800,000	
Administrative costs	100,000	
	1,364,244	1,364,244

The following final adjustments are required:

(1)   the provision for doubtful debts is to be adjusted to 5% of the debtors figure. The charge is to be included in administrative costs;

(2)   corporation tax on the current year profits is estimated at £31,200;

(3)   depreciation at 10% of cost is to be provided. The charge is to be included in cost of sales;

(4)   the directors propose a final dividend of 3 pence per share.

(5)   interest for the year ended 31 March 20X5 was paid on 1 April 20X5. No accrual has been made.

Task

Prepare a profit and loss account for the year ended 31 March 20X5, and a balance sheet as at that date, insofar as information permits.

3   Activity

The following balances have been extracted from the books of the Nimrod Co Ltd as at 30 September 20X7:

	£
Creditors	18,900
Sales	240,000
Land at cost	54,000
Buildings at cost	114,000
Furniture and fittings at cost	66,000
Bank (credit balance)	18,000
Depreciation: Buildings	18,000
Furniture and fittings	30,000
Discounts received	5,292
Unappropriated profit at 1 Oct 20X6	6,000
Provision for doubtful debts	2,448
Goodwill (treat as a fixed asset)	49,200
Cash in hand	696
Stock at 1 Oct 20X6	42,744
Interim dividend on preference shares	1,800
Rates	6,372
Wages and salaries	24,000
Insurance	5,688
Returns inwards	1,116
General expenses	1,308
Debtors	37,920
Purchases	131,568
Debenture interest	1,200
Bad debts	2,028
5% debentures	48,000
6% £1 preference shares	60,000
£1 ordinary shares	60,000
General reserve	30,000
Share premium account	3,000

Additional information:

(1)   stock on hand at 30 September 20X7 was £46,638;

(2)   insurance paid in advance - £300;

(3)   wages owing - £840;

(4)   depreciation is to be provided at 10% on cost of buildings, and at 20% on the written down value of furniture and fittings;

(5)   provision for doubtful debts is to be reduced to 5% of debtors;

(6)   debenture interest outstanding is £1,200;

(7)   the directors propose to pay a 5% ordinary dividend and the final preference dividend, and to transfer £24,000 to general reserve;

(8)   the corporation tax charge for the year is £20,000.

Task

Prepare the trading, profit and loss and appropriation account for the year ended 30 September 20X7 and a balance sheet as at that date.

Chapter 9

PUBLISHED ACCOUNTS

1   Activity

The following profit and loss account for the year to 31 March 20X2 has been prepared for the management of Ople public limited company

	£'000	£'000
Sales		8,500
Cost of sales		
Opening stock	500	
Plus purchases	4,400	
Closing stock	4,900	
	(700)	4200
Gross profit		4,300
Dividends received		240
		4,540
Hire of plant and machinery	15 *COS*	
Wages and salaries	1,200 *BELOW*	
Directors' salaries	95 *A*	
Rent and rates (warehouse)	65 *D*	
Office expenses	190 *A*	
Legal expenses	35 *A*	
Auditors	50 *A*	
Distribution expenses	425 *D*	
Factory expenses	970 *COS*	
Depreciation		
Vans	40 *D*	
Furniture	20 *A*	
Plant and machinery	85 *C.OS*	
		3,190
Profit before taxation		1,350
Taxation (this years 380 – 30 over provision)		350
Profit after taxation ~~last year~~		1,000
Dividends (pref £100, paid £200, proposed £200)		500
Returned profit		500

Additional information

(1)   Wages and salaries (other than those for directors) are to be apportioned as follows

Distribution	80%
Office expenses	20%

(2)   The company's issued and fully paid up share capital is as follows

	£'000
Ordinary shares of £1 each	8,000
10% Preference shares of £1 each	1,000

Task

Insofar as the information permits, prepare Ople plc's profit and loss account for the year to 31 March 20X2 in accordance with the requirements of the Companies Act 1985 and related accounting standards. Ignore the grossing up of dividends received.

2	Activity

The trial balance of Toby Ltd at 31 December 20X8 is as follows.

	£	£
Share capital - £1 ordinary shares		10,000
Profit and loss account		19,000
Sales and purchases	61,000	100,000
Sales returns and purchase returns	2,000	4,000
Sales and purchase ledger control a/cs	20,000	7,000
Land and buildings (at cost)	40,000	
Plant (at cost, and depreciation to 1 January 20X8)	50,000	22,000
Debentures (10% pa interest)		30,000
Opening stock	15,000	
Operating expenses	9,000	
Administration expenses	7,000	
Selling expenses	6,000	
Bank		8,000
Suspense account		10,000
	210,000	210,000

Notes

(a)   5,000 new shares were issued during the year at £1.60 per share. The proceeds have been credited to the suspense account.

(b)   Sales returns of £1,000 have been entered in the sales day book as if they were sales.

(c)   The bookkeeper has included the opening provision for doubtful debts of £800 in the selling expenses account in the trial balance. The provision is required to be 5% of debtors.

(d)   A standing order payment of £1,000 for rates paid in December has not been entered. This payment covered the half-year to 31 March 20X9. Any rates account has been included under operating expenses. The balance in the account is £1,500.

(e)   90% of the buildings is factory space: the remainder is offices.

(f)   Closing stock is £18,000.

(g)   No debenture interest has been paid.

(h)   The remaining balance on the suspense account after the above represents the sales proceeds of a fully depreciated item of plant, costing £10,000. No other entries (except bank) have been made concerning this disposal.

(i)   Depreciation at 10% on cost should be provided on the plant.

(j)   A tax charge of £3,000 is to be provided.

Task

Prepare the trading, profit and loss account for the year, and balance sheet as at 31 December 20X8, to comply with the requirements of the CA 1985, taking account of the above notes.

Chapter 10

TAXATION IN COMPANY ACCOUNTS

1 Activity

Explain the meaning of and accounting treatment of each of the following terms:

(a)   Output VAT;
(b)   Unfranked investment income;
(c)   Over provision of Corporation tax in the previous year;
(d)   Deferred taxation.

2 Activity

The accountant of a company has already prepared the extended trial balance for the 20X5 accounts but has since discovered a number of further items that require accounting for:

(a)   Provision is to be made for Corporation tax for 20X5 of £64,700;

(b)   In the 20X4 accounts provision was made for Corporation tax of £54,000 but during 20X5 when the final settlement was made £57,400 was paid to the Inland Revenue;

(c)   A dividend of £1,000 was received from another company in which shares are held. Tax credits of £111 are available to be added to this dividend.

(d)   A transfer of £800 is to be made to the deferred tax account.

Task 1

Write up journal entries to record each of these further items.

Task 2

Show the make up of the tax charge for 20X5 in the profit and loss account for the year and the Corporation tax creditor that will appear in the balance sheet at the end of the year.

3 Activity

Which tax rates should be used according to FRS 16?

Chapter 11

TANGIBLE FIXED ASSETS

1 Activity

Explain the purpose of providing for depreciation and give details of one method of computing the annual depreciation on an asset.

2 Activity

A company purchased a freehold building on 1 January 20X2 for £120,000. It is being depreciated over an estimated useful economic life of 50 years. At 31 December 20X6 the building is valued at £140,000 and it is decided by the directors of the company to incorporate this valuation into the 20X6 financial statements.

Task 1

Show the journal entries required to effect the revaluation of this building.

Task 2

Determine the annual depreciation charge from 20X7 onwards.

Task 3

Explain the differences in accounting treatment if this building had been classified as an investment property according to SSAP 19.

3 Activity

Explain the accounting treatment for capital based grants as set out in SSAP 4.

4 Activity

What is meant by an impairment review as defined by FRS 11. Explain the **principles** of calculation of an impairment review.

Chapter 12

INTANGIBLE FIXED ASSETS

1   Activity

Task 1

Explain the **three** classifications of research and development expenditure.

Task 2

Discuss the treatment of research and development expenditure with special reference to the fundamental concepts of accounting.

2   Activity

I plc has deferred development expenditure of £600,000 relating to the development of Brand X. It is expected that the demand for the product will stay at a high level for the next three years. Annual sales of 400,000, 300,000 and 200,000 units respectively are expected over this period. Brand X sells for £10.

Task

Suggest two possibilities for writing off the development expenditure.

3   Activity

Give reasons why goodwill may exist in a business.

4   Activity

Explain the circumstances in which development expenditure may be capitalised.

Chapter 13

STOCKS AND LONG TERM CONTRACTS

1 Activity

ABC Ltd purchases and sells the following items in March:

		Units	£ per unit
3 Mar	purchases	600	£20
19 Mar	purchases	300	£23
31 Mar	sells	700	

Task

Find the value of closing stock and the value of the units sold under the following methods of stock valuation:

(a)   FIFO
(b)   LIFO
(c)   Weighted average

2 Activity

What is the correct stock valuation for the following items?

	Cost £	Costs to complete £	Selling costs £	Selling price £	NRV £	Valuation £
Item 1	1,000	nil	50	1,500		
Item 2	2,000	500	100	2,400		
Item 3	3,000	800	200	3,800		
					____	
					____	

3 Activity

A company has the following stock items at the year end

Item	Raw materials costs £	Labour costs £	Production overheads £	NRV £
A	500	800	800	2,600
B	1,000	-	-	1,100
C	500	800	800	1,950

Task

At what amount will stock be stated in the balance sheet?

4   Activity

Task 1

A firm buys and sells two models, P and Q. The following unit costs are available (all figures are in £s and all the costs are borne by the firm):

	P	Q
Purchase cost	100	200
Delivery costs from supplier	20	30
Delivery costs to customers	22	40
Coloured sales packaging costs	15	18
Selling price	150	300

Calculate the figure to be included in closing stock for a unit of each model, according to SSAP 9.

Task 2

A firm has the following transactions with its product R.

Year 1

Opening stock: nil
Buys 10 units at £300 per unit
Buys 12 units at £250 per unit
Sells 8 units at £400 per unit
Buys 6 units at £200 per unit
Sells 12 units at £400 per unit

Year 2

Buys 10 units at £200 per unit
Sells 5 units at £400 per unit
Buys 12 units at £150 per unit
Sells 25 units at £400 per unit.

Calculate on an item by item basis for both year 1 and year 2:

(i)   The closing stock
(ii)   The sales
(iii)   The cost of sales
(iv)   The gross profit

using, separately, the LIFO and the FIFO methods of stock valuation. Present all workings clearly.

5   Activity

Briefly explain the terms cost and net realisable value in relation to stocks.

6   Activity

Explain the problems behind the accounting for long term contract work in progress. Explain the fundamental accounting concepts that apply to accounting for long term contracts. Explain the required accounting for long term contract work in progress per SSAP 9.

Chapter 14

SUBSTANCE OF TRANSACTIONS

1   Activity

In relation to SSAP 17 *Accounting for post balance sheet events*:

(a)   Define 'adjusting events' and 'non-adjusting events';

(b)   Give two examples of each type of event;

(c)   Explain how material post balance sheet events should be incorporated into a company's financial statements.

2   Activity

Steelparts Ltd has entered into an agreement with a finance company to lease a machine for a four year period. Under the terms of the agreement, the machine is to be made available to Steelparts Ltd on 1 January 20X1, when an immediate payment of £15,000 has to be made, followed by seven semi-annual payments of an equivalent amount, payable on 30 June and 31 December.

The fair market price of the machine on 1 January 20X1 is £96,000. The estimated life of such machines is four years. Steelparts Ltd can borrow money from the bank at a rate of 18% pa. The company has a policy of depreciating the machines of this type that it owns over a four year period on a straight line basis.

The company has a calendar year end.

Task 1

Explain the key factors that differentiate a finance lease from an operating lease.

Task 2

If the lease is to be treated as a finance lease show how it would be recorded in the profit and loss account and balance sheet of Steelparts Ltd during the first two years of the lease agreement. The interest charge is to be allocated on the basis of the actuarial method assuming an implicit rate of interest of 7% per six months.

3   Activity

The Accounting Standards Board has issued Financial Reporting Standard 5 *Reporting the substance of transactions*.

Task

State the main provisions of FRS 5 and explain why it was issued.

4   Activity

The ASB has issued FRS 8 *Related Party Disclosures*.

Task

Explain why FRS 8 was issued.

Chapter 15

REPORTING FINANCIAL PERFORMANCE

1	Activity

The ASB has issued FRS 3, Reporting Financial Performance, which has the aim of moving the emphasis from concentrating on a single performance indicator to highlighting a range of important components of financial performance.

Task

Discuss how FRS 3 presents users of financial statements with information that is designed to present clearly the key components of performance.

2	Activity

Topaz Limited makes up its accounts regularly to 31 December each year. The company has operated for some years with four divisions A, B, C and D, but on 30 June 1996 Division B was sold for £8m, realising a profit of £2.5m. During 1996 there was a fundamental reorganisation of Division C, the costs of which were £1.8m.

The trial balance of the company at 31 December 1996 included the following balances:

	Division B		Divisions A, C and D combined	
	Dr £m	Cr £m	Dr £m	Cr £m
Sales		13		68
Costs of sales	8		41	
Distribution costs (including a bad debt of £1.9m - Division D)	1		6	
Administrative expenses	2		4	
Profit on sale of Division B		2.5		
Reorganisation costs, Division C			1.8	
Interest on £10m 10% debenture stock issued in 1990			1	
Taxation			4.8	
Interim dividend paid			2	
Revaluation reserve				10

A final dividend of £4m is proposed.

The balance on the revaluation reserve relates to the company's freehold property and arose as follows:

	£m
Balance at 1.1.96	6
Revaluation during 1996	4
Balance at 31.12.96 per trial balance	10

Task 1

Prepare the profit and loss account of Topaz Limited for the year ended 31 December 1996, complying as far as possible with the provisions of the Companies Act 1985 and FRS 3 *Reporting Financial Performance*.

Task 2

Prepare the statement of total recognised gains and losses for the year as required by FRS 3.

---

3   Activity

The ASB has issued SSAP 25 *Segmental Reporting*.

Task

What is the main purpose of reporting an organisation's results by segment? Explain the type of segment information that must be reported under SSAP 25.

Chapter 16

MISCELLANEOUS ACCOUNTING STANDARDS

1 Activity

Explain the main objectives of the ASB when publishing FRS 4, *Capital Instruments*, and how these objectives have been achieved.

2 Activity

Explain the problems of accounting for a defined benefit pension scheme.

3 Activity

Task 1

Distinguish between foreign currency conversion and foreign currency translation.

Task 2

A company has a year end of 31 December. On 28 October 20X5 the company purchased some stock from a French supplier for FFR 114,000. Payment for these goods was eventually made on 7 January 20X6.

Exchange rates FFR to £:

28 October 20X5	11.4
31 December 20X5	10.0
6 January 20X6	10.3

Write up these transactions in the creditors ledger control account and explain what figures will appear in the 20X5 and 20X6 financial statements for this transaction.

Chapter 17

CASH FLOW STATEMENTS

1 Activity

The balance sheets of Antipodean Enterprises at the end of two consecutive financial years were:

Balance sheets as at

31 December 20X2			31 December 20X3	
£	£		£	£
		Fixed assets (at written down values):		
38,000		Premises	37,000	
17,600		Equipment	45,800	
4,080		Cars	18,930	
	59,680			101,730
	17,000	Investments (long-term)		25,000
		Current assets:		
27,500		Stocks	19,670	
14,410		Debtors and prepayments	11,960	
3,600		Short-term investments	4,800	
1,800		Cash and bank balances	700	
	47,310			37,130
		Current liabilities:		
20,950		Creditors and accruals	32,050	
-		Bank overdraft	28,200	
	(20,950)			(60,250)
	103,040	Net assets employed		103,610
		Financed by:		
67,940		Opening capital	75,040	
4,000		Capital introduced/(withdrawn)	(6,500)	
15,300		Profit/(loss) for year	25,200	
(12,200)		Drawings	(15,130)	
	75,040	Closing capital		78,610
	28,000	Long-term liability - Business development loan		25,000
	103,040			103,610

Profit for the year ended 31 December 20X3 (£25,200) is after accounting for:

	£
Depreciation:	
Premises	1,000
Equipment	3,000
Cars	3,000
Profit on disposal of equipment	430
Loss on disposal of cars	740
Interest payable	3,000

The written down value of the assets at date of disposal was:

		£
Equipment		5,200
Cars		2,010

Interest accrued at 31 December 20X3 is £400.

Task 1

Prepare a cash flow statement for Antipodean Enterprises for the year ended 31 December 20X3 in accordance with FRS 1 (revised) including a reconciliation of operating profit to net cash inflow from operating activities.

Task 2

Comment on the financial position of the business as revealed by your answer to Task 1 above and by the balance sheet as at 31 December 20X3.

---

2   Activity

You are given summarised balance sheets for Aida plc as shown below:

	31 December 20X0		31 December 20X1	
	£'000	£'000	£'000	£'000
Ordinary shares		20		25
Share premium		4		9
Property revaluation reserve		5		8
Profit and loss balance		16		16
Debentures				
10%		40		20
15%		0		40
		85		118
Property		25		45
Plant:				
Cost	30		46	
Depreciation	15		24	
		15		22
Stock		46		44
Debtors		17		33
Bank		7		0
		110		144
Trade creditors	20		13	
Dividends	5		9	
Bank	0		4	
		25		26
		85		118

Note: any issues and redemptions of shares or debentures occurred on 1 January 20X1.

All debenture interest is paid within the accounting year in which it is charged.

Only one dividend is declared each year. Dividends are always paid early in the year following that to which they relate. No sales of fixed assets have occurred during the relevant period.

Task 1

Prepare a statement to show the net cash flow derived from trading operations in the year to 31 December 20X1.

Task 2

Prepare a cash flow statement complying with FRS 1 (revised) to highlight the change in the bank balance during the year to 31 December 20X1.

---

3   Activity

Y Ltd's profit and loss account for the year ended 31 December 20X2 and balance sheets at 31 December 20X1 and 31 December 20X2 were as follows:

Y Ltd
Profit and loss account for the year ended 31 December 20X2

	£'000	£'000
Sales		360
Raw materials consumed	35	
Staff costs	47	
Depreciation	59	
Loss on disposal	9	
	—	150
		—
Operating profit		210
Interest payable		14
		—
Profit before tax		196
Taxation		62
		—
		134
Dividend		36
		—
Profit retained for year		98
Balance brought forward		245
		—
		343

Y Ltd
Balance sheets

	31 December 20X2		31 December 20X1	
	£'000	£'000	£'000	£'000
Fixed assets				
Cost		798		780
Depreciation		159		112
		639		668
Current assets				
Stock	12		10	
Trade debtors	33		25	
Bank	29		32	
	74		67	
Current liabilities				
Trade creditors	6		3	
Taxation	46		39	
Proposed dividend	20		16	
	72		58	
Working capital		2		9
		641		677
Long-term liabilities				
Long-term loans		100		250
		541		427
Share capital		180		170
Share premium		18		12
Profit and loss		343		245
		541		427

During the year, the company paid £45,000 for a new piece of machinery.

Task 1

Prepare a cash flow statement for Y Ltd for the year ended 31 December 20X2 in accordance with the requirements of the revised Financial Reporting Standard 1 (FRS 1).

Task 2

Explain what is meant by the term 'cash' in the context of statements prepared under the requirements of FRS 1 (revised).

Chapter 18

INTERPRETATION OF FINANCIAL STATEMENTS

1   Activity

The following details have been extracted from the accounts of PQR plc for three years of recession. The company's year ends on 31 March.

	20X2 £m	20X3 £m	20X4 £m
Turnover (sales)	100	103	108
Gross profit	33.0	34.0	35.6
Net profit	15	15	15
Fixed assets	64	72	68
Stock	4	4	4
Debtors	8	11	15
Creditors	(5)	(6)	(6)
Cash at bank	5	-	-
Bank overdraft	-	6	5

Task 1

Calculate, for each of the three years:

- gross profit percentage;
- net profit percentage;
- quick ratio (acid test).

Task 2

Comment briefly on the ratios you have calculated.

2   Activity

You are given summarised results of an electrical engineering business, as follows. All figures are in £'000.

Profit and loss account

	Year ended 31.12.X1	Year ended 31.12.X0
Turnover	60,000	50,000
Cost of sales	42,000	34,000
Gross profit	18,000	16,000
Operating expenses	15,500	13,000
	2,500	3,000
Interest payable	2,200	1,300
Profit before taxation	300	1,700
Taxation	350	600

(Loss) profit after taxation	(50)	1,100
Dividends	600	600
Transfer (from) to reserves	(650)	500

Balance sheet

Fixed assets		
Intangible	500	-
Tangible	12,000	11,000
	12,500	11,000
Current assets		
Stocks	14,000	13,000
Debtors	16,000	15,000
Bank and cash	500	500
	30,500	28,500
Creditors due within one year	24,000	20,000
Net current assets	6,500	8,500
Total assets less current liabilities	19,000	19,500
Creditors due after one year	6,000	5,500
	13,000	14,000
Capital and reserves		
Share capital	1,300	1,300
Share premium	3,300	3,300
Revaluation reserve	2,000	2,000
Profit and loss	6,400	7,400
	13,000	14,000

Task 1

Prepare a table of the following ratios, calculated for both years, clearly showing the figures used in the calculations:

current ratio
quick assets ratio
stock turnover in days
debtors turnover in days
creditors turnover in days
gross profit %
net profit % (before taxation)
interest cover
dividend cover
ROCE
gearing

Task 2

Making full use of the information given in the question, of your table of ratios, and your common sense, comment on the actions of the management.

3   Activity

The outline balance sheets of the Nantred Trading Co Ltd were as shown below:

Balance sheets as at 30 September

	20X5			20X6	
	£	£		£	£
			Fixed assets (at written down values):		
	40,000		Premises	98,000	
	65,000		Plant and equipment	162,000	
		105,000			260,000
			Current assets:		
	31,200		Stock	95,300	
	19,700		Trade debtors	30,700	
	15,600		Bank and cash	26,500	
	66,500			152,500	
			Current liabilities:		
	23,900		Trade creditors	55,800	
	11,400		Corporation tax	13,100	
	17,000		Proposed dividends	17,000	
	52,300			85,900	
		14,200	Working capital		66,600
		119,200	Net assets employed		326,600
			Financed by:		
	100,000		Ordinary share capital	200,000	
	19,200		Reserves	26,600	
		119,200	Shareholders' funds		226,600
		-	7% debentures		100,000
		119,200			326,600

The only other information available is that the turnover for the years ended 30 September 20X5 and 20X6 was £202,900 and £490,700, respectively, and that net profit before tax for 20X5 and 20X6 respectively was £21,500 and £37,500.

Task 1

Calculate, for each of the two years, six suitable ratios to highlight the financial stability, liquidity and profitability of the company.

Task 2

Comment on the situation revealed by the figures you have calculated in your answer to Task 1 above.

4   Activity

(a)   Define EPS based on the definition given in FRS 14.

(b)   Calculate the earnings per share based on the following information:

	£'000
Profit on ordinary activities	7,892
Tax on profit on ordinary activities	1,004
Profit after taxation	6,888
Dividends (Note 1)	1,200
Retained profit	5,688

Note 1

Dividends	Ordinary	1,000
	Preference	200
		1,200

There are 10,000,000 shares in issue throughout the year.

Chapter 19

CONSOLIDATED BALANCE SHEET

1   Activity

On 1 January 20X6, Hanson Ltd acquired the following shares in Pickford Ltd:

		£
75,000	Ordinary shares of £1 – cost	93,100
15,000	6% Preference shares of £1 – cost	16,050
		109,150

At the date of acquisition, the accumulated profits of Pickford Ltd amounted to £11,000. The summarised balance sheets of the two companies at 31.12.X8 were as follows:

	Hanson Ltd £	Pickford Ltd £
Ordinary shares of £1	350,000	100,000
6% preference shares of £1	-	60,000
Profit and loss account	348,420	132,700
Sundry creditors	93,400	51,150
	791,820	343,850

	£	£
Fixed assets	431,100	219,350
Investments	109,150	-
Stock	143,070	71,120
Debtors	89,200	36,230
Cash at bank	19,300	17,150
	791,820	343,850

During the year, Hanson Ltd sold goods whose invoice value was £24,000 to Pickford Ltd. These goods were invoiced at cost plus 25%, and one-quarter were still in Pickford's stock at the year end.

Goodwill should be written off over a 5 year period.

Task

Prepare the consolidated balance sheet of Hanson Ltd as at 31 December 20X8.

2   Activity

On 1 January 20X9, Pixie Ltd acquired the following shareholdings in Dixie Ltd. At that date the accumulated profits of Dixie Ltd amounted to £20,000.

	Number of shares	Cost of investment £
£1 Ordinary shares	37,500	58,000
£1 Preference shares	16,000	15,000
		73,000

The balance sheets of the two companies at 31 December 20X9 were as follows:

	Pixie Ltd £	Dixie Ltd £
Ordinary share capital	200,000	50,000
7% Preference share capital	-	40,000
Profit and loss account	120,000	38,000
Sundry creditors	56,100	22,100
Proposed dividends:		
Ordinary	20,000	2,500
Preference	-	1,400
	396,100	154,000
Fixed assets	210,000	110,600
Current assets	113,100	43,400
Investment in Dixie Ltd	73,000	-
	396,100	154,000

You further ascertain that:

• Current assets of Pixie Ltd include £42,000 of goods acquired originally from Dixie Ltd. Dixie Ltd invoiced these goods at cost plus 20%.

• Pixie Ltd has not accounted for dividends receivable from Dixie Ltd.

• Goodwill is to be written off over 9 years.

Task

Prepare the consolidated balance sheet of Pixie Ltd and its subsidiary as at 31 December 20X9.

3   Activity

On 1 January 20X8 HC plc acquired 75% of the ordinary shares of AS plc and on 31 December 20X8 it acquired 80% of the ordinary shares of BS plc. The summarised balance sheets of the three companies at 31 December 20X8 are as follows:

	HC plc £'000	AS plc £'000	BS plc £'000
Sundry net assets	2,300	2,320	1,500
Investment in AS plc	1,500	-	-
Investment in BS plc	1,250	-	-
	5,050	2,320	1,500
£1 ordinary shares, fully paid	2,400	1,200 *75%*	1,000 *80%*
Reserves	2,650	1,000 *-800 pre / -200 post*	500
Proposed dividend	-	120	-
	5,050	2,320	1,500

When HC plc acquired the shares in AS plc, the subsidiary's reserves were £800,000. It is HC plc's policy to write off any goodwill over 5 years. These adjustments have not yet been made in HC plc's books in respect of the acquisitions of AS plc and BS plc. Neither has credit been taken for the proposed dividend of AS plc.

Task 1

Using the above facts, calculate

(i)   the amount of goodwill which arose when HC plc became the holder of the shares in AS plc and BS plc.

(ii)   the figure for consolidated reserves which would be shown in the consolidated balance sheet of the HC plc group,

(iii)   the amount of minority interest for each of the subsidiaries;

Note: workings must be shown.

Task 2

Prepare the consolidated balance sheet at 31 December 20X8.

Chapter 20

CONSOLIDATED PROFIT AND LOSS ACCOUNT

1 Activity

E plc acquired 60% of the ordinary share capital of Y Ltd and 30% of the debentures of Y Ltd on 1 January 20X2. Given below are the profit and loss account figures for E plc and Y Ltd for the year ended 31 December 20X2.

	E plc £	Y Ltd £
Sales	500,000	300,000
Cost of sales	300,000	180,000
Distribution and administrative costs	70,000	30,000
Dividends received/receivable	17,000	4,000
Dividends payable	64,000	20,000
Interest payable (all relating to debentures)	40,000	30,000
Taxation	42,000	20,000
Interest receivable	18,000	-

Task

Prepare the group profit and loss account.

2 Activity

The finance director of R plc has asked you to prepare the consolidated profit and loss account of the R plc group. He has provided you with the following summarised profit and loss accounts and information.

Summarised profit and loss accounts for the year ended 31 March 20X4

	R plc £	S Ltd £	J Ltd £
Profits from trading	728,000	149,000	510,000
Net operating expenses	182,000	37,250	127,500
Operating profit	546,000	111,750	382,500
Investment income	49,500	-	-
Profit before taxation	595,500	111,750	382,500
Taxation	162,250	29,000	89,000
Profit after taxation	433,250	82,750	293,500
Dividends	200,000	20,000	60,000
Retained profit for year	233,250	62,750	233,500
Retained profits b/f	124,000	44,000	100,000
Retained profits c/f	357,250	106,750	333,500

Additional information

(a)   The issued share capital of S Ltd consists of 200,000 ordinary shares of £1 each. R plc acquired 150,000 ordinary shares for £210,000 on 1 October 20X3.

(b)   The issued share capital of J Ltd consists of 120,000 shares of £1 each. R plc acquired 84,000 ordinary shares of J Ltd for £120,000 on 1 April 20X0 when the reserves of J Ltd were £30,000.

(c)   The profits of S Ltd are deemed to accrue evenly throughout the year.

(d)   All of the investment income in R plc's books is dividend income from S Ltd and J Ltd.

(e)   During the year, R plc made sales of £50,000 to J Ltd. The closing stock of J Ltd contains £10,000 of purchases from R plc. R plc has a profit margin of 20% on sales.

(f)   It is the policy of R plc to amortise goodwill over a period of five years from the date of acquisition.

Task

Prepare the consolidated profit and loss account of the R plc group for the year ended 31 March 20X4.

Chapter 21

ASSOCIATED UNDERTAKINGS

1 Activity

Explain what is meant by significant influence of one company over another company. What are the different accounting treatments generally used for a situation where one company controls another and for the situation where one company has significant influence over another?

2 Activity

Task 1

Explain what is meant by equity accounting.

Task 2

X plc acquired 60,000 ordinary £1 shares in Y Ltd for £96,000 on 1 January 20X5 when the reserves of Y Ltd were £90,000.

At 31 December 20X7 the summarised balance sheet and profit and loss account of Y Ltd were as follows:

Balance sheet as at 31 December 20X7

	£
Sundry net assets	410,000
£1 Ordinary share capital	240,000
Profit and loss account	170,000
	410,000

Profit and loss account for the year ended 31 December 20X7

	£
Operating profit	100,000
Taxation	30,000
Profit after tax	70,000
Dividend	20,000
Retained profit	50,000

What figures will appear in X plc's consolidated balance sheet and profit and loss account in respect of Y Ltd? If X plc's policy is to write goodwill off over a four year period what entries would be made in the consolidated profit and loss reserve account in respect of Y Ltd?

3   Activity

A plc owns 30% of the ordinary share capital of B Ltd. A plc acquired this interest 6 years ago for £150,000 when the total net assets of B Ltd amounted to £450,000. Any goodwill arising on acquisitions is written off over a three year period. Since acquisition B Ltd has made profits amounting to £100,000 and at the latest balance sheet date, 31 March 20X4, the total net assets of B Ltd amounted to £550,000.

Task

(a)   Calculate the goodwill arising on the acquisition of B Ltd.

(b)   At what amount will the investment in B Ltd be shown in the group balance sheet at 31 March 20X4?

Chapter 22

CONSOLIDATION PRINCIPLES

1 Activity

Briefly explain the reasons why a subsidiary may be excluded from consolidation.

2 Activity

(a) What is meant by a business combination?

(b) Distinguish between the two types of business combination that can be identified.

(c) What are the two types of accounting that can be used in consolidated financial statements for different types of business combination?

82

PRACTICE CENTRAL ASSESSMENT ACTIVITIES

QUESTIONS

ASSESSMENT ACTIVITIES

These assessment activities have been taken from the June 1996 to December 1998 Central Assessments set by the AAT. The assessments have been split into sections as follows:

UNIT 11 – SECTION 1 – JUNE 1996

You are reminded that competence must be achieved in each section. You should therefore attempt and aim to complete EVERY task in EACH section.

Note: You are advised to spend approximately 54 minutes on section 1.

Data

You have been assigned to assist in the preparation of the financial statements of Dowango Ltd for the year ended 31 March 1996. The company is a cash and carry operation that trades from a large warehouse on an industrial estate.   You have been provided with the extended trial balance of Dowango Ltd on 31 March 1996 which is set out below.

DOWANGO LTD
EXTENDED TRIAL BALANCE 31 MARCH 1996

	TRIAL BALANCE		ADJUSTMENTS		PROFIT & LOSS		BALANCE SHEET	
FOULKS*lynch*	Debit	Credit	Debit	Credit	Debit	Credit	Debit	Credit
	£000	£000	£000	£000	£000	£000	£000	£000
Land–cost	431						431	
Buildings–cost	512						512	
Fixtures & Fittings–cost	389						389	
Motor vehicles–cost	341						341	
Office equipment–cost	105						105	
Buildings–accumulated depreciation		184						184
Fixtures & fittings–accumulated depreciation		181						181
Motor vehicles–accumulated depreciation		204						204
Office equipment–accumulated depreciation		56						56
Stock	298		365	365	298	365	365	
Investment	64						64	
Debtors	619						619	
Provision for doubtful debts		27						27
Prepayments			21				21	
Cash in hand	3						3	
Cash at bank		157						157
Creditors		331						331
Accruals				41				41
Sales		5,391				5,391		
Purchases	2,988				2,988			
Returns inwards	39				39			
Returns outwards		31				31		
Carriage inwards	20				20			
Distribution expenses	1,092		23	11	1,104			
Administrative costs	701		18	10	709			
Interest charges	15				15			
Interim dividend	20				20			
Share capital		500						500
Profit and loss account		275						275
Long term loan		300						300
Profit					594			594
	7,637	7,637	427	427	5,787	5,787	2,850	2,850

You have been given the following further information:

(1)   The authorised and issued share capital of the business consists of ordinary shares with a nominal value of £1.

(2)   The company has paid an interim dividend of 4p per share during the year but has not provided for the final dividend of 6p per share.

(3)   Depreciation has been calculated on all of the fixed assets of the business and has already been entered on a monthly basis into the distribution expenses and administration costs ledger balances as shown on the extended trial balance.

(4)   The tax charge for the year has been calculated as £211,000.

(5)   Interest on the long-term loan has been paid for six months of the year. No adjustment has been made for the interest due for the final six months of the year. Interest is charged on the loan at a rate of 10% per annum.

(6)   An advertising campaign was undertaken during the year at a cost of £19,000. No invoices have yet been received for this campaign and no adjustment for this expense has been made in the extended trial balance.

(7)   The investments consist of shares in a retail company that were purchased with a view to resale at a profit. Dowango Ltd owns 2% of the share capital of the company. At the end of the year a valuation of the shares was obtained with a view to selling the shares in the forthcoming year. The shares were valued at £56,000.

Task 1.1

Make any adjustments you feel to be necessary to the balances in the extended trial balance as a result of the matters set out in the further information above. Set out your adjustments in the form of journal entries. Narratives are not required.

(Ignore any effect of these adjustments on the tax charge for the year as given above.)

Task 1.2

On the answer sheet that follows, draft a profit and loss account for the year ended 31 March 1996 and a balance sheet as at that date using Format 1 in accordance with the Companies Act 1985 as supplemented by FRS 3 'Reporting Financial Performance'.

(You are NOT required to prepare a statement of total recognised gains and losses or the reconciliation of movements in shareholders' funds required under FRS 3.)

Answer sheet for Task 1.2

PROFORMA PROFIT AND LOSS ACCOUNT
(FORMAT 1 AS SUPPLEMENTED BY FRS 3)

	£	£
Turnover		
Continuing operations		
Acquisitions		
	‾‾‾‾‾	
Discontinued operations		
	‾‾‾‾‾	
Cost of sales		
		‾‾‾‾‾
Gross profit (or loss)		
Distribution costs		
Administrative expenses		
Other operating income		
		‾‾‾‾‾
Operating profit (or loss)		
Continuing operations		
Acquisitions		
	‾‾‾‾‾	
Discontinued operations		
	‾‾‾‾‾	
Profit (or loss) on disposal of discontinued operations		
Income from shares in group undertakings		
Income from participating interests		
Income from other fixed asset investments		
Other interest receivable and similar income		
Amounts written off investments		
		‾‾‾‾‾
Profit (or loss) on ordinary activities before interest		
Interest payable and similar charges		
		‾‾‾‾‾
Profit (or loss) on ordinary activities before taxation		
Tax on profit (or loss) on ordinary activities		
Extraordinary items		
		‾‾‾‾‾
Profit (or loss) for the financial year		
Dividends		
		‾‾‾‾‾
Retained profit for the financial year		
		‾‾‾‾‾

PROFORMA BALANCE SHEET (FORMAT 1)

	£	£
Fixed assets		
Intangible assets		
Tangible assets		
Investments		
	────	
Current assets		
Stocks		
Debtors		
Investments		
Cash at bank and in hand		
	────	
Creditors: amounts falling due within one year		
	────	
Net current assets (liabilities)		────
Total assets *less* current liabilities		
Creditors: amounts falling due after more than one year		
Provisions for liabilities and charges		
		────
		────
Capital and reserves		
Called up share capital		
Share premium account		
Revaluation reserve		
Profit and loss account		
		────
		────

UNIT 11 – SECTION 1 – DECEMBER 1996

You are reminded that competence must be achieved in each section. You should therefore attempt and aim to complete EVERY task in EACH section.

You are advised to spend approximately 65 minutes on section 1.

PART 1

Data

You have been assigned to assist in the preparation of the financial statements of Spiraes Ltd for the year ended 30 November 1996. The company is a trading company operating from freehold premises in a large industrial city. You have been provided with the extended trial balance of Spiraes Ltd on 30 November 1996 which is set out on the following page.

SPIRAES LTD
EXTENDED TRIAL BALANCE 30 NOVEMBER 1996

	TRIAL BALANCE		ADJUSTMENTS		PROFIT & LOSS		BALANCE SHEET	
	Debit	Credit	Debit	Credit	Debit	Credit	Debit	Credit
	£000	£000	£000	£000	£000	£000	£000	£000
Trade creditors		2,653						2,653
Accruals				63				63
Cash at bank	375						375	
Interest charges	189				189			
Buildings–accumulated depreciation		810						810
Office equipment–accumulated depreciation		319						319
Motor vehicles–accumulated depreciation		1,912						1,912
Fixtures & fittings–accumulated depreciation		820						820
Sales		18,742				18,742		
Trade debtors	3,727						3,727	
Provision for doubtful debts		68						68
Dividends received		52				52		
Fixed asset investment	866						866	
Profit and loss account		6,192						6,192
9% debentures		4,200						4,200
Prepayments			31				31	
Land–cost	3,570						3,570	
Buildings–cost	2,933						2,933	
Office equipment–cost	882						882	
Motor vehicles–cost	3,485						3,485	
Fixtures & fittings–cost	2,071						2,071	
Purchases	10,776				10,776			
Administrative expenses	1,805		27	12	1,820			
Stock	3,871		4,153	4,153	3,871	4,153	4,153	
Returns inwards	595				595			
Returns outwards		314				314		
Ordinary share capital		1,000						1,000
Share premium		560						560
Distribution costs	2,497		36	19	2,514			
Profit					3,496			3,496
	37,642	37,642	4,247	4,247	23,261	23,261	22,093	22,093

You have been given the following further information:

(1)   The share capital of the business consists of ordinary shares with a nominal value of 25p.

(2)   The company has paid no interim dividend this year but is proposing to provide a final dividend of 2 pence per share for the year.

(3)   Depreciation has been calculated on all of the fixed assets of the business and has already been entered on a monthly basis into the distribution expenses and administration expenses ledger balances as shown on the extended trial balance.

(4)   The tax charge for the year has been calculated as £1,356,000.

(5)   Interest on the 9% debentures has been paid for the first six months of the year only. No adjustment has been made for the interest due for the final six months of the year.

(6)   The land has been valued at market value at the end of the year by a professional valuer at £4,290,000. It is proposed that the valuation be incorporated into the financial statements of the company as at 30 November 1996.

(7)   The fixed asset investment consists of shares in a publicly quoted company and is shown in the extended trial balance at cost. The investment represents 7% of the total issued ordinary share capital of the quoted company and was purchased with the intention of investing in the company on a long-term basis.

(8)   Some items of stock which were included in the stock balance in the extended trial balance at a cost of £405,000 were sold after the year end for £355,000.

Task 1.1

Make any additional adjustments you feel to be necessary to the balances in the extended trial balance as a result of the matters set out in the further information above. Set out your adjustments in the form of journal entries.

Note: Narratives are not required.

Ignore any effect of these adjustments on the tax charge for the year as given above.

Task 1.2

Justify your treatment of items (6) and (8) in the further information above. Refer in your answer, where relevant, to company law, accounting concepts and applicable accounting standards.

Task 1.3

On the answer sheet that follows, draft a profit and loss account for the year ended 30 November 1996 using Format 1 in accordance with the Companies Act 1985 as supplemented by FRS 3 "Reporting Financial Performance".

Note: You are NOT required to prepare a balance sheet or the reconciliation of movements in shareholders' funds required under FRS 3. Ignore tax credits available on dividends received.

Task 1.4

On the answer sheet that follows, prepare a statement of total recognised gains and losses for the year ended 30 November 1996 for Spiraes Ltd as required by FRS 3.

Answer sheet for Task 1.3 and Task 1.4

PROFORMA PROFIT AND LOSS ACCOUNT
(FORMAT 1 AS SUPPLEMENTED BY FRS 3)

	£	£
Turnover		
Continuing operations		
Acquisitions		
	———	
Discontinued operations		
	———	
Cost of sales		
		———
Gross profit (or loss)		
Distribution costs		
Administrative expenses		
Other operating income		
		———
Operating profit (or loss)		
Continuing operations		
Acquisitions		
	———	
Discontinued operations		
	———	
Profit (or loss) on disposal of discontinued operations		
Income from shares in group undertakings		
Income from participating interests		
Income from other fixed asset investments		
Other interest receivable and similar income		
Amounts written off investments		
		———
Profit (or loss) on ordinary activities before interest		
Interest payable and similar charges		
		———
Profit (or loss) on ordinary activities before taxation		
Tax on profit (or loss) on ordinary activities		
Extraordinary items		
		———
Profit (or loss) for the financial year		
Dividends		
		———
Retained profit for the financial year		
		———

Statement of Total Recognised Gains and Losses

	£'000
Profit for the financial year	
Unrealised surplus on revaluation of properties	
	———
Total recognised gains and losses relating to the year	
	———

PART B

Data

You have been asked to assist in the production of a reconciliation between cash flows from operating activities and operating profit for the year ended 31 July 1996 for Poised Ltd. The financial statements of the company drafted for internal purposes are set out below, along with some further information relating to the reporting year:

Poised Ltd
Profit and loss account for the year ended 31 July 1996

		1996
		£000
Turnover		12,482
Opening stock	2,138	
Purchases	8,530	
Closing stock	(2,473)	
Cost of sales		8,195
Gross profit		4,287
Depreciation		1,347
Other expenses		841
Operating profit for the year		2,099
Interest paid		392
Profit before tax		1,707
Taxation on profit		562
Profit after tax		1,145
Ordinary dividend		360
Retained profit		785

Poised Ltd
Balance sheet as at 31 July 1996

	1996 £000	1995 £000
Fixed assets	6,867	6,739
Current assets		
Stocks	2,473	2,138
Trade debtors	1,872	1,653
Cash	1,853	149
	6,198	3,940
Current liabilities		
Trade creditors	1,579	1,238
Dividends payable	240	265
Taxation	562	477
	2,381	1,980
Net current assets	3,817	1,960
Long-term loan	4,200	3,800
	6,484	4,899
Capital and reserves		
Called up share capital	3,000	2,500
Share premium	400	100
Profit and loss account	3,084	2,299
	6,484	4,899

Further information:

(1)   No fixed assets were sold during the year.
(2)   All sales and purchases were on credit. Other expenses were paid for in cash.

Task 1.5

Provide a reconciliation between cash flows from operating activities and operating profit for the year ended 31 July 1996.

Note: You are NOT required to prepare a cash flow statement.

FOULKS*lynch*

UNIT 11 – SECTION 1 – JUNE 1997

You are reminded that competence must be achieved in each section. You should therefore attempt and aim to complete EVERY task in EACH section.

All workings should be shown.

You are advised to spend approximately 60 minutes on section 1.

This section is in two parts.

PART 1

Data

You have been assigned to assist in the preparation of the financial statements of Primavera Fashions Ltd for the year ended 31 March 1997. The company is a trading company which distributes fashion clothing. It has one subsidiary undertaking and one associated company.

Primavera Fashions Ltd recently engaged a financial accountant to manage a team of book-keepers. The book-keepers produced a correct extended trial balance of the company and gave it to the accountant so that he could draft the year end financial statements.

The book-keeping staff have reported that he appeared to have some difficulty with the task and, after several days, apparently gave up the task and has not been seen since. He left behind him a balance sheet and some pages of workings which appear to contain a number of errors.

There is to be a meeting of the Board next week at which the financial statements will be approved. You have been brought in to assist in the production of a corrected balance sheet and to advise the directors on matters concerning the year end accounts. The uncorrected balance sheet, the workings left by the financial accountant and the correct extended trial balance of Primavera Fashions Ltd on 31 March 1997 are set out on the following pages.

PRIMAVERA FASHIONS LTD
EXTENDED TRIAL BALANCE 31 MARCH 1997

	TRIAL BALANCE		ADJUSTMENTS		PROFIT & LOSS		BALANCE SHEET	
	Debit	Credit	Debit	Credit	Debit	Credit	Debit	Credit
	£000	£000	£000	£000	£000	£000	£000	£000
Profit and loss account		2,819						2,819
Land—cost	525						525	
Buildings—cost	1,000						1,000	
Fixtures and fittings—cost	1,170						1,170	
Motor vehicles—cost	1,520						1,520	
Office equipment	350						350	
Sales		12,604				12,604		
Buildings–accumulated depreciation		170		50				220
Fixtures & fittings–accumulated depreciation		229		117				346
Motor vehicles—accumulated depreciation		203		380				583
Office equipment–accumulated depreciation		73		70				143
Stock	1,097		1,178	1,178	1,097	1,178	1,178	
Interest charges	153				153			
Goodwill	128						128	
Trade debtors	857						857	
Purchases	7,604				7,604			
Interim dividend	160				160			
Investments	2,924						2,924	
Cash at bank	152						152	
Distribution costs	1,444		68	17	1,495			
Administrative expenses	1,441		36	20	1,457			
Depreciation–buildings			50		50			
Depreciation–fixtures & fittings			117		117			
Depreciation–motor vehicles			380		380			
Depreciation–office equipment			70		70			
Share capital		1,000						1,000
Provision for doubtful debts		61						61
Trade creditors		483						483
Accruals				104				104
Dividends from subsidiary undertaking		23				23		
Prepayments			37				37	
Dividends from associated company		10				10		
10% Debentures		1,500						1,500
Share premium		800						800
Revaluation reserve		550						550
Profit					1,232			1,232
	20,525	20,525	1,936	1,936	13,815	13,815	9,841	9,841

Primavera Fashions Ltd
Balance sheet as at 31 March 1997

	£'000	£'000
Fixed assets		
Intangible assets		128
Tangible assets		3,948
Investments		2,924
		7,000
Current assets		
Stocks	1,097	
Debtors	924	
Cash at bank and in hand	152	
	2,173	
Creditors: amounts falling due within one year	2,486	
Net current assets (liabilities)		(313)
Total assets less current liabilities		6,687
Creditors: amounts falling due after more than one year		800
		5,887
Capital and reserves		
Called up share capital		1,000
Revaluation reserve		550
Profit and loss account		4,051
		5,601

WORKINGS

1   Fixed assets:

	Cost £'000	Acc. Depn £'000	NBV £'000
Land	525	-	525
Buildings	1,000	50	950
Fixtures & fittings	1,170	117	1,053
Motor vehicles	1,520	380	1,140
Office equipment	350	70	280
	4,565	617	3,948

2   Debtors

	£'000	£'000
Trade debtors	857	
plus Accruals	104	
		961
less Prepayments		(37)
		924

3   Creditors (amounts falling due within one year):

	£'000
Trade creditors	483
Corporation tax payable	382
Dividends payable	60
Provision for doubtful debts	61
10% Debentures	1,500
	2,486

4   Creditors (amounts falling due after more than one year):

	£'000
Share premium	800

5   Profit and loss account:

	£'000
At 1/4/96	2,819
Retained profit for the year	1,232
At 31/3/97	4,051

You have also received the following additional information to assist you in your task:

(1)   The share capital consists of ordinary shares with a nominal value of 25 pence. The company has paid an interim dividend during the year and the directors have recommended a final dividend of 6 pence per share, which has not been provided for in the extended trial balance.

(2)   The tax charge for the year has been estimated at £382,000.

(3)   The investments shown on the extended trial balance relate to long-term investment in the shares of one subsidiary undertaking and one associated company.

Task 1.1

On the answer sheet below, redraft the company balance sheet for Primavera Fashions Ltd as at 31 March 1997. Make any changes that you feel to be necessary to the balance sheet and workings provided by the financial accountant using the information contained in the extended trial balance for the year ended 31 March 1997 and the additional information provided above.

Note: You are NOT required to produce a profit and loss account.

Answer sheet for Task 1.1

PROFORMA BALANCE SHEET (FORMAT 1)

	£	£
Fixed assets		
Intangible assets		
Tangible assets		
Investments		
		____
Current assets		
Stocks		
Debtors		
Investments		
Cash at bank and in hand		
	____	
Creditors: amounts falling due within one year		
	____	
Net current assets (liabilities)		
		____
Total assets *less* current liabilities		
Creditors: amounts falling due after more than one year		
Provisions for liabilities and charges		
		____
		____
Capital and reserves		
Called up share capital		
Share premium account		
Revaluation reserve		
Profit and loss account		
		____
		____

PART B

Data

The directors of Primavera Fashions Ltd have asked you to prepare some answers to certain questions they have relating to the year end financial statements that are due to be considered at next week's meeting of the Board.

The directors are uncertain as to how the balance on the share premium account arose and how it can be used.

The directors have just learned that one of their trade debtors has gone into liquidation owing them £24,000. The liquidator has informed them that it is likely that there will be no assets available to pay off creditors and they wonder whether this will have any effect on the financial statements for the year ended 31 March 1997.

The directors are also uncertain as to the accounting treatment of their investment in shares of an associated company, Spring Ltd. Primavera Fashions Ltd purchased a 35% interest in the company for £400,000 in 1995 when the total net assets of the company amounted to £800,000. (There was no goodwill shown in the associated company's own balance sheet.) Since acquisition Spring Ltd has made profits amounting to £200,000 and, as at 31 March 1997, the total net assets of the company amounted to £1,000,000.

Task 1.2

Reply to the following questions from the directors. Where appropriate, justify your answers by reference to company law, accounting concepts and applicable accounting standards.

(1)　(a)　How did the balance on the "share premium" arise?

　　　(b)　Can it be used to pay dividends to the shareholders?

　　　(c)　Give one use of the share premium account.

(2)　Will the fact that the debtor went into liquidation after the end of the financial year have any impact upon the financial statements for the year ended 31 March 1997?

(3)　(a)　At what amount will the investment in Spring Ltd be shown in the group balance sheet as at 31 March 1997?

　　　(b)　Show how the total investment in Spring Ltd will be analysed in the notes to the group financial statements.

Assume that goodwill arising on acquisition is amortised over four years with a full year's charge in the year of acquisition.

UNIT 11 – SECTION 1 – DECEMBER 1997

You are reminded that competence must be achieved in each section. You should therefore attempt and aim to complete EVERY task in EACH section.

All workings should be shown.

You are advised to spend approximately 35 minutes on section 1.

Data

You have been assigned to assist in the preparation of the financial statements of McTaggart Ltd for the year ended 30 September 1997. The company markets and distributes a board game called 'The Absolute' to a worldwide market from premises in Cambridge. You have been provided with the extended trial balance of McTaggart Ltd on 30 September 1997 which is set out below.

McTAGGART LTD
EXTENDED TRIAL BALANCE 30 SEPTEMBER 1997

	TRIAL BALANCE		ADJUSTMENTS		PROFIT & LOSS		BALANCE SHEET	
	Debit	Credit	Debit	Credit	Debit	Credit	Debit	Credit
	£'000	£'000	£'000	£'000	£'000	£'000	£'000	£'000
Trade creditors		1,891						1,891
Profit and loss account		2,159						2,159
Interim dividend	240				240			
Land–cost	1,820						1,820	
Buildings–cost	2,144						2,144	
Fixtures and fittings–cost	1,704						1,704	
Motor vehicles–cost	1,931						1,931	
Office equipment–cost	236						236	
Trade debtors	2,191						2,191	
Interest charges	166				166			
Sales		15,373				15,373		
Accruals				145				145
Provision for doubtful debts		85						85
Distribution costs	1,951		82		2,033			
Administrative expenses	1,499		63		1,562			
Stock	2,034		4,731	4,731	2,034	4,731	4,731	
Cash at bank and in hand	1,086						1,086	
Long-term loan		2,750						2,750
Returns inwards	95				95			
Returns outwards		157				157		
Buildings–accumulated depreciation		872						872
Fixtures and fittings–accumulated depreciation		898						898
Motor vehicles–accumulated depreciation		1,027						1,027
Office equipment–accumulated depreciation		88						88
Ordinary share capital		3,000						3,000
Purchases	11,166				11,166			
Prepayments	37						37	
Profit					2,965			2,965
	28,300	28,300	4,876	4,876	20,261	20,261	15,880	15,880

You have been given the following further information:

- The authorised share capital of the business, all of which has been issued, consists of ordinary shares with a nominal value of £1.

- Depreciation has been calculated on all of the fixed assets of the business and has already been entered on a monthly basis into the distribution costs and administration expenses ledger balances as shown on the extended trial balance.

- The corporation tax charge for the year has been calculated as £1,113,000.

- The company has paid an interim dividend of 8p per share during the year but has not provided for the proposed final dividend of 12p per share.

- Interest on the long-term loan has not been paid for the last month of the year. The interest charge for September 1997 amounts to £26,000.

Task 1.1

Taking into account the further information provided, draft on the answer sheet that follows, a profit and loss account for the year ended 30 September 1997 and a balance sheet as at that date.

Notes:

(1)   You must show any workings relevant to understanding your calculation of figures appearing in the financial statements.

(2)   You are not required to produce journal entries for any adjustments to the figures in the extended trial balance that are required.

(3)   Ignore any effect of these adjustments on the tax charge for the year as given above.

Answer sheet for Task 1.1

PROFORMA PROFIT AND LOSS ACCOUNT
(FORMAT 1 AS SUPPLEMENTED BY FRS 3)

	£	£
Turnover		
Continuing operations		
Acquisitions	———	
Discontinued operations	———	
Cost of sales		
		———
Gross profit (or loss)		
Distribution costs		
Administrative expenses		
Other operating income		———
Operating profit (or loss)		
Continuing operations		
Acquisitions	———	
Discontinued operations	———	
Profit (or loss) on disposal of discontinued operations		
Income from shares in group undertakings		
Income from participating interests		
Income from other fixed asset investments		
Other interest receivable and similar income		
Amounts written off investments		———
Profit (or loss) on ordinary activities before interest		
Interest payable and similar charges		———
Profit (or loss) on ordinary activities before taxation		
Tax on profit (or loss) on ordinary activities		
Extraordinary items		———
Profit (or loss) for the financial year		
Dividends		———
Retained profit for the financial year		———

PROFORMA BALANCE SHEET (FORMAT 1)

£   £

Fixed assets
  Intangible assets
  Tangible assets
  Investments

                                _____

Current assets
  Stocks
  Debtors
  Investments
  Cash at bank and in hand

                                _____

Creditors: amounts falling due within one year

                                _____

Net current assets (liabilities)

                                        _____

Total assets *less* current liabilities
Creditors: amounts falling due after more than one year
Provisions for liabilities and charges

                                        _____

                                        _____

Capital and reserves
  Called up share capital
  Share premium account
  Revaluation reserve
  Profit and loss account

                                        _____

                                        _____

UNIT 11 – SECTION 1 – DECEMBER 1998

You are reminded that competence must be achieved in each section. You should therefore attempt and aim to complete EVERY task in EACH section, using the answer booklet provided.

All workings should be shown in the answer booklet section.

A pro-forma for journal entries and a pro-forma profit and loss account (Companies Act format 1 as supplemented by FRS 3) are provided in your answer booklet section for your use.

You are advised to spend approximately 55 minutes on Section 1, 70 minutes on Section 2 and 55 minutes on Section 3.

SECTION 1

You are advised to spend approximately 55 minutes on this section.
This section is in two parts.

PART A

Task 1.1

State one type of profit-making and one type of public sector or not-for-profit organisation.

For each type of organisation:

(a)   give one example of an external user of the financial statements, *and*

(b)   describe one type of decision which would be made by the users with the assistance of the financial statements of the organisation.

Task 1.2

The accounting equation is often expressed as:

$$\text{ASSETS} - \text{LIABILITIES} = \text{OWNERSHIP INTEREST}$$

(a)   Explain what each of the terms 'assets', 'liabilities' and 'ownership interest' means.

(b)   Identify, in general terms only, the balances that would appear in the 'ownership interest' section of the balance sheet of one profit-making and one public sector or not-for-profit organisation.

PART B

Data

Bimbridge Hospitals Trust has just lost its supplier of bandages. The company that has been supplying it for the last five years has gone into liquidation. The Trust is concerned to select a new supplier which it can rely on to supply it with its needs for the foreseeable future. You have been asked by the Trust managers to analyse the financial statements of a potential supplier of bandages. You have obtained the latest financial statements of the company, in summary form, which are set out below.

Patch Ltd
Summary Profit and Loss Accounts
for the year ended 30 September 1998

	1998	1997
	£'000	£'000
Turnover	2,300	2,100
Cost of sales	1,035	945
Gross profit	1,265	1,155
Expenses	713	693
Net profit before interest and tax	552	462

Patch Ltd
Summary Balance Sheets
as at 30 September 1998

	1998		1997	
	£'000	£'000	£'000	£'000
Fixed assets		4,764		5,418
Current assets				
Stocks	522		419	
Debtors	406		356	
Cash	117		62	
	1,045		837	
Current liabilities				
Trade creditors	305		254	
Taxation	170		211	
	475		465	
Net current assets		570		372
Long-term loan		(1,654)		(2,490)
		3,680		3,300
Share capital		1,100		1,000
Share premium		282		227
Profit and loss account		2,298		2,073
		3,680		3,300

You have also obtained the industry average ratios which are as follows:

	1998	1997
Return on capital employed	9.6%	9.4%
Net profit percentage	21.4%	21.3%
Quick ratio/acid test	1.0:1	0.9:1
Gearing (Debt/Capital Employed)	36%	37%

Task 1.3

In the answer booklet section, prepare a report for the managers of Bimbridge Hospitals Trust recommending whether or not to use Patch Ltd as a supplier of bandages. Use the information contained in the financial statements of Patch Ltd and the industry averages supplied.

Your answer should:

- comment on the company's profitability, liquidity and financial position;
- consider how the company has changed over the two years;
- include a comparison with the industry as a whole.

The report should include calculation of the following ratios for the two years:

(i)   Return on capital employed;
(ii)   Net profit percentage;
(iii)   Quick ratio/acid test;
(iv)   Gearing.

UNIT 11 – SECTION 2 – JUNE 1996

You are reminded that competence must be achieved in each section. You should therefore attempt and aim to complete EVERY task in EACH section.

Note: You are advised to spend approximately 54 minutes on section 2.

Data

The directors of Dowango Ltd have asked to have a meeting with you. They are intending to ask the bank for a further long-term loan to enable them to purchase a company which has retail outlets. The directors have identified two possible companies to take over and they intend to purchase the whole of the share capital of one of the two targeted companies. The directors have obtained the latest financial statements of the two companies, in summary form, and have also sent you a letter with some questions that they would like you to answer. The financial statements and the letter are set out below.

Summary profit and loss accounts

	Company A £'000	Company B £'000
Turnover	800	2,100
Cost of sales	440	1,050
Gross profit	360	1,050
Expenses	160	630
Net profit before interest and tax	200	420

Summary balance sheets

	Company A £'000	Company B £'000
Fixed assets	620	1,640
Net current assets	380	1,160
Long-term loan	(400)	(1,100)
	600	1,700
Share capital and reserves	600	1,700

DOWANGO LTD

Dear AAT student,

In preparation for discussions about a possible loan to Dowango Ltd, the bank has asked to see the latest financial statements of Dowango Ltd. We wish to ensure that the financial statements show the company in the best light. In particular, we wish to ensure that the assets of the business are shown at their proper value. We would like to discuss with you the following issues:

(1)   The fixed assets of our company are undervalued. We have received a professional valuation of the land and buildings which shows that they are worth more than is stated in our financial statements. The land has a current market value of £641,000 and the buildings are valued at £558,000.

(2)   The investments are recorded in our trial balance at cost. We realise that the market value of the investment is less than the cost, but since we have not yet sold it, we have not made a loss on it and so we should continue to show it at cost.

(3)   Stocks are recorded in our balance sheet at cost. Most of our stock is worth more than this as we could sell it for more than we paid for it. Only a few items would sell for less than we paid for them. We have worked out the real value of our stock as follows:

	Cost £000	Sales price £000
Undervalued items	340	460
Overvalued items	25	15
Total	365	475

We have set out a number of questions we would like answered at our meeting in an appendix to this letter. We would also like you to advise us at that meeting on the profitability and return on capital of the two companies targeted for takeover (whose financial statements we have already sent to you) and on the reporting implications if we purchase one of the companies.

Yours sincerely,

The directors

Task 2.1

The questions from the appendix to the directors' letter are shown below. Write a memo to the directors answering these questions, which relate to the financial statements of Dowango Ltd. Explain your answers, where relevant, by reference to company law, accounting concepts and applicable accounting standards.

(a)   (i)   Can we show the land and buildings at valuation rather than cost?

(ii)   If we did so, how would the valuation of land and buildings be reflected in the financial statements?

(iii)   Would revaluing the land and buildings have any effect upon the gearing ratio of the company and would this assist us in our attempt to get a loan from the bank?

(iv)   What effect would a revaluation have upon the future results of the company?

(b)   Can we continue to show the investments at cost?

(c)   What is the best value for stock that we can show in our balance sheet in the light of the information we have given you about sales price?

Task 2.2

Advise the directors as to which of the two companies targeted for takeover is the more profitable and which one provides the higher return on capital. Your answer should include calculation of the following ratios:

(i)   return on capital employed;
(ii)   net profit margin;
(iii)   asset turnover.

You should also calculate and comment on at least **one** further ratio of your choice, for which you have sufficient information, which would be relevant to determining which of the companies is more profitable or provides the greater return on capital.

Task 2.3

Advise the directors as to whether Dowango Ltd would have any further reporting requirements in the future as a result of the purchase of shares in one of the companies targeted for takeover.

UNIT 11 – SECTION 2 – DECEMBER 1996

You are reminded that competence must be achieved in each section. You should therefore attempt and aim to complete EVERY task in EACH section.

You are advised to spend approximately 45 minutes on section 2.

Data

You have been asked to assist in the preparation of the consolidated accounts of the Thomas Group. Set out below are the balance sheets of Thomas Ltd and James Ltd for the year ended 30 September 1996:

Balance sheet as at 30 September 1996

	Thomas Ltd £'000	James Ltd £'000
Fixed assets	13,022	3,410
Investment in James Ltd	3,760	-
Current assets		
Stocks	6,682	2,020
Debtors	5,526	852
Cash	273	58
	12,481	2,930
Current liabilities		
Trade creditors	3,987	507
Taxation	834	173
	4,821	680
Net current assets	7,660	2,250
Total assets less current liabilities	24,442	5,660
Long-term loan	8,000	1,500
	16,442	4,160
Capital and reserves		
Called up share capital	5,000	1,000
Share premium	2,500	400
Profit and loss account	8,942	2,760
	16,442	4,160

You have been given the following further information:

(1)   The share capital of both Thomas Ltd and James Ltd consists of ordinary shares of £1 each. There have been no changes to the balances during the year.

(2)   Thomas Ltd acquired 800,000 shares in James Ltd on 30 September 1995 at a cost of £3,760,000.

(3)   At 30 September 1995 the balance on the profit and loss account of James Ltd was £2,000,000.

(4)   The fair value of the fixed assets of James Ltd at 30 September 1995 was £3,910,000. The revaluation has not been reflected in the books of James Ltd.

◈ FOULKS*lynch*

(5)   Goodwill arising on consolidation is to be capitalised and amortised over 4 years from the date of acquisition.

Task 2.1

On the answer sheet below, prepare a consolidated balance sheet for Thomas Ltd and its subsidiary undertaking as at 30 September 1996.

PROFORMA BALANCE SHEET (FORMAT 1)

	£	£
Fixed assets		
Intangible assets		
Tangible assets		
Investments		
	____	
Current assets		
Stocks		
Debtors		
Investments		
Cash at bank and in hand		
	____	
Creditors: amounts falling due within one year		
	____	
Net current assets (liabilities)		
		____
Total assets *less* current liabilities		
Creditors: amounts falling due after more than one year		
Provisions for liabilities and charges		
		____
		____
Capital and reserves		
Called up share capital		
Share premium account		
Revaluation reserve		
Profit and loss account		
Minority interest		
		____
		____

UNIT 11 – SECTION 2 – JUNE 1997

You are reminded that competence must be achieved in each section. You should therefore attempt and aim to complete EVERY task in EACH section.

All workings should be shown.

You are advised to spend approximately 50 minutes on section 2.

Data

Botticelli Ltd is a trading company that sells carpets to retail outlets. The shareholders of Botticelli Ltd have some questions about the profitability and liquidity of the company and about how cash flows from operating activities can be reconciled to operating profit. The profit and loss account and balance sheet produced for internal purposes are set out below.

Botticelli Ltd
Profit and loss account for the year ended 31 December 1996

	£'000	1996 £'000	£'000	1995 £'000
Turnover		2,963		1,736
Opening stock	341		201	
Purchases	1,712		1,097	
Closing stock	(419)		(341)	
Cost of sales		1,634		957
Gross profit		1,329		779
Depreciation		247		103
Other expenses		588		334
Profit on the sale of fixed assets		15		-
Operating profit for the year		509		342
Interest paid		78		26
Profit before tax		431		316
Taxation on profit		138		111
Profit after tax		293		205
Ordinary dividend		48		22
Retained profit		245		183

Botticelli Ltd
Balance sheet as at 31 December 1996

	1996 £'000	1995 £'000
Fixed assets	2,800	1,013
Current assets		
Stocks	419	341
Debtors	444	381
Cash	-	202
	863	924
Current liabilities		
Trade creditors	322	197
Dividends payable	48	41
Taxation	158	103
Bank overdraft	194	-
	722	341
Net current assets	141	583
Total assets less current liabilities	2,941	1,596
Long-term loan	970	320
	1,971	1,276
Capital and reserves		
Called up share capital	400	200
Share premium	250	—
Profit and loss account	1,321	1,076
	1,971	1,276

Task 2.1

Prepare a report to the shareholders about the profitability and liquidity of Botticelli Ltd for the two years 1995 and 1996. Your report should include:

(i)   calculation of the following ratios for the two years:

- return on capital employed;
- gross profit ratio;
- net profit ratio;
- current ratio;
- quick ratio (also called acid test);

(ii)   comments on the changes in the ratios from 1995 to 1996.

Task 2.2

Prepare a reconciliation between cash flows from operating activities and operating profit for the year-end 31 December 1996.

UNIT 11 – SECTION 2 – DECEMBER 1997

You are reminded that competence must be achieved in each section. You should therefore attempt and aim to complete EVERY task in EACH section.

All workings should be shown.

You are advised to spend approximately 75 minutes on section 2.

Data

Due to the success of the board game 'The Absolute', McTaggart Ltd is thinking of expanding its operations. It has identified another company, Hegel Ltd, which also distributes board games, as a possible target for take-over. The directors have obtained a set of financial statements of the company for the last two years; these have been prepared for internal purposes. Hegel Ltd's year-end is 30 September.

The directors have established that if they had purchased 80% of the ordinary share capital of Hegel Ltd at 30 September 1997 they would have had to pay £3,300,000. The net assets of Hegel Ltd are shown in the balance sheet at their fair values, except for the fixed assets which have a fair value at 30 September 1997 of £6,672,000.

The directors have a number of questions relating to the company and to the possible take-over which they would like you to answer. The financial statements for Hegel Ltd are set out below.

Hegel Ltd
Profit and loss account for the year ended 30 September 1997

	£'000	1997 £'000	£'000	1996 £'000
Turnover		6,995		3,853
Opening stock	681		432	
Purchases	4,245		2,561	
Closing stock	(729)		(681)	
Cost of sales		4,197		2,312
Gross profit		2,798		1,541
Depreciation		971		311
Other expenses		593		415
Profit on the sale of fixed assets		20		-
Operating profit for the year		1,254		815
Interest paid		302		28
Profit before tax		952		787
Taxation on profit		333		276
Profit after tax		619		511
Ordinary dividend		144		120
Retained profit		475		391

Hegel Ltd
Balance sheet as at 30 September 1997

	1997 £'000	1996 £'000
Fixed assets	6,472	2,075
Current assets		
Stocks	729	681
Debtors	574	469
Cash	-	320
	1,303	1,470
Current liabilities		
Trade creditors	340	424
Dividends payable	144	120
Taxation	333	276
Bank overdraft	158	-
	975	820
Net current assets	328	650
Long-term loan	3,350	350
	3,450	2,375
Capital and reserves		
Called up share capital	1,200	1,000
Share premium	400	-
Profit and loss account	1,850	1,375
	3,450	2,375

Further information

- Fixed assets costing £156,000 with accumulated depreciation of £83,000 were sold in 1997 for £93,000.

- All sales and purchases were on credit. Other expenses were paid for in cash.

Task 2.1

Provide a reconciliation between cash flows from operating activities and operating profit for the year ended 30 September 1997.

Task 2.2

Using the answer sheet that follows, prepare a cash flow statement for Hegel Ltd, for the year ended 30 September 1997, in accordance with the requirements of FRS 1 (Revised).

PROFORMA CASH FLOW STATEMENT AS PER FRS 1 (REVISED)
(INDIRECT METHOD)

£

Net cash inflow from operating activities

Returns on investments and servicing of finance

Taxation

Capital expenditure

_____

Equity dividends paid

_____

Management of liquid resources

Financing

_____

Increase/(decrease) in cash

_____

Task 2.3

Calculate the goodwill on consolidation that would have arisen on acquisition if McTaggart Ltd had purchased 80% of the shares in Hegel Ltd on 30 September 1997.

Note: You are not required to produce a consolidated balance sheet for the group.

Task 2.4

Prepare a report for the directors of McTaggart Ltd which covers the relevant calculations and questions set out below

(a)   Calculate the current and quick ratios (also known as the "acid test") of Hegel Ltd for the two years. Using this information and that provided in the cash flow statement state how the liquidity of Hegel Ltd has changed from 1996 to 1997.

(b)   Calculate the gearing ratio for Hegel Ltd for 1996 and 1997 and comment on the results. Explain whether the level of borrowings in Hegel Ltd would have any impact on the level of gearing in the group accounts of McTaggart Ltd.

(c)   Set out the permitted accounting treatments for the goodwill arising on consolidation in the group accounts of McTaggart Ltd.

Note: You are not required to attempt to calculate the gearing ratio of the group.

UNIT 11 – SECTION 2 – DECEMBER 1998

You are advised to spend approximately 70 minutes on this section. This section is in two parts.

PART A

Data

You have been asked to assist in the preparation of the financial statements of Fun Ltd for the year ended 30 September 1998. The company is a distributor of children's games. You have been provided with the extended trial balance of Fun Ltd as at 30 September 1998 which is set out below.

Fun Ltd
Extended trial balance as at 30 September 1998

DESCRIPTION	TRIAL BALANCE	
	DEBIT	CREDIT
	£'000	£'000
Trade debtors	2,863	
Bank overdraft		316
Interest	300	
Profit and loss account		3,811
Provision for doubtful debts		114
Distribution costs	2,055	
Administration expenses	1,684	
Returns inwards	232	
Sales		14,595
Land–cost	2,293	
Buildings–cost	2,857	
Fixtures and fittings–cost	1,245	
Motor vehicles–cost	2,524	
Office equipment–cost	872	
Stock	1,893	
Purchases	6,671	
Interim dividend	480	
Trade creditors		804
Buildings–accumulated depreciation		261
Fixtures and fittings–accumulated depreciation		309
Motor vehicles–accumulated depreciation		573
Office equipment–accumulated depreciation		184
Prepayments	63	
Carriage inwards	87	
Returns outwards		146
Accruals		
Investments	2,244	
Loan		3,600
Ordinary share capital		2,000
Share premium		1,300
Revaluation reserve		350
Profit		
Total	**28,363**	**28,363**

ADJUSTMENTS		PROFIT AND LOSS		BALANCE SHEET	
DEBIT	CREDIT	DEBIT	CREDIT	DEBIT	CREDIT
£'000	£'000	£'000	£'000	£'000	£'000
				2,863	
					316
		300			
					3,811
					114
614		2,669			
358		2,042			
		232			
			14,595		
				2,293	
				2,857	
				1,245	
				2,524	
				872	
2,041	2,041	1,893	2,041	2,041	
		6,671			
		480			
					804
	51				312
	124				433
	603				1,176
	81				265
				63	
		87			
			146		
	113				113
				2,244	
					3,600
					2,000
					1,300
					350
		2,408			2,408
3,013	**3,013**	**16,782**	**16,782**	**17,002**	**17,002**

◈ FOULKS*lynch*

You have been given the following further information:

- The share capital of the business consists of ordinary shares with a nominal value of 25 pence.

- The company has paid an interim dividend of 6 pence per share this year and is proposing a final dividend of 10 pence per share.

- Depreciation has been calculated on all of the fixed assets of the business and has already been entered into the distribution costs and administrative expenses ledger balances as shown on the extended trial balance.

- The corporation tax charge for the year has been calculated as £972,000.

- Interest on the loan has been paid for the first eleven months of the year only, but no interest has been paid or charged for the final month of the year. The loan carries a rate of interest of 8% per annum of the balance outstanding on the loan.

Answer tasks 2.1–2.5 in the answer booklet section provided.

Task 2.1

In the answer booklet section, make any additional adjustments you feel to be necessary to the balances in the extended trial balance as a result of the matters set out in the further information above. Using the pro-forma provided, set out your adjustments in the form of journal entries.

Note:

(1)   Narratives and dates are not required.

(2)   Ignore any effect of these adjustments on the tax charge for the year as given above.

Task 2.2

Using the pro-forma profit and loss account in the answer booklet section, and taking account of any adjustments made in Task 2.1, draft a profit and loss account for the year ended 30 September 1998 using Format 1 in accordance with the Companies Act 1985 as supplemented by FRS 3 'Reporting Financial Performance'.

Note: You are **NOT** required to produce notes to the accounts.

Data

The directors are interested in expanding operations next year. They wish to be clear about the constituents of the equity on the balance sheet and on the impact that leasing equipment, rather than purchasing equipment, might have on the company's balance sheet. They would like you to attend the next meeting of the Board.

Task 2.3

Prepare notes to bring to the Board meeting dealing with the following matters.

(a)   How the balances on the share premium and the revaluation reserve arose;

(b)   The recommendation of one of the directors is to lease the assets as he says that this means that the asset can be kept off the balance sheet. Comment on this recommendation.

PART B

Data

The directors of Fun Ltd have a number of questions relating to the financial statements of their recently acquired subsidiary undertaking, Games Ltd. Fun Ltd acquired 75% of the ordinary share capital of Games Ltd on 30 September 1998 for £2,244,000. The fair value of the fixed assets in Games Ltd as at 30 September 1998 was £2,045,000. The directors have provided you with the balance sheet of Games Ltd as at 30 September 1998 along with some further information:

Games Ltd
Balance sheet as at 30 September 1998

	1998 £'000	1997 £'000
Fixed assets	1,845	1,615
Current assets		
Stocks	918	873
Trade debtors	751	607
Cash	23	87
	1,692	1,567
Current liabilities		
Trade creditors	583	512
Dividends payable	52	48
Taxation	62	54
	697	614
Net current assets	995	953
Long-term loan	560	420
	2,280	2,148
Capital and reserves		
Called up share capital	1,000	1,000
Share premium	100	100
Profit and loss account	1,180	1,048
	2,280	2,148

Further information:

- No fixed assets were sold during the year. The depreciation charge for the year amounted to £277,000.

- All sales and purchases were on credit. Other expenses were paid for in cash.

- The profit on ordinary activities before taxation was £246,000. Interest of £56,000 was charged in the year.

Task 2.4

Provide a reconciliation between cash flows from operating activities and operating profit for Games Ltd for the year ended 30 September 1998.

Note: You are **NOT** required to prepare a cash flow statement.

Task 2.5

Prepare notes to take to the Board meeting to answer the following questions of the directors:

(a)   what figure for the minority interest would appear in the consolidated balance sheet of Fun Ltd as at 30 September 1998?

(b)   where in the balance sheet would the minority interest be disclosed?

(c)   what is a 'minority interest'?

Task 2.1

Pro-forma Journal Entries

	Debit £'000	Credit £'000

Workings for Task 2.1

Workings for Task 2.1

Task 2.2

Pro-forma Profit and Loss Account
(Format 1 as supplemented by FRS 3)

	£'000	£'000
Turnover		
Continuing operations		
Acquisitions	_____	
Discontinued operations	_____	
Cost of sales		_____
Gross profit (or loss)		
Distribution costs		
Administrative expenses		
Other operating income		
Operating profit (or loss)		
Continuing operations		
Acquisitions	_____	
Discontinued operations	_____	
Profit (or loss) on disposal of discontinued operations		_____
Income from shares in group undertakings		
Income from participating interests		
Income from other fixed asset investments		
Other interest receivable and similar income		
Amounts written off investments		_____
Profit (or loss) on ordinary activities before interest		
Interest payable and similar charges		_____
Profit (or loss) on ordinary activities before taxation		
Tax on profit (or loss) on ordinary activities		_____
Profit (or loss) on ordinary activities after taxation		_____
Extraordinary items		
Profit (or loss) for the financial year		
Dividends		_____
Retained profit for the financial year		_____

Workings for Task 2.2

UNIT 11 – SECTION 3 – JUNE 1996

You are reminded that competence must be achieved in each section. You should therefore attempt and aim to complete EVERY task in EACH section.

Note: You are advised to spend approximately 27 minutes on Section 3.

Data

You have been asked to advise Jonathan Brown, a sole trader, on the accounting treatment of certain transactions which he feels might affect his financial statements for the year ended 31 December 1995. The matters on which he would like your advice are set out below:

(1)   The business paid for an advertising campaign during the year at a cost of £2,800. It is estimated by Jonathan Brown that this will lead to an overall increase in sales of 15%. Half of this increase was achieved in 1995 and the other half is expected to be achieved in 1996.

(2)   Jonathan Brown took stock costing £500 from the business at the end of the year for his own use. He removed the stock on 31 December 1995 after the year-end stock count had taken place. No adjustment was made to the stock balance to take account of this action.

(3)   During the year a word processor, which had a written down value of £850, was accidentally dropped out of the window during an office party and destroyed. The asset has been written out of the books of the business. The insurance company has refused to meet the cost of the loss. The solicitors of the business are currently pursuing the matter through the courts and say that the company has a reasonable chance of success.

(4)   Jonathan Brown has put his own house up as security for a loan made by the bank to his business. The loan was made specifically for the business and not for the personal use of Jonathan Brown.

Task 3.1

Advise Jonathan Brown on the accounting treatment of these transactions in his financial statements for the year ended 31 December 1995. Explain your treatment, where relevant, by reference to accounting concepts and generally accepted accounting principles.

UNIT 11 – SECTION 3 – DECEMBER 1996

You are reminded that competence must be achieved in each section. You should therefore attempt and aim to complete EVERY task in EACH section.

You are advised to spend approximately 70 minutes on section 3.

Data

You have been asked by Pride and Co, a partnership, to assist in the preparation of the financial statements for the year ended 31 October 1996 and to give advice on partnership matters. From your initial discussions with the book-keeper you have constructed a summarised profit and loss account which is set out below:

Pride and Co
Profit and loss account for the year ended 31 October 1996

	£
Sales	600,000
Cost of sales	360,000
Gross profit	240,000
Expenses	150,000
Net profit	90,000

You have obtained the following information about the partnership of Pride and Co:

(1)   The partners of Pride and Co are Jane, Elizabeth and Lydia. They share profits and losses in the following proportions:

Jane	five-tenths
Elizabeth	three-tenths
Lydia	two-tenths

(2)   Jane receives a salary of £15,000, Elizabeth a salary of £10,000 and Lydia a salary of £5,000.

(3)   Partners receive interest on their capital accounts of 8% per annum on the balance outstanding at the end of the year. No interest is to be allowed on the balances of current accounts.

(4)   The balances on the capital and current accounts at 1 November 1995 were as follows:

	Capital £	Current £
Jane	25,000	5,700 CR
Elizabeth	22,000	4,200 CR
Lydia	3,000	2,300 DR

There were no injections or withdrawals of capital by the partners during the year to 31 October 1996.

(5)   Jane, in addition to her balance on the capital account, has loaned the partnership £10,000. She is entitled to interest on this loan at a rate of 10% per annum.

(6)   The partners' drawings during the year were as follows:

	£
Jane	15,600
Elizabeth	14,700
Lydia	18,900

The partners have been negotiating with Asmah, a sole trader, with a view to admitting her as a partner on 1 November 1996. If Asmah is admitted into the partnership she will bring into it as her capital contribution the net assets of her business at a fair value of £35,000. She will bring with her the existing customers of her business. Her summarised profit and loss account for the year ended 31 October 1996 is set out below:

Asmah
Profit and loss account for the year ended 31 October 1996

	£
Sales	200,000
Cost of sales	110,000
Gross profit	90,000
Expenses	70,000
Net profit	20,000

If Asmah is admitted into the partnership an adjustment for goodwill, which is currently not shown as an asset in the books of the partnership, is to be made in the books of Pride and Co.

Goodwill has been valued at £60,000.

No account for goodwill will be maintained in the books of the new partnership. Any adjustment affecting the partners is to be made in the capital accounts of the partners.

An adjustment will have to be made in order to reflect the fair values of the assets in the existing partnership. The fixed assets of the partnership are currently included in the books of the partnership at a net book value of £88,000. The current market value of the assets is £128,000. Any adjustment affecting the partners is to be made in the capital accounts of the partners.

In the new partnership the profit sharing ratios will be as follows:

Jane	five-twelfths
Elizabeth	three-twelfths
Lydia	two-twelfths
Asmah	two-twelfths

Task 3.1

Draw up the appropriation account for the partnership of Pride and Co for the year ended 31 October 1996.

Task 3.2

Write a report to the existing partners of Pride and Co covering the following matters:

(a)   Using appropriate profitability ratios, compare the performance of the existing partnership of Pride and Co with that of Asmah. On the basis of your calculations and any other matters you consider relevant, advise the existing partners on the desirability of admitting Asmah into the partnership.

Note: You can assume that a similar level of sales, cost of sales and expenses will be achieved in the next financial year.

(b)   What legal formalities would you recommend as a result of the admission of a new partner into the business?

(c)   Show what entries would have to be made in the capital accounts of the partnership if, taking into account your advice, the partnership were to go ahead and admit Asmah into the partnership on 1 November 1996.

UNIT 11 – SECTION 3 – JUNE 1997

You are reminded that competence must be achieved in each section. You should therefore attempt and aim to complete EVERY task in EACH section.

All workings should be shown.

You are advised to spend approximately 45 minutes on Section 3.

Data

You have been asked by Sandro Venus to assist in the preparation of the year end financial statements of his business. He is a sole trader who runs a trading business which specialises in ornaments decorated with sea shells. The extended trial balance as at 31 March 1997 is set out on the following page.

SANDRO VENUS
EXTENDED TRIAL BALANCE 31 MARCH 1997

	TRIAL BALANCE		ADJUSTMENTS		PROFIT & LOSS		BALANCE SHEET	
	Debit	Credit	Debit	Credit	Debit	Credit	Debit	Credit
	£	£	£	£	£	£	£	£
Wages and National Insurance Contribution	28,996		348		29,344			
Capital as at 1 April 1996		83,696						83,696
Postage and stationery	524				524			
Accumulated depreciation–Motor vehicles		8,125		6,094				14,219
Accumulated depreciation–Office equipment		1,375		1,375				2,750
Accumulated depreciation–Fixtures & fittings		2,780		2,780				5,560
Purchases	103,742				103,742			
Trade creditors		17,725						17,725
Carriage inwards	923				923			
Motor vehicles (cost)	32,500						32,500	
Office equipment (cost)	13,745						13,745	
Fixtures & fittings (cost)	27,800						27,800	
Sales		187,325				187,325		
Returns outwards		1,014				1,014		
Trade debtors	18,740						18,740	
Drawings	14,400						14,400	
Depreciation–Motor vehicles			6,094		6,094			
Depreciation–Office equipment			1,375		1,375			
Depreciation–Fixtures & fittings			2,780		2,780			
Prepayments			320				320	
Accruals				1,131				1,131
Stock	27,931		30,229	30,229	27,931	30,229	30,229	
Returns inwards	1,437				1,437			
Cash at bank	9,473						9,473	
Cash in hand	166						166	
Bank deposit interest		972				972		
Carriage outwards	657				657			
Rent, rates and insurance	8,041			320	7,721			
Bad debts	830				830			
Discounts allowed	373				373			
Bank charges	693				693			
Telephone	3,524		783		4,307			
Lighting and heating	3,755				3,755			
Motor expenses	4,762				4,762			
Profit					22,292			22,292
	303,012	303,012	41,929	41,929	219,540	219,540	147,373	147,373

◆ **FOULKS**lynch

You are given the following further information:

(1)   A general provision for doubtful debts is to be set up at 5% of the year end debtors' balance.

(2)   During the year Sandro Venus took goods which had cost £500 for his own personal use in decorating his flat.

(3)   At the end of the year, one of the motor vehicles which had cost £5,500 and on which there was accumulated depreciation of £2,400 was sold for £3,500. Payment for the vehicle sold has not yet been received by Sandro Venus and no entry to reflect the sale has been made in the extended trial balance.

Task 3.1

Make any additional adjustments you feel necessary to the balances in the extended trial balance as a result of the matters set out in the further information above. Set out your adjustments in the form of journal entries.

Note: Narratives are not required.

Task 3.2

On the answer sheet that follows, draft a profit and loss account for the year ended 31 March 1997.

Task 3.3

Sandro Venus is considering whether to incorporate the business and has said that he will telephone you tomorrow for advice.

Prepare notes for the telephone conversation that will enable you to explain the difference between the legal status of a sole trader and that of a company in respect of:

(i)   the liability of the owners for the debts of the business;
(ii)   the legal identity of the business;
(iii)   the regulation of the production of financial statements for the business.

Sandro Venus
Profit and loss account for the year ended 31 March 1997

		£	£
Sales			
Less:	Returns inwards		
Less:	Cost of Sales		
	Opening Stock		
	Purchases		
	Carriage inwards		
Less:	Returns outwards		
Less:	Closing stock		
Gross profit			
Plus:	Profit on the sale of motor vehicle		
	Interest on bank deposit		
Less:	Expenses		
	Wages and NIC		
	Rent, rates & insurance		
	Depreciation - Motor vehicles		
	- Office equipment		
	- Fixtures and fittings		
	Bad debts		
	Increase in provision for doubtful debts		
	Motor expenses		
	Bank charges		
	Lighting & heating		
	Postage and stationery		
	Telephone		
	Carriage outwards		
	Discounts allowed		
Net profit			

UNIT 11 – SECTION 3 – DECEMBER 1997

You are reminded that competence must be achieved in each section. You should therefore attempt and aim to complete EVERY task in EACH section.

All workings should be shown

You are advised to spend approximately 70 minutes on section 3.

Data

Georgina Moore, Bob Russell, Jeremy Ward and Louise Dickenson are in partnership together running a wholesale book trading operation called 'Apostles & Co' from a small industrial unit. Georgina keeps the books of the partnership. She has produced a draft profit and loss account for the partnership for the year ended 30 June 1997, but is not clear how to treat certain items in the year end accounts. She has asked you to assist her in making the necessary adjustments to the profit and loss account and in finalising the partnership accounts. She would also like you to explain some matters to the partners that have arisen out of the transactions during the year.

Georgina supplies you with the following information which is relevant to the year in question:

(1)   Bob had removed books, which were purchased at a cost of £1,500 during the year for use in his own personal library. No adjustment has yet been made for these items.

(2)   One customer who had owed the partnership £5,595 went into liquidation during the year, and the liquidators have said that there is no money available to pay creditors. Georgina estimates that, in addition to this, a provision for doubtful debts of £4,350 is required. A provision for doubtful debts of £1,750 has been brought forward from last year.

(3)   Georgina received the partnership's electricity bill for £1,758, which related to the quarter to 30 June 1997. She ignored this in preparing her accounts as the bill was received after the year end.

(4)   Interest on capital is to be paid at a rate of 10% on the balance at the year end on the capital accounts. No interest is paid on the current accounts.

(5)   Cash drawings in the year amounted to:
Georgina   £13,000
Bob   £11,000
Jeremy   £12,000
Louise   £9,000

(6)   The partners are entitled to the following salaries per annum:

Georgina   £13,000
Bob   £11,000
Jeremy   £10,500
Louise   £8,000

(7)   On 1 July 1996, the partners admitted Louise Dickenson into the partnership. She paid £35,000 cash into the partnership on that date. The profit sharing ratios in the old partnership were:

Georgina   4/10
Bob   3/10
Jeremy   3/10

The new profit sharing ratios are now:

Georgina	4/12
Bob	3/12
Jeremy	3/12
Louise	2/12

On the day that Louise was admitted into the partnership the goodwill in the partnership was valued at £180,000. No goodwill is to be kept in the accounts of the new partnership. Adjustments for goodwill are to be made in the capital accounts of the partners.

(8)   The balances on the current and capital accounts at the beginning of the year, before any adjustments have been made for the admission of Louise into the partnership, were as follows:

Capital accounts:

Georgina	£34,000
Bob	£22,000
Jeremy	£14,000

Current accounts:

Georgina	£6,000
Bob	£4,000
Jeremy	£1,000

(9)   The net profit per the accounts given to you by Georgina amounted to £145,453.

Task 3.1

Make any adjustments to the ledger balances used in the calculation of the net profit figure that are appropriate given the information above. Set out your adjustments in the form of journal entries.

Notes:

(1)   Narratives are not required.

(2)   Journals are not required for any of the appropriations of profit.

Task 3.2

Draft a letter to the partners explaining why you have made the adjustments in task 3.1 by reference, where relevant, to accounting concepts, accounting standards or generally accepted accounting principles.

Task 3.3

Show the new net profit figure taking into account the adjustments made in task 3.1.

Task 3.4

Prepare the partners' capital accounts for the year ended 30 June 1997 from the information provided above.

Task 3.5

Prepare an appropriation account for the partnership for the year ended 30 June 1997, starting with your adjusted net profit prepared in task 3.3.

Task 3.6

Prepare the partners' current accounts for the year ended 30 June 1997 from the information provided above and in your answers to the above tasks.

UNIT 11 – SECTION 3 – DECEMBER 1998

You are advised to spend approximately 55 minutes on this section.

Data

Jack Locke, Jane Berkeley and Sreela Hume were in partnership together selling and distributing scientific equipment. On 1 October 1997 they admitted Bhatti Ayer into the partnership. You have been asked to finalise the partnership accounts for the year ended 30 September 1998 and to make the entries necessary to account for the admission of Bhatti into the partnership. You have been given the following information.

(1)   On 1 October 1997 Bhatti paid £50,000 into the partnership. The profit-sharing ratios in the old partnership were:

Jack   5/12
Jane   4/12
Sreela   3/12

The new profit-sharing ratios are now:

Jack   5/15
Jane   4/15
Sreela   3/15
Bhatti   3/15

On the day that Bhatti was admitted into the partnership, the goodwill in the partnership was valued at £180,000. No goodwill is to be kept in the accounts of the new partnership. Adjustments for goodwill are to be made in the capital accounts of the partners.

(2)   Jack has produced a set of accounts which shows a profit of £164,100 for the year ended 30 September 1998.

On further enquiry you discover that one of the debtors, who had owed the business £12,500, had gone into liquidation during the year ended 30 September 1998 and the liquidators have said that there are no funds available to meet creditor balances. No adjustment has yet been made for this item.

An invoice for £4,200 was received on 13 November 1998 relating to delivery costs of equipment sold to customers during the year to 30 September 1998. It had not been included in the accounts as it had been received after the year end.

(3)   Interest on capital is to be paid at the rate of 10% on the balance at the year end on the capital accounts. No interest is paid on the current accounts.

(4)   Cash drawings in the year amounted to:

Jack   £48,200
Jane   £39,300
Sreela   £29,800
Bhatti   £25,400

(5)   The partners are entitled to the following salaries per annum:

    Jack   £15,000
    Jane   £12,000
    Sreela   £8,000
    Bhatti   £8,000

(6)   The balances on the current and capital accounts at the beginning of the year, before any adjustments had been made for the admission of Bhatti into the partnership, were as follows:

Capital accounts: *Current accounts:*

    Jack   £37,000   Jack   £5,300
    Jane   £31,000   Jane   £4,200
    Sreela   £26,000   Sreela   £3,100

Answer tasks 3.1–3.5 in the answer booklet section provided.

Task 3.1

Produce a statement adjusting the profit figure given to you by Jack, taking into account the matters set out in the data above, and calculate the net profit figure for appropriation.

*   You do not need to set out your adjustments in the form of journal entries.

Task 3.2

Justify any adjustments made to the profit figure in task 3.1 by referring, where relevant, to accounting concepts.

Task 3.3

Prepare the partners' capital accounts for the year ended 30 September 1998.

Task 3.4

Prepare an appropriation account for the partnership for the year ended 30 September 1998.

Task 3.5

Prepare the partners' current accounts for the year ended 30 September 1998.

UNIT 11 – SECTION 4 – JUNE 1996

You are reminded that competence must be achieved in each section. You should therefore attempt and aim to complete EVERY task in EACH section.

Note: You are advised to spend approximately 45 minutes on Section 4.

Data

You have been asked to take over work on finalising the accounts of the partnership of Stooge & Co. An extended trial balance for the year ended 31 March 1996 has already been produced and is set out on the following page.

STOOGE & CO.
EXTENDED TRIAL BALANCE 31 MARCH 1996

	TRIAL BALANCE		ADJUSTMENTS		PROFIT AND LOSS A/C		PROFIT & LOSS APPROPRIATION A/C		BALANCE SHEET	
	Debit	Credit	Debit	Credit	Debit	Credit	Debit	Credit	Debit	Credit
	£000	£000	£000	£000	£000	£000	£000	£000	£000	£000
Motor vehicles–cost	61								61	
Office equipment–cost	14								14	
Purchases	199				199					
Cash at bank	26								26	
Sales		382				382				
Debtors	79								79	
Stock	28		33	33	28	33			33	
Expenses	36		8	6	38					
Drawings–Curly	30								30	
–Larry	24								24	
–Mo	32								32	
Motor vehicles–accumulated depreciation		20								20
Office equipment–accumulated depreciation		6								6
Creditors		19								19
Accruals				8						8
Current accounts–Curly		6								6
–Larry	4								4	
Capital accounts –Curly		40								40
–Larry		20								20
–Mo		40								40
Prepayments			6						6	
Net profit					150			150		
Partners' salaries–Curly							30			30
–Larry							20			20
–Mo							20			20
Balance of net profit							80			80
	533	533	47	47	415	415	150	150	309	309

You are given the following further information:

(1)   Mo was admitted into the partnership on 1 April 1995. Before he entered the partnership the profit-sharing ratio was as follows:

Curly	6/10
Larry	4/10

After the admission of Mo into the partnership the profit-sharing ratio became:

Curly	5/10
Larry	3/10
Mo	2/10

(2)   Goodwill was valued at £60,000 at the time of admission of Mo into the partnership. An adjustment for goodwill should have been made in the accounts of the partnership on the admission of Mo, but this has yet to be done. Although goodwill must be taken into account, no balance of goodwill is to be kept in the final accounts of the partnership.

(3)   No adjustment has yet been made for interest on capital. The partnership deed states that interest is to be allowed on the balance of the capital accounts of the partners at the end of the year at a rate of 10%.

Task 4.1

Prepare an appropriation account for the partnership, starting with the balance of net profit in the profit and loss appropriation account on the extended trial balance.

Task 4.2

Prepare the partners' current and capital accounts for the year ended 31 March 1996 from the balances in the extended trial balance, taking into account the further information provided above.

UNIT 11 – SECTION 4 – JUNE 1997

You are reminded that competence must be achieved in each section. You should therefore attempt and aim to complete EVERY task in EACH section.

All workings should be shown.

You are advised to spend approximately 25 minutes on Section 4.

Data

You are required to attend a meeting of the partners Alice Grace, Ethel Grace and Isabella Grace. They are three sisters who are in partnership together selling gardening equipment. They share profits in the ratio:

Alice	5/12
Ethel	4/12
Isabella	3/12

They will admit a fourth partner, Flora Bundi, into the business on 1 June 1997. She will put £30,000 into the partnership. The profit sharing ratios will then become:

Alice	4/10
Ethel	3/10
Isabella	2/10
Flora	1/10

You have been given the following additional information:

(1)   The business has freehold land and buildings which had originally cost £120,000 and on which, at 31 May 1997, there is accumulated depreciation of £25,000. The land and buildings have recently been revalued at £179,000.

(2)   Motor vehicles which had originally cost £24,000 and on which, at 31 May 1997, there is accumulated depreciation of £8,400 are now thought to be worth only £6,000.

(3)   The new values of the freehold and buildings and the motor vehicles are to be incorporated into the partnership on admission of the new partner with any adjustment being made in the capital accounts of the partners.

(4)   Goodwill has been valued at £144,000 and it has been agreed to adjust the capital balances of the partners to reflect the goodwill that exists in the business. A goodwill account is to be maintained in the new partnership.

The capital account balances for the existing partnership at 31 May 1997 are as follows:

	£
Alice	55,000
Ethel	45,000
Isabella	40,000

Task 4.1

Make the necessary entries in the capital accounts of the partners to reflect the admission of Flora into the partnership on 1 June 1997 taking into account the terms of entry given in the information supplied above.

Task 4.2

Draft notes to take to the meeting to explain why adjustments to the partners' capital accounts are necessary to take into account the new values of the land and buildings and the motor vehicles.

PRACTICE CENTRAL ASSESSMENTS

QUESTIONS

TECHNICIAN STAGE

NVQ/SVQ LEVEL 4 IN ACCOUNTING

PRACTICE CENTRAL ASSESSMENT 1

DRAFTING FINANCIAL STATEMENTS
(ACCOUNTING PRACTICE, INDUSTRY AND COMMERCE)

(UNIT 11)

Time allowed: 3 hours plus 15 minutes' reading time

This central assessment is in three sections. You are required to attempt EVERY task in EACH section, using the answer booklet provided, immediately following these questions.

Note: A balance sheet proforma, two profit and loss account proformas, a proforma for journal entries and a proforma report are provided in the answer booklet for you to use.

You are advised to spend approximately 55 minutes on Section 1, 70 minutes on Section 2 and 55 minutes on Section 3.

SECTION 1

This section is in two parts.

PART A

Task 1.1

(a)   Distinguish between the purpose of a set of financial statements for a company and for a public sector body.

(b)   Briefly discuss the needs of the main users of a set of company financial statements.

Task 1.2

Distinguish between the different types of ownership interest in companies and public sector and not-for-profit organisations.

PART B

Data

You have been asked by the management of Metre Ltd to analyse the performance and financial position of the company over the last two years. The summarised financial statements for the company are given below:

Metre Ltd
Summary Profit and Loss Accounts for the years ended 31 December

	1997 £'000	1996 £'000
Turnover	940	800
Cost of sales	790	648
Gross profit	150	152
Expenses	103	88
Net profit before interest and tax	47	64
Interest	19	10
Net profit before tax	28	54

Metre Ltd
Summary Balance Sheets as at 31 December

	1997		1996	
	£'000	£'000	£'000	£'000
Fixed assets		1,133		901
Current assets	200		120	
Current liabilities	100		70	
Net current assets		100		50
		1,233		951
Bank loans		(300)		(180)
		933		771
Ordinary share capital		700		600
Share premium		74		40
Profit and loss account		159		131
		933		771

A number of industry average ratios have also been provided for your use:

	1997	1996
Gross profit margin	21%	18%
Net profit margin (before interest and tax)	8%	6%
Return on capital employed (profit before tax)	5%	4%
Asset turnover	1.2	1.2
Current ratio	2.0:1	2.5:1
Gearing ratio	26%	38%
Interest cover	8.0	5.2

Task 1.3

In the answer booklet, prepare a report for the directors of the company on the performance and position of the company over the last two years and in comparison to the industry average performance. Your answer should comment on the profitability, liquidity and level of gearing in the company and in particular should comment on the likely reaction of the company's bank if approached for a further bank loan.

SECTION 2

This section is in two parts.

PART A

Data

You have been assigned to assist in the preparation of the financial statements of Fanta Ltd for the year ended 31 December 1997. You have been provided with the draft trial balance of the company as at 31 December 1997 and this is set out below.

Draft trial balance of Fanta Ltd as at 31 December 1997

	£'000	£'000
Ordinary share capital (50 pence shares)		2,000
6% Debentures	800	
Sales		10,320
Trade creditors		1,204
Cash at bank	93	
Purchases	6,112	
Stock	2,749	
Trade debtors	1,760	
Provision for doubtful debts		64
Land and buildings at cost	1,972	
Fixtures and fittings at cost	987	
Motor vehicles at cost	841	
Buildings - accumulated depreciation		214
Fixtures and fittings - accumulated depreciation		225
Motor vehicles - accumulated depreciation		289
Interim dividend	200	
Distribution costs	1,516	
Administration expenses	1,188	
Share premium		1,340
Investment	2,007	
Profit and loss account		4,569
	20,225	20,225

You have been given the following further information:

(a)   the directors propose a final dividend of 6 pence per share;

(b)   the debentures were issued on 1 April 1997 but the interest due for the year has not yet been accounted for;

(c)   the corporation tax charge for the year has been calculated as £380,000;

(d)   the company's land is to be revalued upwards by £104,000;

(e)   on 31 December 1997 a further 600,000 50 pence shares were issued by the company at a premium of 30 pence per share. These shares are not eligible for the final proposed dividend;

(f)   the directors have decided that a provision of £98,000 should be set up for deferred tax.

Task 2.1

Using the proforma provided in the answer booklet produce the journal entries necessary to adjust the draft trial balance for the additional information given above.

Notes: Ignore any effect of these adjustments on the tax charge for the year as given above.

Task 2.2

Using the proforma provided in the answer booklet produce the profit and loss account for the year ended 31 December 1997 taking into account the adjustments made in Task 2.1 and on the assumption that stock was valued at £3,421,000 at 31 December 1997.

Notes:

(a)   You must show any workings relevant to understanding your calculation of figures appearing in the profit and loss account.

(b)   A balance sheet is not required.

Task 2.3

In your answer booklet prepare a statement of total recognised gains and losses for the year ended 31 December 1997.

PART B

Data

The investment shown in the trial balance of Fanta Ltd represents the cost of acquiring 80% of the ordinary share capital of Orange Ltd on 31 December 1997.

The summarised balance sheet of Orange Ltd as at 31 December 1997 is given below:

Orange Ltd balance sheet as at 31 December 1997

	£'000
Fixed assets	1,964
Net current assets	342
Long term loans	(588)
	1,718
Ordinary share capital	1,000
Share premium	500
Profit and loss account	218
	1,718

All of the assets and liabilities in the balance sheet are shown at their fair values except for the fixed assets that have a fair value of £2,121,000 at 31 December 1997.

Task 2.4

In your answer booklet calculate the goodwill on consolidation that arose on the acquisition of the shares in Orange Ltd on 31 December 1997. State how FRS 10 would require this goodwill to be dealt with in the consolidated financial statements.

Note: You are not required to produce a consolidated balance sheet for the group.

Task 2.5

In your answer booklet calculate the figure that would appear in the consolidated balance sheet at 31 December 1997 for minority interest. State whether this would be a debit or a credit balance and where it would appear in the consolidated balance sheet.

Note: You are not required to produce a consolidated balance sheet for the group.

SECTION 3

Data

You have been asked by Harry Turner, a sole trader, to assist in the preparation of his final accounts for the year ended 31 March 1998. So far Harry has produced a draft extended trial balance, which is given below.

Draft extended trial balance for Harry Turner
for the year ended 31 March 1998

	Trial balance £	Trial balance £	Adjustments £	Adjustments £	Profit and loss £	Profit and loss £	Balance sheet £	Balance sheet £
Capital		43,212						43,212
Provision for doubtful debts		213						213
Sales		193,277				193,277		
Office expenses	5,118		7,203		12,321			
Fixtures and fittings at cost	4,320						4,320	
Fixtures and fittings - accumulated depreciation		2,160		432				2,592
Purchases	115,967				115,967			
Motor vehicles at cost	47,300						47,300	
Motor vehicles - accumulated depreciation		20,694		6,651				27,345
Debtors	17,420						17,420	
Stock	8,996		9,487	9,487	8,996	9,487	9,487	
Creditors		9,532						9,532
Bank	1,263						1,263	
Sundry expenses	2,138		3,210		5,348			
Wages	20,389				20,389			
Bank loan		5,000						5,000
Suspense account	24,912				24,912			
Returns inwards	1,441				1,441			
Returns outwards		970				970		
Machinery at cost	48,200						48,200	
Machinery - accumulated depreciation		22,406		3,159				25,565
Accruals				1,740				1,740
Prepayments			1,569				1,569	
Profit					14,360			14,360
	297,464	297,464	21,469	21,469	203,734	203,734	129,559	129,559

Harry has also provided you with the following additional information:

(a)   he has forgotten to increase the doubtful debt provision for the year and wishes it to be 3% of his debtors after writing off a further bad debt of £220. The bad and doubtful debt expense is to be included in office expenses.

(b)   the suspense account balance has been investigated and it appears to be made up of the following:

(i)   during the year a piece of machinery was purchased for £6,200. This attracted a 50% government grant but when the £3,100 was received the only accounting entry to be made was to debit the bank account. The piece of machinery is expected to have a useful economic life of 5 years. The deferred credit method of accounting is to be used for this grant.

(ii)   during the year some fixtures and fittings which had originally cost £1,240 but now had a book value of £640 were sold for £830. The only entry to be made in the accounts for this sale was to debit the bank account with the proceeds.

(iii)   the remaining balance on the suspense account was the amount of cash drawings that Harry Turner had taken during the year. These had been credited to the bank account but no other entries had been made in the accounts.

(c)   the interest due to the bank on the bank loan of £560 has been completely omitted from the accounting records.

(d)   as well as cash drawings Harry Turner also took £440 of goods out of the business for his own private use.

(e)   when the stocktake was carried out on 31 March 1998 it was noted that goods which had cost £1,580 but only had a net realisable value of £870 had been included in the closing stock figure at their cost.

Task 1

In your answer booklet prepare a short note explaining what is meant by the deferred credit method of accounting for the government grant.

Task 2

For each item of additional information given above, in your answer booklet, explain the accounting treatment that is required to correct or include the information.

Task 3

Using the proformas in your answer booklet and taking account of the further information provided, draft a profit and loss account for the year ended 31 March 1998 and a balance sheet as at that date.

DRAFTING FINANCIAL STATEMENTS

(ACCOUNTING PRACTICE, INDUSTRY AND COMMERCE)

ANSWER BOOKLET

SECTION 1

PART A

Task 1.1

(a)

(b)

Task 1.2

Part B

Task 1.3

REPORT

SECTION 2

PART A

Task 2.1

JOURNAL

	Debit £'000	Credit £'000
Dividends payable (P&L)		
Proposed dividend creditor		
Interest payable (P&L)		
Interest payable creditor		
Corporation tax (P&L)		
Corporation tax creditor		
Land and buildings at cost		
Revaluation reserve		
Cash		
Ordinary share capital		
Share premium		
Corporation tax (P&L)		
Provision for deferred tax		

Task 2.2

PROFORMA PROFIT AND LOSS ACCOUNT
(FORMAT 1 AS SUPPLEMENTED BY FRS 3)

	£	£
Turnover		
Continuing operations		
Acquisitions		
	———	
Discontinued operations		
	———	
Cost of sales		
		———
Gross profit (or loss)		
Distribution costs		
Administrative expenses		
Other operating income		
		———
Operating profit (or loss)		
Continuing operations		
Acquisitions		
	———	
Discontinued operations		
	———	
Profit (or loss) on disposal of discontinued operations		
Income from shares in group undertakings		
Income from participating interests		
Income from other fixed asset investments		
Other interest receivable and similar income		
Amounts written off investments		
		———
Profit (or loss) on ordinary activities before interest		
Interest payable and similar charges		
		———
Profit (or loss) on ordinary activities before taxation		
Tax on profit (or loss) on ordinary activities		
Extraordinary items		
		———
Profit (or loss) for the financial year		
Dividends		
		———
Retained profit for the financial year		
		———

WORKINGS

Task 2.3

Statement of total recognised gains and losses for the year ended 31 December 1997

£'000

Task 2.4

Task 2.5

SECTION 3

Task 1

Task 2

Task 3

Trading and profit and loss account for the year ended 31 March 1998

	£	£
Sales		
Less: Returns inwards		
Opening stock		
Purchases		
Less: returns outwards		
Less: closing stock		
Cost of sales		
Gross profit		
Office expenses		
Sundry expenses		
Wages		
Bank interest		
Profit on sale of fixtures and fittings		
Government grant		
Net profit		

Balance sheet as at 31 March 1998

	Cost	Acc Depr'n	NBV
	£	£	£

Fixed assets:
Machinery
Fixtures and fittings
Motor vehicles

Current assets:
Stock
Debtors
Less: provision

Prepayments
Bank

Creditors: amounts falling
due within one year
Trade creditors
Accruals

Creditors: amounts falling
due after more than one year
Bank loan
Deferred credit

Opening capital
Profit for the year
Less: drawings

TECHNICIAN STAGE

NVQ/SVQ LEVEL 4 IN ACCOUNTING

PRACTICE CENTRAL ASSESSMENT 2

DRAFTING FINANCIAL STATEMENTS
(ACCOUNTING PRACTICE, INDUSTRY AND COMMERCE)

(UNIT 11)

Time allowed: 3 hours plus 15 minutes' reading time

This central assessment is in three sections. You are required to attempt EVERY task in EACH section, using the answer booklet provided, immediately following these questions.

Note: A Companies Act 1985 Balance Sheet proforma (format 1), a proforma profit and loss account (format 1 as supplemented by FRS 3) and a proforma memorandum are provided in the answer booklet for you to use.

You are advised to spend approximately 60 minutes on section 1, 80 minutes on section 2 and 40 minutes on section 3.

SECTION 1

This section is in two parts.

PART A

Task 1.1

The objective of financial statements has been described as to provide information about the financial position, performance and financial adaptability of an enterprise that is useful to a wide range of users for assessing the stewardship of management and for making economic decisions.

(a)   In this context explain what is meant by each of the following terms:

   (i)   financial position of the enterprise;
   (ii)   financial performance of the enterprise;
   (iii)   financial adaptability of the enterprise;
   (iv)   stewardship of management.

   Which of the financial statements will provide information about each of these four elements?

(b)   Chapter 3 of the ASB's Draft Statement of Principles considers the qualitative characteristics of information and determines that there are four primary characteristics for financial statements, being relevance, reliability, comparability and understandability.

   What is meant by each of these four characteristics?

Task 1.2

Explain what is meant by the accounting concept of recognising the substance of transactions. Illustrate the conflict using the example of a finance lease and an operating lease.

PART B

Data

You work for a small private manufacturing company that has been approached by two other companies in the same line of business, A Ltd and B Ltd, with offers to buy the shares of your company. The most recent financial statements of A Ltd and B Ltd have been obtained and are set out below in summary form.

Summary profit and loss accounts for the year ending 31 March 1998

	A Ltd £'000	B Ltd £'000
Turnover	1,000	240
Cost of sales	670	144
Gross profit	330	96
Expenses	220	70
Net profit	110	26

Summary balance sheets as at 31 March 1998

	A Ltd £'000	A Ltd £'000	B Ltd £'000	B Ltd £'000
Fixed assets		1,532		373
Current assets	470		100	
Current liabilities	280		20	
		190		80
		1,722		453
Long term loans		(500)		(20)
		1,222		433
Ordinary share capital		800		300
Share premium		100		-
Revaluation reserve		100		-
Profit and loss account		222		133
		1,222		433

Task 1.3

In the answer booklet, prepare a report to the directors of your company regarding the performance and position of A Ltd and B Ltd given the information contained in the summary financial statements. Your answer should comment upon the profitability, liquidity and level of gearing in the two companies and should include the calculation of the following ratios for the two companies:

(a)   Gross profit percentage
(b)   Net profit percentage
(c)   Return on capital employed
(d)   Asset turnover
(e)   Current ratio
(f)   Gearing

SECTION 2

This section is in two parts.

PART A

Data

You have been asked to assist in the preparation of the financial statements of Craig Ltd for the year ended 31 March 1998. You have been provided with the draft extended trial balance of Craig Ltd at that date which is set out below.

Craig Ltd - Draft extended trial balance for the year ended 31 March 1998

	Trial balance		Adjustments		Profit and loss		Balance sheet	
	Debit £'000	Credit £'000	Debit £'000	Credit £'000	Debit £'000	Credit £'000	Debit £'000	Credit £'000
Share capital		5,000						5,000
Sales		25,625				25,625		
Debtors	4,232						4,232	
Land and buildings - at cost	4,670						4,670	
Fixtures and fittings - at cost	1,750						1,750	
Motor vehicles - at cost	2,625						2,625	
Returns inwards	182				182			
Cash at bank	395						395	
Purchases	15,217				15,217			
Carriage outwards	146				146			
Carriage inwards	118				118			
6% debentures		4,100						4,100
Returns outwards		126				126		
Stock	5,625		5,941	5,941	5,625	5,941	5,941	
Provision for doubtful debts		137		75				212
Accruals				140				140
Prepayments			78				78	
Buildings - accumulated depreciation		516		60				576
Fixtures and fittings - accumulated depreciation		525		175				700
Motor vehicles - accumulated depreciation		650		494				1,144
Interim dividend	300				300			
Distribution costs	4,118		598		4,716			
Administrative expenses	2,996		268		3,264			
Interest	123				123			
Share premium		2,250						2,250
Trade creditors		2,576						2,576
Investment	2,410						2,410	
Profit and loss account		3,402						3,402
Profit						2,001		2,001
	44,907	44,907	6,885	6,885	31,692	31,692	22,101	22,101

You have also been given the following additional information:

(a)   the corporation tax charge for the year has been calculated as £927,000.

(b)   the share capital of Craig Ltd is made up of 50 pence ordinary shares. On 31 March 1998 a further issue of 1,000,000 ordinary shares was made for a total of £1,200,000 in cash. This has not yet been accounted for and these additional shares do not qualify for the final proposed dividend.

(c)   the directors propose a final dividend of 2 pence per share.

(d)   the interest on the 6% debentures has been paid for the first six months of the year only.

(e)   the land is to be revalued upwards at 31 March 1998 by £240,000.

Task 2.1

Using the pro-formas provided in the answer booklet and taking into account the further information provided, draft a profit and loss account for the year ended 31 March 1998 and a balance sheet as at that date.

Notes:

(a)   You must show any workings relevant to understanding your calculation of figures appearing in the financial statements.

(b)   You are not required to produce journal entries for any necessary adjustments to the figures in the extended trial balance.

(c)   Ignore any effect of these adjustments on the tax charge for the year as given above.

PART B

Data

The investment shown in Craig Ltd's extended trial balance is a holding of 40% of the ordinary share capital of another company, Pepter Ltd. The summarised profit and loss account for the year ended 31 March 1998 for Pepter Ltd and the summarised balance sheet at that date are both given below.

Pepter Ltd
Summarised profit and loss account for the year ended 31 March 1998

	£'000
Turnover	1,000
Cost of sales	600
Gross profit	400
Expenses	240
Profit before tax	160
Corporation tax	60
Profit after tax	100
Dividends	70
Retained profit	30

Pepter Ltd
Summarised balance sheet as at 31 March 1998

	£'000
Fixed assets	5,500
Net current assets	800
	6,300
Share capital	4,500
Profit and loss account	1,800
	6,300

The ordinary shares in Pepter Ltd were acquired when the profit and loss reserve of Pepter Ltd totalled £800,000.

The directors of Craig Ltd are considering purchasing approximately 90% of the share capital of another company, Freesia Ltd, in the next few weeks. They realise that if they do purchase the shares in this company then they may need to prepare consolidated financial statements in subsequent accounting periods.

Task 2.2

Distinguish between the concepts of control over another company and significant influence over another company and describe the different accounting that would be required in each situation. Refer to relevant accounting standards where necessary.

Task 2.3

Explain what is meant by:

(a)   an associated undertaking;
(b)   equity accounting.

Task 2.4

Supposing that Craig Ltd were in fact preparing consolidated accounts for the year ended 31 March 1998 show what figures would appear in the consolidated financial statements for the investment in Pepter Ltd if equity accounting is used. The particular figures that you should calculate are:

(a)   the investment in the associated undertaking to appear in the balance sheet;
(b)   the premium on acquisition (goodwill arising);
(c)   the figures that would appear in the consolidated profit and loss account for Pepter Ltd.

Task 2.5

If the directors of Craig Ltd do purchase the shares in Freesia Ltd explain what criteria must be satisfied if they were to treat the purchase as a merger and use merger accounting.

SECTION 3

Data

Peter Blades, Daphne Millington, Ken Gordon and Francis Pie are in partnership together.   Francis has produced a draft profit and loss account for the partnership for the year ended 31 March 1998 and has then asked you to finalise the partnership accounts. He has given you the following information that is relevant to the year in question:

(a)   The balances on the capital and current accounts for the partners at the beginning of the year were as follows:

Capital accounts:
Peter	£41,000
Daphne	£35,800
Ken	£31,200
Francis	£26,600

Current accounts:
Peter	£2,100
Daphne	£3,400
Ken	£1,100
Francis	£1,000

(b)   The net profit for the year from the draft accounts supplied by Francis is £235,572.

(c)   Interest on capital is to be paid to the partners at a rate of 8% on the balance on their capital accounts at the start of the year. No interest is to be paid on current accounts.

(d)   Cash drawings in the year amounted to:

Peter	£64,000
Daphne	£71,000
Ken	£39,000
Francis	£31,000

(e)   The partners are entitled to the following salaries per annum:

Peter	£10,000
Daphne	£12,000
Ken	£14,000
Francis	£ 8,000

(f)   The partnership profit sharing ratio for the year was:

Peter	2/6
Daphne	2/6
Ken	1/6
Francis	1/6

(g)   On 31 March 1998 Daphne announced that she was to retire from the partnership. She would require a cash payment on retirement of £20,000 but any further amounts due to her would remain as a loan to the partnership at a rate of 10% per annum.

On 31 March 1998 the goodwill in the partnership was valued at £108,000. No goodwill is to be kept in the accounts of the partnership and the adjustments for goodwill are to take place in the partners' capital accounts.

The profit-sharing ratio of the new partnership is to be:

Peter	4/10
Ken	3/10
Francis	3/10

Task 3.1

Prepare an appropriation account for the partnership for the year ended 31 March 1998.

Task 3.2

Prepare the partners' capital accounts and current accounts for the year ended 31 March 1998.

DRAFTING FINANCIAL STATEMENTS

(ACCOUNTING PRACTICE, INDUSTRY AND COMMERCE)

ANSWER BOOKLET

SECTION 1

PART A

Task 1.1

(a)

(b)

Task 1.2

PART B

Task 1.3

REPORT

To:
From:
Date:
Re:

Task 2.1

PROFORMA PROFIT AND LOSS ACCOUNT
(FORMAT 1 AS SUPPLEMENTED BY FRS 3)

	£	£
Turnover		
Continuing operations		
Acquisitions		
	____	
Discontinued operations		
	____	
Cost of sales		
	____	
Gross profit (or loss)		
Distribution costs		
Administrative expenses		
Other operating income		
	____	
Operating profit (or loss)		
Continuing operations		
Acquisitions		
	____	
Discontinued operations		
	____	
Profit (or loss) on disposal of discontinued operations		
Income from shares in group undertakings		
Income from participating interests		
Income from other fixed asset investments		
Other interest receivable and similar income		
Amounts written off investments		
	____	
Profit (or loss) on ordinary activities before interest		
Interest payable and similar charges		
	____	
Profit (or loss) on ordinary activities before taxation		
Tax on profit (or loss) on ordinary activities		
Extraordinary items		
	____	
Profit (or loss) for the financial year		
Dividends		
	____	
Retained profit for the financial year		
	____	

PROFORMA BALANCE SHEET (FORMAT 1)

	£	£
Fixed assets		
Intangible assets		
Tangible assets		
Investments		
	____	
Current assets		
Stocks		
Debtors		
Investments		
Cash at bank and in hand		
	____	
Creditors: amounts falling due within one year		
	____	
Net current assets (liabilities)		____
Total assets *less* current liabilities		
Creditors: amounts falling due after more than one year		
Provisions for liabilities and charges		
		____
		____
Capital and reserves		
Called up share capital		
Share premium account		
Revaluation reserve		
Profit and loss account		
		____
		____

WORKINGS

◆ FOULKS*lynch*

Task 2.2

Task 2.3

Task 2.4

Task 2.5

Task 3.1

Appropriation account for the year ended 31 March 1998

	£	£

Task 3.2

Partners' Capital Accounts

	Peter	Daphne	Ken	Francis		Peter	Daphne	Ken	Francis
	£	£	£	£		£	£	£	£

Partners' Current Accounts

	Peter	Daphne	Ken	Francis		Peter	Daphne	Ken	Francis
	£	£	£	£		£	£	£	£

ANSWERS

Chapter 1

FINANCIAL STATEMENTS AND FRAMEWORK

1 SOLUTION

(a) The fundamental objective of financial reporting is to provide information about the financial position, performance and financial adaptability of an entity that is useful to a wide range of users for assessing the stewardship of management and for making economic decisions.

(b) The information in the financial statements is to be communicated to:

(i) **Shareholders** - the owners of the company: existing and potential, including persons or groups interested in take-overs and mergers.

(ii) **Providers of external finance**, long and short term, such as debenture holders and finance companies, both existing and potential.

(iii) **Employees** past, present and potential.

(iv) **Suppliers of goods and services, and customers,** past, present and prospective.

(v) **Tax authorities.**

(vi) **Trade agencies, local authorities, environmental pressure groups, ratepayers** and any other members of the public who may require such information as is normally and legally contained in the report.

(vii) **Analysts and advisers**, both of investors (stockbrokers, economists, statisticians and journalists) and of employees (trade unions).

(c) The information contained in the financial statements should be:

(i) **Reliable** - so that conclusions drawn may be 'true and fair'.

(ii) **Understandable** - material matters should be disclosed without unnecessary complex detail.

(iii) **Complete** - if an unbalanced or biased report is presented, readers will be unable to make sound judgements.

(iv) **Comparable** - the information contained in one period's report should be, as far as possible, calculated and presented on the same bases as in previous periods, so that comparisons are relevant.

(v) **Objective** - an unbiased view of the company's affairs, without regard to the interests of particular groups of interested parties, should be put forward.

(vi) **Up-to-date** - companies are required to prepare their reports annually, and this is important from the point of view of investors and those advising them, for evaluation purposes.

(d) The kind of information required by two of the groups is:

(i) **Shareholders** - Shareholders are interested in the future performance of the business but require past figures as a guide to the future. Therefore, all financial information in the report is needed.

In addition, any general indication given in the report as to future prospects is relevant.

(ii) **Tax authorities** - require past figures as a basis for computing tax liabilities.

2   SOLUTION

The Companies Acts, now consolidated in Companies Acts 1985 and 1989, lay down the basic framework for the keeping of books of accounts and the preparation of published accounts for quoted companies. As far as the preparation of the published accounts is concerned the Companies Acts set out the formats for the financial statements that should be followed, together with some details of information that should be disclosed in the financial statements. However much of the detail of which accounting techniques should be used and exactly what information should be disclosed is left to the accountancy bodies themselves to decide.

The accountancy bodies in the UK publish accounting standards to fill in the details of methods of accounting that are preferred and the precise information that should be disclosed in financial statements. These standards were, for many years, issued as Statements of Standard Accounting Practice (SSAPs) but under the new regulatory system are now published as Financial Reporting Standards (FRSs). A company's financial statements should comply with SSAPs and FRSs and if they do not the company risks investigation and possible disciplinary proceedings.

The Financial Reporting Review Panel aims to monitor the accounts of quoted companies and instigate disciplinary proceedings against those that do not prepare their accounts in line with SSAPs and FRSs. There is also some debate as to whether accounting standards should be given legal backing in order to strengthen their position in the regulatory framework.

3   SOLUTION

The capital structures of a sole trader, a partnership and a limited company are likely to have some similarities. It is likely that all three types of business entity will be financed by a mixture of debt capital, or loans, and owners capital. However the detail and accounting will differ depending upon the type of business entity.

A sole trader may have loans outstanding from a bank or from friends or family however it is likely that the majority of the capital provided for the business has come from the sole trader himself. This is described as owners capital and all belongs to the sole trader. Any profits made by the business are additions to this owners capital and any drawings taken from the business are reductions of capital.

A partnership's capital structure is in many ways similar to that of a sole trader as a partnership is simply a number of sole traders trading as a single entity together. A partnership is likely to have loan capital from banks and it is also possible that a former or even current partner may make a loan to the partnership. Again however most of the capital will have been provided by the partners and this will be shown in their capital accounts. Each partner will have an individual capital account in order to record precisely how much capital the business owes to each partner. Any profits that the partnership makes is an increase in the partners' capital and any drawings that each partner removes from the business a reduction in capital. In most partnerships the profits and drawings relating to each partner are recorded in separate current accounts.

The capital structure of a limited company is altogether more complex. Companies may have loan capital not only in the form of bank loans but also in the form of debentures issued to the public. The owners capital of a company is known as share capital and the most usual form is the issue of ordinary shares to investors. There are also preference shares that can be issued to investors which give a fixed rate of dividend each year. The profits of a company all belong to the ordinary shareholders but are split into a variety of reserves. This may include statutory reserves such as the share premium account or revaluation reserve and other reserves for the accumulation of retained profits such as a general reserve and the profit and loss account reserve.

Chapter 2
GAAPS AND CONCEPTS

1   SOLUTION

(a)   Objectivity, as related to accountants and accountancy, is that in solving accounting problems or preparing financial statements or accounting records there should be freedom from bias, subjectivity and uncertainty as far as possible. This is to ensure that accounting information would be presented in the same manner no matter who was preparing the information.

(b)   As shareholders may not be the managers of the company in which they hold shares they need to read accounts in order to evaluate the strength of their investment in terms of the profitability and liquidity of the company they have invested in. This information will help them to decide whether to maintain their existing investment, to invest further or to disinvest in whole or in part.

(c)   With the application of objectivity to accounts they are likely to be more free from bias and therefore more reliable. However, in order to arrive at objectivity accounts are prepared under the historical cost convention, which means that the information they disclose, based on historic costs of assets and liabilities, may not faithfully represent that which it purports to represent, such costs often being out of date. If shareholders wish to look to the future of their investment, then historic cost accounts, while reliable, may not in fact be relevant.

2   SOLUTION

The going concern concept is an assumption that the business for which accounts are being prepared will continue for the foreseeable future and that the financial statements of the business will reflect this assumption. If the business is to be assumed to be continuing for the foreseeable future then any long-term assets that are remaining at the end of the accounting period, such as fixed assets, can validly be valued based on their original cost. If however there is evidence that the business will not continue for the foreseeable future then such assets should be written down to their net realisable values.

As an example under the going concern concept it is valid to value fixed assets at their historical cost less any accumulated depreciation. However if there were evidence to suggest that the business would soon cease then it would be more appropriate to value fixed assets at the amount at which they could be sold on the open market. This may involve writing off intangible fixed assets (eg goodwill) entirely.

The accruals concept means that when preparing financial statements costs and revenues should be matched wherever possible and dealt with in the period in which they are earned or incurred rather than the period in which the cash is received or paid.

As an example of this concept the amount of telephone expense that is charged to the profit and loss account for the period should be the telephone expense used in the period. This may exclude some rental paid in advance which will be treated as a prepayment and may include an accrual for calls that have been made but for which perhaps the bill has not yet been received or paid.

The consistency concept is an assumption that similar items in the financial statements will be treated in the same manner within a period and from one period to another. This assumption means that it is possible to compare an organisation's results from period to period in a meaningful manner. If an organisation does change its accounting treatment of an item between one accounting period and another enough information about this change, the old policy and the new policy should be given for users to be able to appreciate the effect of the change of policy.

An area where there is a need for a consistent accounting policy in order for the accounts to be validly compared from period to period is the valuation of items of stock. The stock valuation method chosen, such as first in first out or average cost, should be used consistently from period to period.

The prudence concept is a concept that the figures used in the financial statements should never overstate profits made or the assets shown in the balance sheet. Therefore any losses that are anticipated should be written off immediately and any profits should not be recognised in the financial statements until there is reasonable certainty that they have been earned. If an item in the financial statements is uncertain then the figure taken for that item will be that which will give the lower profit.

An example of the prudence concept is that any item of stock that is expected to realise less than its original cost should be written down to its net realisable value thus recognising the expected loss immediately. However items of stock that are expected to realise more than their original cost are still only valued at their cost thus deferring the recognition of profit until the items are actually sold.

Chapter 3

SOLE TRADERS AND THE TRIAL BALANCE

1   SOLUTION

Cash

20X4 Jul	Details	£	20X4 Jul	Details	£
1	Capital	4,000	2	Purchases	1,130
31	Debtors ledger control	190	8	Wages	13
			8	Sundry expenses	2
			22	Fixtures & fittings	350
			25	Wages	38
			26	Drawings	80
			31	Rent	500
			31	Balance c/d	2,077
		4,190			4,190
Aug					
1	Balance b/d	2,077			

Capital

20X4 Jul	Details	£	20X4 Jul	Details	£
31	Balance c/d	5,750	1	Cash	4,000
			1	Motor car	1,750
		5,750			5,750
			Aug		
			1	Balance b/d	5,750

Motor car

20X4 Jul	Details	£	20X4	Details	£
1	Capital	1,750			

Purchases

20X4 Jul	Details	£	20X4 Jul	Details	£
12	Cash account	1,130			
18	Creditors ledger control	85	31	Balance c/d	1,215
		1,215			1,215
Aug					
1	Balance b/d	1,215			

Wages

20X4 Jul	Details	£	20X4 Jul	Details	£
8	Cash	13	31	Balance c/d	51
25	Cash	38			
		51			51
Aug					
1	Balance b/d	51			

Sundry expenses

20X4 Jul	Details	£	20X4	Details	£
8	Cash	2			

Sales

20X4 Jul	Details	£	20X4 Jul	Details	£
31	Balance c/d	430	9	Debtors ledger control	190
			14	Debtors ledger control	240
		430			430
			Aug		
			1	Balance b/d	430

Debtors ledger control

20X4 Jul	Details	£	20X4 Jul	Details	£
9	Sales	190	31	Cash	190
14	Sales	240	31	Balance c/d	240
		430			430
Aug					
1	Balance b/d	240			

Rent

20X4 Jul	Details	£	20X4	Details	£
31	Cash	500			

Creditors ledger control

20X4	Details	£	20X4 Jul	Details	£
			18	Purchases	85

Fixtures and fittings

20X4 Jul	Details	£	20X4	Details	£
22	Cash	350			

Drawings

20X4 Jul	Details	£	20X4	Details	£
26	Cash	80			

Trial balance as at 31 July 20X4

	Dr £	Cr £
Cash	2,077	
Capital		5,750
Motor car	1,750	
Purchases	1,215	
Wages	51	
Sundry expenses	2	
Sales		430
Debtors ledger control	240	
Rent	500	
Creditors ledger control		85
Fixtures and fittings	350	
Drawings	80	
	6,265	6,265

2   SOLUTION

Task 1

Cash at bank

	£		£
Capital	10,000	Rent	140
Sales	380	Purchases	730
Debtors	2,575	Van	4,050
		Wages	370
		Drawings	700
		Balance c/d	6,965
	12,955		12,955
Balance b/d	6,965		

Capital

	£		£
		Cash at bank	10,000

Rent

	£		£
Cash at bank	140		

Purchases

	£		£
Cash at bank	730	Balance c/d	2,642
Creditors	1,912		
	2,642		2,642
Balance b/d	2,642		

Van

	£		£
Cash at bank	4,050		

Sales

	£		£
Balance c/d	5,271	Debtors	2,575
		Debtors	2,316
		Cash at bank	380
	5,271		5,271
		Balance b/d	5,271

Debtors

	£		£
Sales	2,575	Cash at bank	2,575
Sales	2,316	Balance c/d	2,316
	4,891		4,891
Balance b/d	2,316		

Creditors

	£		£
		Purchases	1,912

Wages

	£		£
Cash at bank	370		

Drawings

	£		£
Cash at bank	700		

Task 2

Samantha Wright
Trial balance

	Debit £	Credit £
Cash at bank	6,965	
Capital		10,000
Rent	140	
Purchases	2,642	
Van	4,050	
Sales		5,271
Debtors	2,316	
Creditors		1,912
Wages	370	
Drawings	700	
	17,183	17,183

3   SOLUTION

Suspense account

	£		£
Trial balance difference	86,000		

Van disposal

Step 1   The entries should be:

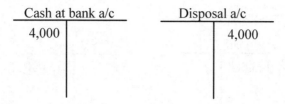

Step 2   The entries actually made:

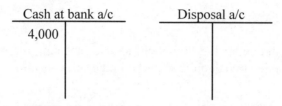

Step 3   Work out the difference

There should be a £4,000 credit to disposal account, there was no entry at all, therefore a £4,000 credit is required in the disposal account.

Bank a/c		Disposal a/c	
4,000			**4,000**

Step 4   Post the opposite entry to the suspense account

Suspense a/c		Disposal a/c	
b/d 86,000			
4,000		4,000	

Step 5   Journal entry

Dr	Suspense a/c	£4,000	
Cr	Disposal a/c		£4,000

Being correction of posting error from the cash receipts book

Sales figure transposition

Step 1   The entries should be:

Debtors a/c		Sales a/c	
123,000			123,000

Step 2   The entries actually made:

Debtors a/c		Sales a/c	
123,000			213,000

Step 3   Work out the difference

There should be a £123,000 credit to sales account, there was a £213,000 credit entry, therefore a £90,000 debit is required in the sales account.

Debtors a/c		Sales a/c	
123,000		**90,000**	213,000

Step 4   Post the opposite entry to the suspense account

Suspense a/c		Sales a/c	
86,000	**90,000**	90,000	213,000
4,000			

Step 5   Journal entry

Dr	Sales account	£90,000	
Cr	Suspense account		£90,000

Being the correction of a transposition error in posting the sales day book.

Notice that the suspense account now balances and the trial balance would be correct

4   SOLUTION

Suspense account

	£		£
Balance b/d	1,075	Trial balance - difference	957
Postage (trial balance		Creditors control (b)	500
only) (a)	675	Fixed asset - cost (c)	1,575
Sundry income (trial balance			
only) (d)	162		
Cash (e)	620		
Capital account - ETT (f)	500		
	3,032		3,032

Explanatory notes:

The £1,075 debit balance is already included in the books, whilst the £957 is entered on the credit side of the suspense account because the trial balance, as extracted, shows debits exceeding credits by £957. Although the two amounts arose in different ways they are both removed from suspense by the application of double entry

(a)   The incorrect extraction is corrected by amending the balance on the trial balance and debiting the suspense account with £675. In this case the 'credit' entry is only on the trial balance, as the postages account itself shows the correct balance, the error coming in putting that balance on the trial balance.

(b)   The non-entry of the £500 to the debit of X's account causes the account to be incorrectly stated and the trial balance to be unbalanced. To correct matters Dr X, Cr Suspense, amending both X's ledger account and the trial balance.

(c)   The suspense entry here arose from adherence to double entry procedures, rather than a numerical error. In this case the bookkeeper should have Dr Fixed asset - cost, Cr Bank instead of Dr Suspense, Cr Bank, so to correct matters the entry Dr Fixed asset - cost, Cr Suspense is made.

(d)   Is similar to (a), but note that the incorrect extraction of a credit balance as a debit balance means that twice the amount involved has to be amended on the trial balance and debited to suspense account.

(e)   Is similar to (b) - on this occasion Dr Suspense, Cr Cash, and amend the cash account balance on the trial balance.

(f)   Is similar to (c). The bookkeeper should have Dr Bank, Cr ETT - capital, but has instead Dr Bank, Cr Suspense, so to correct matters Dr Suspense, Cr Capital.

(g)   Item (g) does not appear in the suspense account as the error does not affect the imbalance of the trial balance. As *no* entry has been made for the cheque, the correcting entry is

	£	£
Dr Cash at bank account	120	
Cr Debtors control account		120

(h)   Item (h) also does not appear in the suspense account. Although an entry has been made in the books which was wrong, the entry was incorrect for both the debit and credit entry. The correcting entry is

	£	£
Dr Cash at bank account	45	
Cr Debtor control account		45

5   SOLUTION

Task 1

Suspense account

	£		£
Sales ledger control	3,200	Trial balance difference	
Cash - bank charges	23	(103,457 – 102,113)	1,344
		Travel expenses	9
		Purchase ledger control	1,870
	3,223		3,223

Task 2

	£
Draft net profit	97,499
Travel expenses	(9)
Returns outwards undercast	100
Electricity accrued expense	(154)
Overdraft interest	(28)
Machinery incorrectly charged to repairs	1,450
Depreciation on machinery (20% × 1,450)	(290)
Discounts allowed	(30)
Adjusted profit	98,538

WORKINGS

(W1)   The journal entries for each of the errors are as follows:

			£	£
(1)	Travel expenses		9	
	Suspense			9
(2)	Purchase ledger control		100	
	Returns outwards/purchases returns			100
(3)	Electricity		154	
	Accruals			154
(4)	Purchase ledger control		1,870	
	Suspense			1,870
(5)	Interest payable		28	
	Bank			28
(6)	Machinery at cost		1,450	
	Machinery repairs			1,450
	Depreciation charge (20% × 1,450)		290	
	Provision for depreciation			290
(7)	Discount allowed		30	
	Sales ledger control			30

(8)	Suspense		3,200	
	Sales ledger control			3,200
(9)	Suspense		23	
	Bank			23

6   SOLUTION

Task 1

TD - Journal

			Dr £	Cr £
(i)	Dr	Suspense	1,000	
		Cr Sales		1,000
(ii)	Dr	Plant (at cost)	240	
		Cr Delivery and installation costs		240
(iii)	Dr	Discounts received	150	
		Cr Creditors (JW a/c)		150
(iv)	Dr	Stationery stock	240	
		Cr Stationery		240
(v)	Dr	Suspense	500	
		Cr Purchases		500
(vi)	Dr	Sales returns (returns inwards)	230	
		Purchase returns (returns outwards)	230	
		Cr Suspense		460

Task 2

Suspense

		£			£
(i)	Sales	1,000		Balance b/f	1,040
(v)	Purchases	500	(vi)	Sales and purchase returns	460
		1,500			1,500

Chapter 4

SOLE TRADERS – THE ACCOUNTS

1   SOLUTION

Task 1

Profit or loss on disposal:

	£
Cost	12,000
Depreciation	(5,000)
NBV	7,000

Comparing the net book value of £7,000 with the sale proceeds of £4,000, there is a loss of (7,000 – 4,000) £3,000.

Task 2

T-account entries

Disposal of fixed assets account

	£		£
Car cost	12,000	Car provision for dep'n a/c	5,000
		Balance c/d	7,000
	12,000		12,000
		Cash at bank a/c (sales proceeds)	4,000
Balance b/d	7,000	Loss on disposal	3,000
	7,000		7,000

Car account

	£		£
Balance b/d	12,000	Disposal a/c	12,000

Car provision for depreciation account

	£		£
Disposals a/c	5,000	Balance b/d	5,000

Cash at bank account

	£		£
Disposals a/c	4,000		

2   SOLUTION

Motor vehicles cost account

		£			£
20X3			20X3		
1 June	Cash at bank	17,000	31 Dec	Balance c/d	17,000
20X4			20X4		
1 Jan	Balance b/d	17,000			
1 Aug	Cash at bank	12,500	31 Dec	Balance c/d	29,500
		29,500			29,500
20X5			20X5		
1 Jan	Balance b/d	29,500	5 Sept	Disposals	12,500
2 Feb	Cash at bank	19,400	31 Dec	Balance c/d	36,400
		48,900			48,900
20X6					
1 Jan	Balance b/d	36,400			

Motor vehicles - provision for depreciation account

		£			£
20X3			20X3		
31 Dec	Balance c/d	3,825	31 Dec	Depreciation expense $\left(\frac{17,000-1,700}{4}\right)$	3,825
20X4			20X4		
			1 Jan	Balance b/d	3,825
31 Dec	Balance c/d	10,463	31 Dec	Depreciation expense $\left(\frac{29,500-2,950}{4}\right)$	6,638
		10,463			10,463
20X5			20X5		
5 Sept	Disposals $\left(\frac{12,500-1,250}{4}\right)$	2,813	1 Jan	Balance b/d	10,463
31 Dec	Balance c/d	15,840	31 Dec	Depreciation expense $\left(\frac{36,400-3,640}{4}\right)$	8,190
		18,653			18,653
			20X6		
			1 Jan	Balance b/d	15,840

Disposals

		£			£
20X5			20X5		
5 Sept	Motor vehicle cost	12,500	5 Sept	Motor vehicles provision for dep'n	2,813
			5 Sept	Cash at bank	7,600
			31 Dec	P&L a/c (loss)	2,087
		12,500			12,500

3   SOLUTION

Motor van - cost

20X2	£	20X2	£
Cash	2,400	Balance c/d	2,400
	2,400		2,400
20X3		20X3	
Balance b/d	2,400	Balance c/d	2,400
	2,400		2,400
20X4		20X4	
Balance b/d	2,400	Disposals	2,400
	2,400		2,400

Motor van - accumulated depreciation

20X2	£	20X2	£
Balance c/d	210	Profit and loss	210
	210		210
20X3		20X3	
Balance c/d	630	Balance b/d	210
		Profit and loss	420
	630		630
20X4		20X4	
Disposal	735	Balance b/d	630
		Profit and loss	105
	735		735

Motor van disposals

20X4	£	20X4	£
Cost	2,400	Accumulated depreciation	735
Profit and loss (bal fig)	135	Cash	1,800
	2,535		2,535

WORKINGS

$$\text{Depreciation charge pa} \quad = \quad \frac{£2,400 - £300}{5}$$

$$= \quad £420 \text{ pa}$$

Charge for 20X2	=	(6m) 6/12 × £420	=	**£210**
Charge for 20X3	=	(12m)	=	**£420**
Charge for 20X4	=	(3m) 3/12 × £420	=	**£105**

Effect on financial statements:

(a)   Profit and loss account:

	£
20X2 Depreciation charge (Dr)	210
20X3 Depreciation charge (Dr)	420
20X4 Depreciation charge (Dr)	105
20X4 Depreciation over provided (Cr)	135

Note: the net effect of the two items in 20X4 would be combined with the depreciation charge on other fixed assets.

(b)   Balance sheet:

	20X2	20X3	31 Dec 20X4
	£	£	£
Cost	2,400	2,400	-
Less: Accumulated depreciation	210	630	-
Net book value	2,190	1,770	-

4   SOLUTION

Step 1   Write off the bad debt in 20X0.

Dr   Bad debts expense account
Cr   Debtors account

Bad debts expense

20X0	£	20X0	£
31 Dec Debtors	370		

Step 2   Calculate the provision required.

	£
Provision for doubtful debts $((6{,}570 - 370) \times 4\%)$	248

Step 3   Write up the provision for doubtful debts account.

Dr   Bad debts expense account
Cr   Provision for doubtful debts account

This will be the full amount of the provision as this is the first year that the provision has been set up.

Bad debts expense

20X0	£	20X0	£
31 Dec Debtors	370		
31 Dec Provision for doubtful debts	248		

Provision for doubtful debts

20X0	£	20X0	£
		31 Dec Bad debts expense	248

Step 4   Write off the balance on the bad debts expense account to the profit and loss account and carry down the balance on the provision account into 20X1.

Bad debts expense

20X0		£	20X0		£
31 Dec	Debtors	370			
31 Dec	Provision for doubtful debts	248	31 Dec	P&L a/c	618
		618			618

Provision for doubtful debts

20X0		£	20X0		£
31 Dec	Bal c/d	248	31 Dec	Bad debts expense	248
		248			248
			20X1		
			1 Jan	Bal b/d	248

Step 5   For 20X1 write off the bad debt to the bad debts expense account and set up the provision required.

	£
20X1 doubtful debts provision required $((8,400 - 1,500) \times 2\%)$	138

As the provision required is a decrease of £110 over the 20X0 provision the double entry is

Dr	Provision for doubtful debts account
Cr	Bad debts expense account

Bad debts expense

20X1		£	20X1		£
31 Dec	Debtors	1,500	31 Dec	Provision for doubtful debts	110

Provision for doubtful debts

20X0		£	20X0		£
31 Dec	Bal c/d	248	31 Dec	Bad debts expense	248
		248			248
20X1			20X1		
31 Dec	Bad debts expense	110	1 Jan	Bal b/d	248

Step 6   Balance off the bad debts expense account transferring the balance to the profit and loss account and carry down the required balance on the provision for doubtful debts account.

Bad debts expense

20X1		£	20X1		£
31 Dec	Debtors	1,500	31 Dec	Provision for doubtful debts	110
			31 Dec	P&L a/c	1,390
		1,500			1,500

Provision for doubtful debts

20X0		£	20X0		£
31 Dec	Bal c/d	248	31 Dec	Bad debts expense	248
		248			248
20X1			20X1		
31 Dec	Bad debts expense	110	1 Jan	Bal b/d	248
31 Dec	Bal c/d	138			
		248			248
			20X2		
			1 Jan	Bal b/d	138

Step 7 Calculate the provision required for 20X2.

	£
Specific provision	350
General provision ((6,250 – 350) × 2%)	118
	468

Step 8 Write up the provision account and the bad debts expense account. The increase in provision required is (468 – 138) £330 and the double entry for this increase is

Dr Bad debts expense account
Cr Provision for doubtful debts account

Bad debts expense

20X2		£	20X2		£
31 Dec	Provision for doubtful debts	330			

Provision for doubtful debts

20X0		£	20X0		£
31 Dec	Bal c/d	248	31 Dec	Bad debts expense	248
		248			248
20X1			20X1		
31 Dec	Bad debts expense	110	1 Jan	Bal b/d	248
31 Dec	Bal c/d	138			
		248			248
			20X2		
			1 Jan	Bal b/d	138
			31 Dec	Bad debts expense	330

Step 9   Transfer the balance on the bad debts expense account to the profit and loss account and carry down the required balance on the provision account.

Bad debts expense

20X2		£	20X2		£
31 Dec	Provision for doubtful debts	330	31 Dec	P&L a/c	330
		330			330

Provision for doubtful debts

20X0		£	20X0		£
31 Dec	Bal c/d	248	31 Dec	Bad debts expense	248
		248			248
20X1			20X1		
31 Dec	Bad debts expense	110	1 Jan	Bal b/d	248
31 Dec	Bal c/d	138			
		248			248
20X2			20X2		
			1 Jan	Bal b/d	138
31 Dec	Bal c/d	468	31 Dec	Bad debts expense	330
		468			468
			20X3		
			1 Jan	Bal b/d	468

5   **SOLUTION**

Alpha
Trading and profit and loss account for year to 31 December

	£	£
Sales		39,468
Opening stock	3,655	
Purchases (working 2)	27,101	
	30,756	
Less: Closing stock	3,123	
		27,633
Gross profit		11,835
Insurance	580	
Plant repairs	110	
Rent and rates	1,782	
Wages	3,563	
Discount allowed	437	
Motor van expenses	1,019	
General expenses	522	
		8,013
Net profit		3,822

Alpha
Balance sheet as at 31 December

	£	£	£
Fixed assets:			
Motor van			980
Plant			2,380
Shop fittings			1,020
			4,380
Current assets:			
Stock		3,123	
Debtors		3,324	
Cash on hand		212	
		6,659	
Current liabilities:			
Bank overdraft (working 1)	3,424		
Creditors	4,370		
		7,794	
			(1,135)
			3,245
Capital:			
Balance at 1 Jan			2,463
Add: Profit for year			3,822
			6,285
Less: Drawings (working 2)			3,040
			3,245

WORKINGS:

(W1)   Trial balance at 31 December

	Dr £	Cr £
Sales		39,468
Insurance	580	
Plant repairs	110	
Rent and rates	1,782	
Motor van	980	
Plant	2,380	
Purchases	27,321	
Wages	3,563	
Stock at 1 Jan (opening)	3,655	
Discount allowed	437	
Motor van expenses	1,019	
Shop fittings	1,020	
General expenses	522	
Capital account at 1 Jan		2,463
Sundry debtors	3,324	
Sundry creditors		4,370
Cash on hand	212	
Personal drawings	2,820	
	49,725	46,301
Bank overdraft (balancing figure)		3,424
	49,725	49,725

(W2)   Goods for own use:

	£
Drawings per trial balance	2,820
Add: Goods for own use	220
	3,040
Purchases per trial balance	27,321
Less: Goods for own use	220
	27,101

Note: if stock is taken from the business by the proprietor for his personal use, the double entry is to debit drawings and credit purchases. No entry is made in the stock account.

6   SOLUTION

Delta
Trading and profit and loss account for the year to 31 December 20X9

	£	£	£
Sales			124,450
Less: Returns			186
			124,264
Opening stock		8,000	
Add: Purchases	86,046		
Less: Returns	135		
	85,911		
Carriage inwards	156		
Wages	8,250		
		94,317	
Less: Closing stock		(7,550)	
			94,767
Gross profit			29,497
Discount received			138
			29,635
Salaries		3,500	
Travellers' salaries		5,480	
Travelling expenses		1,040	
Discounts allowed		48	
General expenses		2,056	
Gas, electricity and water		2,560	
Rent (W2)		1,750	
Carriage outwards		546	
Printing and stationery		640	
Bad debts (W4)		485	
Loan interest (W1)		100	
Depreciation (W3)		575	
Bank charges		120	
			18,900
Net profit			10,735

Delta - Balance sheet as at 31 December 20X9

	Cost £	Dep'n £	£
Fixed assets			
Premises	8,000	-	8,000
Plant and machinery	5,500	550	4,950
Furniture and fittings	500	25	475
	14,000	575	13,425
Current assets			
Stock		7,550	
Debtors	20,280		
Less: Provision (W4)	1,014		
		19,266	
Prepayments		250	
Cash at bank		650	
		27,716	
Current liabilities			
Creditors	10,056		
Accruals - loan interest	100		
		10,156	
			17,560
			30,985
Loan - Omega			2,000
			28,985
Capital: balance at 1 Jan 20X9			20,000
Add: Profit for the year			10,735
			30,735
Less: Drawings			1,750
			28,985

WORKINGS

(W1)   Loan interest

Accrual required   =   5% × £2,000

=   £100

Interest payable account			
	£		£
Balance c/d	100	Profit and loss account	100
	100		100
		Balance b/d	100

Note: it is not necessary to show the writing up of the ledger account as above where there have been no previous expenses stored up in the ledger account during the year.

It is more important to see the effect of the adjustment - a Dr to profit and loss account and a Cr on the balance sheet.

(W2)

Rent

	£		£
Cash	2,000	Profit and loss account	1,750
		Prepayment c/d	250
	2,000		2,000
Prepayment b/d	250		

(W3)   Depreciation

	£
Plant and machinery 10% × £5,500	550
Furniture and fittings 5% × £500	25
	575

Note: as with working (1) it is not necessary to write up the ledger accounts. The effect of the calculations can be inserted into the profit and loss account and the balance sheet.

Dr   Depreciation (Profit and loss account) = Expense
Cr   Accumulated depreciation (Balance sheet) = Reduction in asset)

(W4)   Bad debts

Bad debts account

	£		£
Balance b/d (per trial balance)		Balance b/d (per trial balance)	
Bad debts	256	Bad debts recovered	45
Provision for doubtful debts	274	Profit and loss account	485
	530		530

Provision for doubtful debts account

	£		£
Balance required c/d 5% × £20,280	1,014	Balance b/d (per trial balance)	740
		Bad debts account	274
	1,014		1,014

Note: no workings/ledger accounts have been shown for stock as the opening and closing stock figures can be inserted into the final accounts without further adjustments.

Chapter 5

THE EXTENDED TRIAL BALANCE – SOLE TRADERS

1   SOLUTION

Step 1   Enter the trial balance amounts onto the extended trial balance. Note that the opening stock had been omitted and must be put in on the debit side. Note also that the drawings had been entered onto the wrong side of the original trial balance. Once this is corrected and the drawings are included on the debit side of the trial balance the trial balance columns then balance.

Step 2   Enter the year end adjustments for bad debts, depreciation and errors into the adjustments column.

Step 3   Enter the year end accruals and prepayments in the adjustments column.

Step 4   Enter the opening and closing stock adjustments in the adjustments column ready to transfer across to the profit and loss account and balance sheet columns.

Step 5   Cross cast the extended trial balance into the profit and loss account and balance sheet columns as appropriate.

Step 6   Balance off the profit and loss account columns. In this case the missing figure is a loss for the year (on the credit side) of £9,600. This must be shown on the debit side of the balance sheet columns (a reduction in capital) in order for the balance sheet columns to balance.

PG Trading
Extended trial balance
at 31 December 20X6

Account	Trial balance		Adjustments		Profit and loss		Balance sheet	
	Dr £	Cr £	Dr £	Cr £	Dr £	Cr £	Dr £	Cr £
Capital account		63,000						63,000
Stock	22,500		25,500	22,500			25,500	
Sales		150,000				150,000		
Purchases	105,000				105,000			
Rent and rates	15,000			300 + 1,200	13,500			
Drawings	18,000						18,000	
Electricity	3,000				3,000			
Motor van cost	12,000						12,000	
Motor van provision for depreciation		6,000		750				6,750
Bank balance	6,750						6,750	
Trade debtors	30,000			1,500			28,500	
Trade creditors		31,500						31,500
Sundry expenses	750		75		825			
Wages and salaries	37,500		300 + 225		38,025			
Depreciation expenses			750		750			
Bad debt expense			1,500		1,500			
Accruals				300				300
Prepayments			1,200				1,200	
Stock (profit and loss)			22,500	25,500	22,500	25,500		
Loss for year						9,600	9,600	
	250,500	250,500	52,050	52,050	185,100	185,100	101,550	101,550

Chapter 6

BASIC PARTNERSHIP ACCOUNTING

1 SOLUTION

Task 1

Trial balance as at 31 December

	Dr £	Cr £
Capital account:		
Owen		9,000
Steel		10,000
10% loan account:		
Steel		5,000
Williams		6,000
Current account balance on 1 January:		
Owen		1,000
Steel		2,000
Drawings:		
Owen	6,500	
Steel	5,500	
Sales		113,100
Sales returns	3,000	
Closing stock	17,000	
Cost of goods sold	70,000	
Sales ledger control account	30,000	
Purchase ledger control account		25,000
Operating expenses	26,100	
Fixed assets at cost	37,000	
Provision for depreciation		18,000
Bank overdraft		3,000
Suspense (bal fig)		3,000
	195,100	195,100

*(**Tutorial note:** the information in the question refers to 'closing stock' and 'cost of goods sold'. Both of these imply that the year-end adjustments for stock have already been made.)*

Task 2

Adjustments to trial balance

Ref to question			Dr £	Cr £
(a)	(i)	Sales returns	100	
		Sales ledger control		100
	(ii)	Purchase ledger control	200	
		Sales ledger control		200
	(iii)	Sales ledger control	1,800	
		Sales		1,800
(b)		Disposal	5,000	
		Fixed asset cost		5,000
		Accumulated depreciation	5,000	
		Disposal		5,000
		Suspense	3,000	
		Disposal		3,000

(Tutorial note:

The last entry arises as the transaction was originally inserted into the books as a one-sided transaction (Dr Bank). The missing credit entry must therefore make up the £3,000 suspense account balance.*)*

(c)	Expenses	500	
	Drawings - Steel		500
	Drawings - Owen	1,000	
	Cost of goods sold		1,000
(d)	Interest expense	1,100	
	Interest accrual		1,100

Task 3

Owen and Steel
Profit and loss account for the year

	£	£
Sales (113,100 + 1,800)		114,900
Less: Returns (3,000 + 100)		3,100
		111,800
Cost of sales (70,000 – 1,000)		(69,000)
Gross profit		42,800
Operating expenses (26,100 – 3,000 + 500)	23,600	
Loan interest	1,100	
		(24,700)
Net profit for year		18,100

Appropriations:
  Interest
    Owen   900
    Steel   1,000

  Salary - Owen   (1,900)
                                                             (5,000)
                                                            ───────
                                                             11,200
Balance of profit:
  Owen   5,600
  Steel   5,600
                                            ───────
                                                            (11,200)
                                                            ───────

Owen and Steel
Balance sheet as at 31 December

	£	£	£
Fixed assets:			
Cost (37,000 – 5,000)		32,000	
Depreciation (18,000 – 5,000)		13,000	
		───────	
			19,000
Current assets:			
Stock		17,000	
Debtors (30,000 – 100 – 200 + 1,800)		31,500	
		───────	
		48,500	
Current liabilities:			
Creditors (25,000 – 200)	24,800		
Interest	1,100		
Bank overdraft	3,000		
	───────		
		28,900	
		───────	
Net current assets			19,600
			───────
			38,600
Loans			(11,000)
			───────
			27,600
			───────

	Capital £	Current £	Total £
Owen (see working)	9,000	5,000	14,000
Steel (see working)	10,000	3,600	13,600
	───────	───────	───────
	19,000	8,600	27,600
	───────	───────	───────

WORKING

Current accounts

	Owen £	Steel £		Owen £	Steel £
Drawings	6,500	5,500	Balance b/d	1,000	2,000
Adjustment to drawings	1,000		Adjustment to drawings		500
			Interest on capital	900	1,000
			Salary	5,000	
Balance c/d	5,000	3,600	Profit	5,600	5,600
	12,500	9,100		12,500	9,100

Chapter 7

ACCOUNTING FOR PARTNERSHIP CHANGES

1 SOLUTION

Task 1

River, Stream and Pool
Profit and loss appropriation account
for the year ended 30 September 20X7

	£	£
Net profit (see working)		47,300
Partner's salary - Pool		(11,000)
Interest on capital (see part (b))		
River	950	
Stream	1,230	
Pool	470	
		(2,650)
		33,650
Balance in PSR		
River	16,825	
Stream	10,095	
Pool	6,730	
		(33,650)

WORKINGS

	£
Net profit for the year per draft accounts	46,300
Reduction in valuation of opening stock	2,000
	48,300
Interest on River's loan account 10% × £10,000	1,000
	47,300

*(**Tutorial note:** it is necessary to work out the adjustments to the partner's capital accounts for Task 2 before the interest can be computed for Task 1.)*

Task 2

Smart and Swift
Partners' capital accounts year ended 30 September 20X7

	R £	S £	P £		R £	S £	P £
Adjustment				Balance b/d	30,000	20,000	15,000
Stock valuation	1,000	1,000		Goodwill	14,000	14,000	
Goodwill	14,000	8,400	5,600	(see working)			
(see working)							
Transfer to loan							
account	10,000						
Balances c/d	19,000	24,600	9,400				
	44,000	34,000	15,000		44,000	34,000	15,000
				Balances b/d	19,000	24,600	9,400

(Tutorial note: stock at 1 October 20X7 represents an asset of the business into which Pool is being admitted as a partner. A change in an asset value from its book value creates a revaluation surplus or deficit which must be reflected in the existing partners' capital accounts.)

Partners' current accounts year ended 30 September 20X7

	R £	S £	P £		R £	S £	P £
Drawings	21,000	13,000	11,000	Balance b/d	1,000	700	-
Balance c/d			7,200	Loan interest	1,000		
				Salary			11,000
				Interest on			
				capital	950	1,230	470
				Balance of			
				profit	16,825	10,095	6,730
				Balance c/d	1,225	975	-
	21,000	13,000	18,200		21,000	13,000	18,200
Balances b/d	1,225	975		Balance b/d			7,200

Goodwill

	£			£
Goodwill written up in old PSR			Goodwill written down in new PSR	
River ½	14,000		River 5	14,000
Stream ½	14,000		Stream 3	8,400
			Pool 2	5,600
	28,000			28,000

2   SOLUTION

Task 1

Smart and Swift
Profit and loss account for the year ended 31 December 20X8

	£	£	£
Hotel receipts			5,100
Catering and hotel expenses:			
Foodstuffs (2,600 + 420 - 300)	2,720		
Wages	2,200		
General expenses (810 + 60)	870		
		5,790	
Depreciation:			
Motor vehicle	200		
Fittings	100		
		300	
Loan interest		180	
			6,270
Net loss for the year			1,170
Allocated:			
Smart (three-fifths)			702
Swift (two-fifths)			468
			1,170

Task 2

Step 1   Enter all of the partnership assets into the realisation account at their book value.

Step 2   Account for the assets taken over by the partners in their capital accounts.

Step 3   Account for the assets realised and dissolution expenses through the cash account.

Step 4   Determine any profit on realisation and credit to partners' capital accounts.

Realisation account

	£	£		£	£
Sundry assets:			Assets taken over:		
Debtors		600	Smart:		
Fittings and fixtures			Stock of foodstuffs	250	
(1,800 - 100)		1,700	Fittings and fixtures		
Stocks of foodstuffs		300	(part)	600	
Freehold premises		6,000	Sundry items	40	
Motor vehicle (700 - 200)		500			890
Dissolution expenses		120	Swift:		
Profit on realisation:			Motor vehicle	400	
Smart (three-fifths)	462		Sundry items	20	
Swift (two-fifths)	308				420
		770	Assets realised:		
			Freehold		6,800
			Debtors		480
			Fittings and fixtures		1,400
		9,990			9,990

Task 3

Cash account for January 20X9

	£		£
Proceeds of:		Balance b/d	4,590
Freehold	6,800	Dissolution, etc expenses	120
Debtors	480	Sundry creditors (210 + 60)	270
Fittings and fixtures	1,400	Loan - Smart	3,000
Cash paid in by Swift	830	Cash withdrawn by Smart	1,530
	9,510		9,510

Task 4

Capital accounts

	Smart £	Swift £		Smart £	Swift £
Drawings	520	750	Balances b/d	3,000	500
Net loss for 20X8	702	468	Loan interest	180	
Assets taken over	890	420	Profit on realisation	462	308
Cash withdrawn	1,530		Cash paid in		830
	3,642	1,638		3,642	1,638

Chapter 8

LIMITED COMPANIES – INTRODUCTION

1 SOLUTION

Aysgarth Ltd
Trading, profit and loss and appropriation account for year ended 31 December 20X6

	£	£
Sales		80,000
Opening stock	10,000	
Purchases	49,000	
Carriage inwards	1,000	
	60,000	
Less: Closing stock	15,000	
Cost of sales		45,000
Gross profit		35,000
Discount received		200
		35,200
Discount allowed	400	
Carriage outwards	800	
Administrative expenses	4,000	
Staff salaries	4,000	
Directors' salaries	5,000	
Audit fee	1,000	
Depreciation	4,600	
Debenture interest	5,000	
		24,800
Net profit before tax		10,400
Corporation tax (W1)		5,000
Net profit after tax		5,400
Transfer to plant replacement reserve (W3)	1,000	
Preference dividend of 5% (paid)	1,000	
Ordinary dividend of 5% (proposed) (W2)	3,000	
		5,000
Retained profit		400
Profit and loss account b/d		8,000
Profit and loss account c/d		8,400

Aysgarth Ltd
Balance sheet as at 31 December 20X6

	£	£	£
Fixed assets:			
Tangible assets:			
Freehold land and buildings			
(£230,000 – (100,000 + 4,600))			125,400
Current assets:			
Stock		15,000	
Trade debtors		10,000	
Cash at bank		5,000	
		30,000	
Creditors - Amounts falling due within one year:			
Trade creditors	2,000		
Current taxation (W1)	5,000		
Dividend proposed (W2)	3,000		
Accruals (£5,000 + £1,000)	6,000		
		16,000	
Net current assets			14,000
Total assets less current liabilities			139,400
Creditors - Amounts falling due after more than one year:			
10% debentures 20X9			50,000
			89,400
Capital and reserves:			
Called up share capital:			
Ordinary 50p shares			60,000
5% £1 preference shares			20,000
Plant replacement reserve (W3)			1,000
Profit and loss account			8,400
			89,400

(W1)   Corporation tax

Current taxation

	£		£
Balance c/d	5,000	Corporation tax (profit and loss)	5,000

(W2)   Proposed ordinary dividend

Note that the figure of 2.5 pence per share relates to the number of shares in issue (£60,000 of 50p shares = 120,000 shares) × 2.5 pence = £3,000. Thus:

Dividend payable

	£		£
Balance c/d	3,000	Profit and loss appropriation	3,000

(W3) **Creation of plant replacement reserve**

The creation thereof is an appropriation of profit, and is accordingly shown on the profit and loss account after the profit after taxation figure.

Plant replacement reserve			
	£		£
Balance c/d	1,000	Profit and loss appropriation	1,000

2 SOLUTION

Floyd Ltd
Profit and loss account for year ended 31 March 20X5

	£	£
Sales		998,600
Cost of sales (W1)		830,740
Gross profit		167,860
Administrative costs (W1)		100,741
Debenture interest (9% × 75,000)		6,750
Profit before taxation		60,369
Corporation tax		31,200
Profit after taxation		29,169
Dividends:		
Paid	2,500	
Proposed (W4)	12,000	
		14,500
Retained profit for year		14,669
Profit and loss account b/d		45,910
Profit and loss account c/d		60,579

Floyd Ltd
Balance sheet as at 31 March 20X5

	Cost £	Dep'n £	£
Fixed assets:			
Tangible assets - plant (W3)	307,400	115,340	192,060
Current assets:			
Stock (W5)		61,070	
Debtors	52,030		
Less: Provision	2,601		
		49,429	
Cash at bank		41,118	
Cash in hand		126	
		151,743	
Creditors: Amounts falling due within one year:			
Creditors		38,274	
Current taxation		31,200	
Dividend payable (W4)		12,000	
Debenture interest accrued		6,750	
		88,224	
Net current assets			63,519
Total assets less current liabilities			255,579
Creditors: Amounts falling due after more than one year:			
9% debentures 20X9			75,000
			180,579
Capital and reserves:			
Called up share capital: 25p ordinary shares			100,000
Share premium account			20,000
Profit and loss account			60,579
			180,579

WORKINGS

(W1)

	Cost of sales £	Administrative costs £
Per question	800,000	100,000
Bad debts (W2)		741
Depreciation (W3)	30,740	
	830,740	100,741

FOULKS*lynch*

(W2)

Provision for doubtful debts account

	£		£
Profit and loss account:		Balance b/d	1,860
Balance c/d 5% × 52,030	2,601	Administrative costs - increase	
		in provision	741
	2,601		2,601

(W3)

Accumulated depreciation account

	£		£
		Balance b/d	84,600
		Profit and loss account:	
		Cost of sales	
Balance c/d	115,340	10% × 307,400	30,740
	115,340		115,340

(W4) **Final dividend**

Number of 25p shares = £100,000 × 4 = 400,000 shares

Hence dividend of 3p per share amounts to

3 pence × 400,000   = **£12,000**

(W5) The trial balance figure for stock must be closing stock as 'cost of sales' has also been determined and is shown on the trial balance.

3   SOLUTION

Nimrod Co Ltd
Trading, profit and loss, and appropriation account
for year ended 30 September 20X7

	£	£
Sales		240,000
Less: Returns		1,116
		238,884
Stock at 1 October 20X6	42,744	
Purchases	131,568	
	174,312	
Less: Closing stock at 30 September 20X7	46,638	
		127,674
Gross profit		111,210
Discount received		5,292
		116,502
Rates	6,372	
Wages and salaries (24,000 + 840))	24,840	
Insurance (5,688 - 300)	5,388	
General expenses	1,308	
Bad debts (W2)	1,476	
Depreciation: Buildings (W1)	11,400	
Fixtures and fittings (W1)	7,200	
Debenture interest (W3)	2,400	
		60,384
Profit before tax		56,118
Taxation		20,000
Profit after taxation		36,118
Dividends:		
Preference: Paid	1,800	
Proposed (W4)	1,800	
Ordinary: Proposed (W4)	3,000	
		6,600
Retained for the year		29,518
Transfer to general reserve		24,000
		5,518
Profit and loss account b/d		6,000
Profit and loss account c/d		11,518

Nimrod Co Ltd
Balance sheet as at 30 September 20X7

	Cost £	Dep'n £	£
Fixed assets:			
Intangible assets:			
Goodwill	49,200	-	49,200
Tangible assets:			
Land	54,000	-	54,000
Buildings	114,000	29,400	84,600
Furniture and fittings	66,000	37,200	28,800
	283,200	66,600	216,600
Current assets:			
Stock		46,638	
Debtors	37,920		
Less: Provision (W4)	1,896		
		36,024	
Prepayments (insurance)		300	
Cash in hand		696	
		83,658	
Creditors: Amounts falling due within one year:			
Bank overdraft		18,000	
Creditors		18,900	
Dividend payable (W4)		4,800	
Accruals (W5)		2,040	
Corporation tax		20,000	
		63,740	
Net current assets			19,918
Total assets less current liabilities			236,518
Creditors: Amounts falling due after more than one year:			
5% debentures			48,000
			188,518
Capital and reserves:			
Called up share capital:			
60,000 £1 ordinary shares			60,000
60,000 6% £1 preference shares			60,000
Share premium account			3,000
General reserve (30,000 + 24,000)			54,000
Profit and loss account			11,518
			188,518

(W1)

Accumulated depreciation account

	Build-ings £	Furn-iture £		Build-ings £	Furn-iture £
Balance c/d	29,400	37,200	Balance per trial balance	18,000	30,000
			Profit and loss account:		
			10% × 114,000	11,400	
			20% × (66,000		
			– 30,000)		7,200
	29,400	37,200		29,400	37,200

(W2)

Bad debts account

	£		£
Per trial balance	2,028	Decrease in provision for doubtful debts	552
		Profit and loss account	1,476
	2,028		2,028

Provision for doubtful debts account

	£		£
Bad debts account - decrease in provision	552	Per trial balance	2,448
Balance c/d 5% × 37,920	1,896		
	2,448		2,448

(W3)

Debenture interest account

	£		£
Per trial balance	1,200	Profit and loss account	2,400
Balance c/d - accrual	1,200		
	2,400		2,400

(W4)   **Dividends**

	£
Ordinary 5% × £60,000	3,000
Preference 3% × £60,000	1,800
	4,800

(W5)   **Accruals**

	£
Wages	840
Debenture interest (W3)	1,200
	2,040

Chapter 9

PUBLISHED ACCOUNTS

1   SOLUTION

Ople plc
Profit and loss account for year to 31 March 20X2

	£'000	£'000
Turnover		8,500
Cost of sales (working)		(5,270)
Gross profit		3,230
Distribution costs (working)		(1,490)
Administration expenses (working)		(630)
Operating profit		1,110
Income from fixed asset investments - Dividends		240
Profit on ordinary activities before taxation		1,350
Tax on profit on ordinary activities		
Corporation tax based on profit for year	380	
Over-provision of last year's corporation tax charge	(30)	
		(350)
Profit after taxation		1,000
Dividends		
Preference - Paid 10p per share	100	
Ordinary		
Interim paid 2.5p per share	200	
Final proposed 2.5p per share	200	
		(500)
Retained profit for year		500

(*Tutorial note:* the adjustment for any over/under provision of corporation tax is made in the year in which it occurs rather than treating it as a prior period adjustment.)

WORKING

Analysis of costs

	Cost of sales £'000	Distribution £'000	Admin-istration £'000
Purchases (500 + 4,400 – 700)	4,200		
Audit			50
Depreciation	85	40	20
Salaries			95
Distribution		425	
Factory expenses	970		
Hire	15		
Office expenses			190
Legal expenses			35
Warehouse rent		65	
Wages 0 : 80 : 20		960	240
	5,270	1,490	630

2   SOLUTION

Toby Ltd
Profit and loss account for year to 31 December 20X8

	£	£
Turnover (100 – 1) – (4 – 1)		96,000
Cost of sales (W1)		(65,300)
Gross profit		30,700
Distribution costs	6,800	
Administrative expenses	7,300	
Interest payable (10% × 30,000)	3,000	
		(17,100)
Profit on ordinary activities before taxation		13,600
Tax on profit on ordinary activities		(3,000)
Profit on ordinary activities after taxation and amount set aside to reserves		10,600

Toby Ltd
Balance sheet as at 31 December 20X8

	Cost £	Depr. £	£
Fixed assets			
Tangible assets			
Land and buildings	40,000	-	40,000
Plant and machinery	40,000	16,000	24,000
			64,000
Current assets			
Stocks		18,000	
Debtors (18,000 – 900 (W3))		17,100	
Prepayment (W4)		500	
		35,600	
Creditors: Amounts falling due within one year			
Bank overdraft (W4)	9,000		
Creditors and accruals	7,000		
Interest payable	3,000		
Taxation	3,000		
		22,000	
Net current assets			13,600
Total assets less current liabilities			77,600
Creditors: Amounts falling due after more than one year			
Debentures			30,000
			47,600
Capital and reserves			
Share capital - £1 ordinary shares			15,000
Share premium account			3,000
Profit and loss account (19,000 + 10,600)			29,600
			47,600

WORKINGS

(W1)   **Analysis of costs**

	Cost of sales £	Dist. £	Admin. £
Opening stock	15,000		
Purchases	61,000		
Returns	(4,000)		
Closing stock	(18,000)		
Operating expenses	9,000		
Admin			7,000
Selling		6,000	
Provision netted off against selling expenses		800	
Bad debts (W3)			100
Rates £500 (W3)	450		50
Rates in operating expenses	(150)		150
Depreciation (W5)	4,000		
Profit on sale of plant (W5)	(2,000)		
	65,300	6,800	7,300

(Tutorial note: as the cost classification headings are not defined in the legislation there is some choice as to how various costs are allocated. Bad debts for example could be shown under any heading.

What is important is the production of a working paper showing where you have allocated items.)

(W2)

Suspense account

	£		£
Share capital	5,000	Balance b/d	10,000
Share premium (5,000 × 0.6)	3,000		
Disposal proceeds	2,000		
	10,000		10,000

(W3)

Provision for doubtful debts

	£		£
		Reversal of error - selling expenses	800
Balance c/d 5% × (20,000 – 2,000)	900	Profit and loss	100
	900		900

(Tutorial note: care is needed with the sales returns incorrectly entered. As the company has control accounts, totals are entered from the various books of prime entry to the sales account and sales ledger control account etc. Sales are overstated by £1,000 and thus debtors are overstated by £1,000 (ie, debit to the control account was overstated). In addition sales returns are understated by £1,000 and thus debtors are again overstated by £1,000.)

(W4)   **Standing order for rates**

		Expense account £	Bank overdraft £
(a)			8,000
	Enter into books	1,000	1,000
			9,000
(b)	Prepayment	(500)	
		500	

(W5)   **Disposal - plant**

	Per trial balance	
	Plant cost £	Depreciation £
	50,000	22,000
Eliminated on disposal	(10,000)	(10,000)
	40,000	12,000
Depreciation charge for year 10% × 40,000		4,000
		16,000
Profit on sale = cash proceeds =		2,000

Chapter 10

TAXATION IN COMPANY ACCOUNTS

1   SOLUTION

(a)   Output VAT is the VAT that is charged by VAT registered businesses on their sales. This VAT is collected on behalf of Customs and Excise and paid over to them by the business normally every three months. The sales of the business are shown in the profit and loss account net of VAT and the VAT on those sales is recorded as a creditor due to Customs and Excise.

(b)   Unfranked investment income is the receipt of income such as debenture interest by a company from another company. The receiving company receives it net of income tax and this can be reclaimed by the company from the Inland Revenue. When the debenture interest is included in the profit and loss account then it is included at its gross amount and the related income tax shown as a debtor receivable from the Inland Revenue.

(c)   When the Corporation tax charge for a year is included in the year end accounts in the profit and loss account and balance sheet the amount that is shown is an estimate of the final amount of Corporation tax for that year. When the Corporation tax is paid to the Inland Revenue 9 months later the actual amount paid could be greater or smaller than the estimate included in the previous years accounts. If the amount actually paid is less than the charge estimated in the previous year's profit and loss account then there has been an over provision in the previous year. In accounting terms this is dealt with by crediting the amount of the over provision to the current year's profit and loss account through the current year tax charge.

(d)   Deferred taxation is any additional tax that is thought will be likely to be payable in the future due to timing differences caused by items appearing in the financial statements in one accounting period and in the tax computation in a different accounting period.

2   SOLUTION

Task 1

(a)   DR Corporation tax charge (P&L account)   £64,700
       CR Corporation tax creditor (Balance sheet)   £64,700

       being provision for the 20X5 Corporation tax charge.

(b)   DR Corporation tax charge (P&L account)   £3,400
       CR Corporation tax creditor (Balance sheet)   £3,400

       being adjustment for the under provision for Corporation tax in the previous year.

(c)   DR Corporation tax charge (P&L account)   £111
       CR Dividend income   £111

       being the grossing up of the dividend receipt with its available tax credit.

(d)   DR Corporation tax charge (P&L account)   £800

       CR Deferred tax account (Balance sheet)   £800

being the increase in deferred tax provision for the year.

Task 2

Profit and loss account tax charge:

	£
Corporation tax charge for the year	64,700
Under provision in previous year	3,400
Tax credit on dividend income	111
Transfer to deferred tax account	800
	69,011
Balance sheet Corporation tax creditor	£64,700

3   SOLUTION

The tax rates that should be used are those that have been enacted or substantively enacted by the balance sheet date.

Chapter 11

TANGIBLE FIXED ASSETS

1 SOLUTION

Usually, with the exception of land (providing that it is not a mine, quarry or other wasting asset), fixed assets have a limited number of years of useful life. When a fixed asset is purchased and later scrapped or disposed of by the firm, that part of the original cost not recovered on disposal is called depreciation. Depreciation is thus the part of the cost of the fixed asset consumed during its working life. Accordingly, it is a cost for services in the same way as an expense incurred is a cost for those goods or services received. Depreciation is, therefore, a revenue expense item and will be charged annually in the profit and loss account. The depreciation cost apportionable to each year of the asset's life is estimated in advance of disposal and accounted for by making annual provisions to reduce the asset from cost to the written down value, at the end of each year of its life.

An example of a method of computing the annual depreciation of an asset is the **straight-line method** which is outlined below:

$$\frac{\text{Cost} - \text{Residual value}}{\text{Number of years of expected use}} = \text{Depreciation charge pa}$$

$$\text{eg} \quad \frac{£1,000 - \text{Nil}}{10 \text{ years}} = £100 \text{ pa}$$

2 SOLUTION

Task 1

	£	£
DR Freehold building at cost	20,000	
DR Freehold building - accumulated depreciation	12,000	
(5 years of depreciation at £2,400 per year)		
CR Revaluation reserve		32,000

Task 2

From 20X7 the annual depreciation charge is based upon the revalued amount. Therefore the valuation of £140,000 is to be spread over the remaining useful life of the building of 45 years.

$$\text{Annual depreciation} \quad = \quad \frac{£140,000}{45 \text{ years}}$$

$$= \quad £3,111 \text{ per year}$$

Task 3

If the property were an investment property as per SSAP 19 then it would not be depreciated each year. Instead it would be revalued on an annual basis and included in the balance sheet at its current valuation. Any changes in that valuation are taken to an Investment Revaluation Reserve.

3   SOLUTION

SSAP 4 permits two possible treatments of capital based grants in financial statements:

(a)   to write off the grant against the cost of the fixed asset to which it relates. This has the effect of reducing the annual depreciation charge to the profit and loss account as this is based upon the net cost of the fixed asset.

(b)   to treat the grant as a deferred credit and to transfer a portion of the grant to the profit and loss account each year of the related fixed asset's life. The depreciation charge is based upon the original cost of the fixed asset but this is partially offset by the annual credit for the grant.

Although both methods are acceptable CA85 requires that fixed assets should be stated at their purchase price, therefore ruling out the first method for companies. Therefore a company should use the second method and set up a deferred credit account for its capital based grants.

4   SOLUTION

Firstly an impairment review does not apply to

- derivatives
- investment properties
- goodwill that was written off to reserves under SSAP 22 and has not been restated.

An impairment review is performed on fixed assets and goodwill to ensure that they are not recorded in the Financial Statements at a level above their recoverable amounts.

An impairment review is generally carried out when there is an indication that an impairment has occurred.

The principles of an impairment review can be shown by the following diagram:

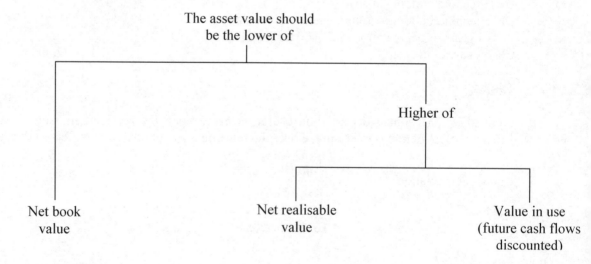

Chapter 12

INTANGIBLE FIXED ASSETS

1 SOLUTION

Task 1

Pure research

Original work which is not primarily directed towards any specific aim or application.

Applied research

Original work directed towards a specific practical aim or objective.

Development

The use of scientific or technical knowledge to produce new or substantially improved products.

Taэk 2

The two fundamental accounting concepts which are particularly relevant here are the accruals concept and the prudence concept.

The accruals concept requires costs to be matched with the relevant revenue. This implies that costs which have been incurred but have not resulted in sales should be carried forward as assets at the year end so that they can be matched with sales when they do arise.

Under this concept all development costs would be carried forward.

The prudence concept, however, requires costs to be written off unless it is reasonably certain that sales will be made in the future which will fully cover those costs.

Under this concept research expenditure would be written off as there is no clear link between the expenditure and the commercial sale of a product. Some development expenditure would also be written off if by the end of the accounting period it is not reasonably certain that profitable production will ensue. Only part of development expenditure would thus be carried forward.

Where there is conflict between the accruals and prudence concepts, the prudence concept normally prevails. Thus development expenditure should only be carried forward if the conditions in SSAP 13 are met.

2   SOLUTION

(a)   In equal instalments over the three year period, ie, £200,000 pa; or

(b)   In relation to total sales expected (900,000 units):

$$£$$

$$\text{Year 1} \quad \frac{400,000}{900,000} \quad \times £600,000 \quad = \quad 266,667$$

$$\text{Year 2} \quad \frac{300,000}{900,000} \quad \times £600,000 \quad = \quad 200,000$$

$$\text{Year 3} \quad \frac{200,000}{900,000} \quad \times £600,000 \quad = \quad 133,333$$

3   SOLUTION

Goodwill may exist because of any combination of a number of possible factors, for example:

- reputation for quality and/or service;
- good physical location;
- technical know-how and experience;
- possession of favourable contracts;
- good management, key personnel, technical personnel etc.

4   SOLUTION

According to SSAP 13, development expenditure **may** be capitalised if **all** the following criteria are met. (Please note that this is optional: if all criteria are met, the business may decide not to capitalise).

The criteria are:

- the project must be clearly defined
- expenditure must clearly distguishable and measurable
- the project must be commercially viable
- it must be technically feasible
- expected future revenue should exceed expected future costs
- adequate resources must exist to enable the project to be completed.

Chapter 13

STOCKS AND LONG TERM CONTRACTS

1 SOLUTION

(a) FIFO

Cost per unit		Units	Sold value £	Stock value £
@ £20 per unit	purchased	600		
	sold	(600)	12,000	
@ £23 per unit	purchased	300		
	sold	(100)	2,300	
	remaining stock	200		4,600
			14,300	4,600

(b) LIFO

Cost per unit		Units	Sold value £	Stock value £
@ £20 per unit	purchased	600		
	sold	(400)	8,000	
	remaining stock	200		4,000
@ £23 per unit	purchased	300		
	sold	(300)	6,900	
			14,900	4,000

(c) Weighted average

		Units	£ per unit	Value £
3 Mar	purchases	600	£20	12,000
19 Mar	purchases	300	£23	6,900
	balance	900		18,900
31 Mar	sells	700	at avge. £21 (£18,900 ÷ 900 units)	14,700
	stock	200	£21	4,200

2 SOLUTION

	Cost £	Costs to complete £	Selling costs £	Selling price £	NRV £	Valuation £
Item 1	1,000	nil	50	1,500	1,450	1,000
Item 2	2,000	500	100	2,400	1,800	1,800
Item 3	3,000	800	200	3,800	2,800	2,800
						5,600

3 SOLUTION

Item	Raw materials costs £	Labour costs £	Production overheads £	NRV £	Balance sheet £
A	500	800	800	2,600	2,100 (cost)
B	1,000	-	-	1,100	1,000 (cost)
C	500	800	800	1,950	1,950 (NRV)
					5,050

4 SOLUTION

Task 1

Model P

Cost	100 + 20 + 15	= 135
Net realisable value	150 - 22	= 128
Lower of cost and net realisable value		£128

Model Q

Cost	200 + 30 + 18	= 248
Net realisable value	300 - 40	= 260
Lower of cost and net realisable value		£248

Task 2

LIFO

Year 1	Purchases £	Cost of sales £	Stock £	Sales £
buy 10 at 300	3,000		3,000	
buy 12 at 250	3,000		6,000	
sell 8 at 400		2,000 (W1)	4,000	3,200
buy 6 at 200	1,200		5,200	
sell 12 at 400		2,800 (W2)	2,400	4,800
	7,200	4,800	2,400	8,000

Year 2

		Cost of sales	Stock	Sales
Opening stock			2,400	
buy 10 at 200	2,000		4,400	
sell 5 at 400		1,000 (W3)	3,400	2,000
buy 12 at 150	1,800		5,200	
sell 25 at 400		5,200 (W4)	0	10,000
	3,800	6,200	0	12,000

FIFO

Year 1	*Purchases* £	*Cost of sales* £	*Stock* £	*Sales* £
buy 10 at 300	3,000		3,000	
buy 12 at 250	3,000		6,000	
sell 8 at 400		2,400 (W5)	3,600	3,200
buy 6 at 200	1,200		4,800	
sell 12 at 400		3,100 (W6)	1,700	4,800
	7,200	5,500	1,700	8,000

Year 2

	£	£	£	£
Opening stock			1,700	
buy 10 at 200	2,000		3,700	
sell 5 at 400		1,100 (W7)	2,600	2,000
buy 12 at 150	1,800		4,400	
sell 25 at 400		4,400 (W8)	0	10,000
	3,800	5,500	0	12,000

WORKINGS

		£
1	8 × 250	2,000
2	6 × 200	1,200
	4 × 250	1,000
	2 × 300	600
		2,800
3	5 × 200	1,000
4	12 × 150	1,800
	5 × 200	1,000
	8 × 300	2,400
		5,200
5	8 × 300	2,400
6	2 × 300	600
	10 × 250	2,500
		3,100

7	2 × 250	500
	3 × 200	600
		1,100

8	3 × 200	600
	10 × 200	2,000
	12 × 150	1,800
		4,400

Trading accounts	LIFO		FIFO	
	£	£	£	£
Year 1				
Sales		8,000		8,000
Opening stock	0		0	
Purchases	7,200		7,200	
	7,200		7,200	
Closing stock	2,400		1,700	
Cost of sales		4,800		5,500
Gross profit		3,200		2,500
Year 2				
Sales		12,000		12,000
Opening stock	2,400		1,700	
Purchases	3,800		3,800	
	6,200		5,500	
Closing stock	0		0	
Cost of sales		6,200		5,500
Gross profit		5,800		6,500

5   SOLUTION

SSAP 9 defines cost as that expenditure which has been incurred in the normal course of business in bringing the product or service to its present location and condition. Thus cost should include both costs of purchase and such costs of conversion (for example direct costs and production overheads) as are appropriate to the location and condition.

Net realisable value should be taken as the actual or estimated selling price (net of trade but before settlement discounts) less all further costs to completion and all costs to be incurred in marketing, selling and distribution.

6   SOLUTION

A long term contract is one that lasts for more than one accounting period. The fundamental problem with accounting for such long term contracts is therefore whether to wait until the end of the contract before any profit on the contract is recognised in the financial statements or whether to recognise some of the profit as it is earned in each accounting period.

The fundamental accounting concepts that apply here are the matching concept and the prudence concept. Under the matching concept, the costs and revenue, and therefore profit, from the contract should be recognised in the periods in which the work is done on the contract. Therefore profit should be recognised as the contract progresses. However the prudence concept is that profits should not be anticipated in the financial statements but only recognised when they are reasonably certain.

SSAP 9 recognises both of these fundamental accounting concepts in its required treatment for long term contract work in progress. In each accounting period, if a final profitable outcome on the contract is reasonably certain, then the attributable profit for the period should be recognised in the profit and loss account. This is done by including the attributable element of turnover and costs for the period therefore resulting in attributable profit. Alternatively if the contract appears to be likely to make a loss then this foreseeable loss should be recognised in full, according to the prudence concept, as soon as it is determined.

Chapter 14

SUBSTANCE OF TRANSACTIONS

1   SOLUTION

(a)   SSAP 17 *Accounting for post balance sheet events* gives the following definitions of events occurring between the balance sheet date and the date on which the financial statements are approved by the board of directors:

- Adjusting events are post balance sheet events which provide additional evidence of conditions existing at the balance sheet date;

- Non-adjusting events are post balance sheet events which concern conditions that did not exist at the balance sheet date.

(b)   Examples can include any two from the following lists:

Adjusting events

The following are examples of post balance sheet events that would normally be classified as adjusting events:

Fixed assets. The subsequent determination of the purchase price or of the proceeds of sale of assets purchased or sold before the year end.

Property. A valuation which provides evidence of an impairment in value.

Investments. The receipt of a copy of the financial statements or other information in respect of an unlisted company which provides evidence of an impairment in the value of a long-term investment.

Stocks and work-in-progress

(i)   The receipt of proceeds of sales after the balance sheet date or other evidence concerning the net realisable value of stocks.

(ii)   The receipt of evidence that the previous estimate of accrued profit on a long-term contract was materially inaccurate.

Debtors. The renegotiation of amounts owing by debtors, or the insolvency of a debtor.

Dividends receivable. The declaration of dividends by subsidiaries and associated companies relating to periods prior to the balance sheet date of the holding company.

Taxation. The receipt of information regarding rates of taxation.

Claims. Amounts received or receivable in respect of insurance claims which were in the course of negotiation at the balance sheet date.

Discoveries. The discovery of errors or frauds which show that the financial statements were incorrect.

Non-adjusting events

The following are examples of post balance sheet events which normally should be classified as non-adjusting events:

Mergers and acquisitions.
Reconstructions and proposed reconstructions.
Issues of shares and debentures.
Purchases and sales of fixed assets and investments.
Losses of fixed assets or stocks as a result of a catastrophe such as fire or flood.
Opening new trading activities or extending existing trading activities.
Closing a significant part of the trading activities if this was not anticipated at the year end.
Decline in the value of property and investments held as fixed assets, if it can be demonstrated that the decline occurred after the year end.
Changes in rates of foreign exchange.
Government action, such as nationalisation.
Strikes and other labour disputes.
Augmentation of pension benefits.

(c)   A material post balance sheet event requires changes in the amounts to be included in financial statements where:

(i)   It is an adjusting event; or

(ii)   it indicates that application of the going concern concept to the whole or a material part of the company is not appropriate.

A material post balance sheet event should be disclosed where:

(i)   it is a non-adjusting event of such materiality that its non-disclosure would affect the ability of the users of financial statements to reach a proper understanding of the financial position; or

(ii)   it is the reversal or maturity after the year end of a transaction entered into before the year end, the substance of which was primarily to alter the appearance of the company's balance sheet (window dressing).

In respect of each post balance sheet event which is required to be disclosed as above, the following information should be stated by way of notes in financial statements:

(i)   the nature of the event; and

(ii)   an estimate of the financial effect, or a statement that it is not practicable to make such an estimate.

The estimate of the financial effect should be disclosed before taking account of taxation, and the taxation implications should be explained where necessary for a proper understanding of the financial position.

The date on which the financial statements are approved by the board of directors should be disclosed in the financial statements.

2   SOLUTION

Task 1

The terms 'operating lease' and 'finance lease' are defined in SSAP 21: *Accounting for leases and hire purchase contracts.*

A finance lease is a lease that transfers substantially all the risks and rewards of ownership of an asset to the lessee. Normally a lease will be treated as a finance lease if the present value of the lease payments is equal to 90% or more of the cash price of the leased asset. In practice a finance lease provides a similar situation to that which exists where a business purchases an asset and obtains a loan to finance the acquisition.

An operating lease is a lease other than a finance lease. The commercial substance of an operating lease is similar to that which exists where a business rents an asset.

Task 2

Actuarial method

Balance sheet extracts

Notes		*Years ending 31 Dec.*	
		20X1	*20X2*
		£	£
2	Fixed assets:		
	Tangible assets:		
	Leased machine under finance lease	72,000	48,000
3	Creditors: amounts falling due within one year:		
	Obligation under finance lease (W2)	22,112	25,316
3	Creditors: amounts falling due after more than one year:		
	Obligation under finance lease (W2)	39,575	14,259

Profit and loss account extracts

	Years ending 31 Dec.	
	20X1	*20X2*
	£	£
Depreciation charge	24,000	24,000
Finance charge under finance lease (W1)	10,687	7,888

Notes to the accounts (required by SSAP 21: Accounting for leases and hire purchase contracts)

1.   Accounting policies note

An amount equivalent to the cost of certain machinery leased under a finance lease is included in fixed assets and depreciated in accordance with the company's normal rates.

Outstanding lease instalments, excluding interest, are shown under creditors. Interest is charged to the profit and loss account by half-annual instalments over the term of the finance lease.

2.   Tangible fixed assets

	20X1 £	20X2 £
Leased machine at cost	96,000	96,000
Less: Accumulated depreciation		
(1/4 × 96,000 pa)	24,000	48,000
	72,000	48,000

WORKINGS

(W1)   Interest (actuarial method)

Half-year	Capital £	Interest 7% £	Sub-total £	Cash £	Balance £
1	81,000	5,670	86,670	15,000	71,670
2	71,670	5,017	76,687	15,000	61,687
		10,687			
3	61,687	4,318	66,005	15,000	51,005
4	51,005	3,570	54,575	15,000	39,575
		7,888			
5	39,575	2,770	42,345	15,000	27,345
6	27,345	1,914	29,259	15,000	14,259
		4,684			
7	14,259	741	15,000	15,000	Nil

(W2)   Creditors

	20X1 £	20X2 £
Capital outstanding at end of year	61,687	39,575
Less: Capital outstanding at end		
of next year	39,575	14,259
Capital repayable within one year	22,112	25,316

3   SOLUTION

The objective of FRS 5 is to ensure that the substance of an entity's transactions is reported in its financial statements. Accounting for substance is a development of the traditional 'substance over form' concept which has long been applied in accounts, eg, to require assets acquired under finance leases to be capitalised in the lessee's balance sheet.

To determine the substance of a transaction it is necessary to identify whether the transaction has given rise to new assets or liabilities for the business and whether it has changed the existing assets or liabilities. Assets and liabilities are defined in the FRS as follows.

Assets are rights or other access to future economic benefits controlled by an entity as a result of past transactions or events.

Liabilities are an entity's obligations to transfer economic benefits as a result of past transactions or events.

Once identified, an asset or liability should be recognised (ie, included) in the balance sheet, provided that it can be measured at a monetary amount with sufficient reliability.

The Companies Act 1985 requires financial statements to give a true and fair view of the state of affairs of the company as at the end of the financial year and of the profit or loss of the company for the financial year. This requirement over-rides all others but nowhere is there a definition of 'true and fair'.

Some preparers of accounts over recent years have developed methods of accounting which comply with the detailed rules of the Companies Acts, but arguably do not give a true and fair view.

For example, assets acquired under hire purchase agreements are sometimes excluded from the purchaser's balance sheet until the final instalment is paid on the argument that title has not yet passed to the purchaser until that moment. However it is now agreed that such accounting, although it accords with the legal form of the situation, does not reflect the actual commercial substance. If accounts are to give a true and fair view, surely they should reflect the reality of the underlying transactions. Thus the concept of substance over form was born, and assets acquired under finance leases and hire purchase agreements had to be shown on the acquirer's balance sheet.

Leasing and HP is a simple situation. In practice clever accountants came up with more and more complex arrangements to test the boundaries of the substance over form concept. The ASB decided that it was time to return to basics and issue an FRS which defined an asset and a liability and required entities to account for transactions according to how assets and liabilities were affected, thus applying a simple solution to a complex problem.

4   SOLUTION

If a company reports a transaction in its financial statements then the assumption that a user of the financial statements would normally make is that this transaction is a normal, arms length transaction. However if there were circumstances that meant that this transaction was taking place between parties that were closely related and therefore this was not a normal arms length transaction then it would be important for the user of the financial statements to know about this.

Therefore the main aim of FRS 8 and the reason that it was issued was to ensure that this disclosure takes place. The FRS requires that companies should disclose material transactions with all related parties in the notes to their financial statements in order to assist users in a fuller understanding of the financial statements.

Chapter 15

REPORTING FINANCIAL PERFORMANCE

1 SOLUTION

Before the publication of Financial Reporting Standard 3 **Reporting financial performance**, companies produced profit and loss accounts which emphasised the 'bottom' line profit achieved from all the operations and activities of the enterprise. This conglomeration concealed important aspects of the periodic financial performance of distinctive components of the enterprise. FRS 3 was issued to help remedy this problem, the objective of the standard being to require entities within its scope to highlight a **range** of important components of financial performance, to aid users in understanding the performance achieved by a reporting entity in a period and to assist them in forming a basis for their assessment of future results and cashflows.

The standard requires a changed format to the profit and loss account to help achieve this objective. A 'layered' format is required showing

(i)   results of continuing operations (including the results of acquisitions),

(ii)   results of discontinued operations,

(iii)   profits or losses on the sale or termination of an operation, costs of a fundamental reorganisation or restructuring and profits or losses on the disposal of fixed assets, and

(iv)   extraordinary items.

Items (i) and (iii) result in all cases in a split of turnover and operating profit on the face of the profit and loss account, and an analysis of cost of sales and net operating expenses in the notes (although these items may be split on the face of the profit and loss account). In an effort to solve the problems of extraordinary items, the standard restricts such items to those being (very) unusual items outside ordinary activities. In addition the earnings per share figure is to be calculated after extraordinary items thus removing the anomaly of comparative EPS figures caused by extraordinary items.

Also as an aid to measuring periodic performance, entities are now to provide a statement of total recognised gains and losses (including unrealised surpluses on revaluation of properties) and a reconciliation of movements in shareholders' funds.

Overall FRS 3 should be helpful to readers of published accounts, making interpretations of the financial performance of an enterprise more meaningful.

2 SOLUTION

Task 1

Topaz Limited
Profit and loss account for the year ended 31 December 1996

	Continuing operations £m	Discontinued operations £m	Total £m
Turnover	68	13	81
Cost of sales	(41)	(8)	(49)
Gross profit	27	5	32
Distribution costs *(Note 1)*	(6)	(1)	(7)
Administrative expenses	(4)	(2)	(6)
Operating profit	17	2	19
Profit on sale of discontinued operations		2.5	2.5
Costs of fundamental reorganisation	(1.8)		(1.8)
Profit on ordinary activities before interest	15.2	4.5	19.7
Interest payable			(1)
Profit on ordinary activities before taxation			18.7
Taxation			(4.8)
Profit on ordinary activities after taxation			13.9
Dividends			
Interim paid			(2.0)
Final proposed			(4.0)
Retained profit for the financial year			7.9

Note 1

Distribution costs include a bad debt of £1.9m which arose on the continuing operations.

Task 2

Topaz Limited
Statement of total recognised gains and losses

	£m
Profit for the financial year	13.9
Unrealised surplus on revaluation of properties	4
Total gains recognised since last annual report	17.9

3   SOLUTION

Many enterprises carry on several different types of business or operate in a number of different geographical areas. These will often have different rates of profitability, different degrees of risk and different opportunities for growth. The purpose of reporting an entity's results by each of these segments is that users of the financial statements can then appreciate more thoroughly the overall results and financial position of the entity and be aware of the impact that changes in significant components of the business may have on the business as a whole.

SSAP 25 leaves the job of determining reportable segments to the directors of a company. These segments however will be either different classes of business or geographical segments. For each class of business and geographical segment the following should be disclosed:

- turnover from external customers;
- turnover from other segments;
- profit before tax;
- net assets.

The total amount that is disclosed by segment should agree with the total in the financial statements otherwise a reconciliation of the two totals is required.

Chapter 16

MISCELLANEOUS ACCOUNTING STANDARDS

1 SOLUTION

The ASB had two main aims when issuing FRS 4 *Capital instruments*:

- to ensure that all capital instruments were correctly categorised on the balance sheet as either debt or shareholders' funds

- to ensure that the full cost of all capital instruments is charged to the profit and loss account over the life of the capital instrument.

The first of these objectives was met by stating that all capital instruments that meet the definition in FRS 4 of a liability must be shown as such on the balance sheet. This means in particular that convertible debentures must be shown as debt and not equity on the balance sheet. However as convertible debentures are somewhat different in nature to other liabilities then they must be disclosed as a separate category of debt.

Any capital instruments that are not shown as debt on the balance sheet are part of shareholders' funds. These shareholders' funds in turn must be split between equity and non-equity. Any shares with any debt characteristics are to be classified as non-equity and the remainder, normally ordinary shares and reserves, as equity.

The second aim of the ASB is met by FRS 4 by detailing the method by which the full finance cost of all capital instruments is to be allocated over the life of the capital instrument in order to give a constant charge each year based upon the outstanding amount of the instrument on the balance sheet.

2 SOLUTION

In a defined benefit scheme, the benefits to be paid depend upon either the average pay of the employee during his or her career or, more typically, the final pay of the employee. It is impossible to be certain in advance that the contributions to the pension scheme, together with the investment return thereon, will equal the benefits to be paid. The employer may have a legal obligation to make good any shortfall; alternatively, if a surplus arises the employer may be entitled to a refund of, or reduction in, contributions paid into the pension scheme.

The amounts involved are frequently material. Typically, many years elapse between making contributions and actually meeting the liabilities.

The pension funds of defined benefit schemes must be regularly valued by a qualified actuary (this normally takes place at three-yearly intervals). The valuation should reveal any surplus or deficit of assets over liabilities. The level of contributions is adjusted so that the fund will be adequate to meet the estimated eventual liability or, alternatively, to take advantage of a surplus.

Valuing a pension fund is a complicated exercise requiring specialist knowledge. The actuary must make estimates of matters such as the rate of return on new investments, salary increases and the estimated future service lives of employees.

In almost all cases, the pension fund is held separately from the assets and liabilities of the company. Therefore neither its assets nor the pension liability appear on the balance sheet. The cost of providing pensions is represented by the charge to the profit and loss account.

Until the introduction of SSAP 24, the pension cost was simply the amount of contributions paid in the year. However, the level of contributions is dependent on the results of the valuation and in practice the actual amount paid can fluctuate wildly. Because of these fluctuations, the actual contribution paid in a period does not necessarily represent the true cost of providing pensions in that period. To account for pensions on that basis would be to contravene the fundamental concept of accruals.

SSAP 24 requires entities to recognise the expected cost of providing pensions on a systematic and rational basis over the period during which they derive benefit from the employees' services. (In practice, variations are spread over the average remaining service lives of employees.) This means that surpluses and deficits are spread over a number of years and their impact on profits is 'smoothed'.

3 SOLUTION

Task 1

Foreign currency conversion is the process of buying or selling one currency for another. For example if a company requires US dollars for a purchase then it will sell pounds to a bank in exchange for a certain number of US dollars.

Foreign currency translation is the accounting procedure that states one foreign currency value in terms of another for accounting purposes.

Task 2

Creditors ledger control account

		£			£
31 Dec	Bal c/d (FFR 10.0)	11,400	28 Oct	Purchases (FFR 11.4)	10,000
			31 Dec	P&L a/c - exchange loss	1,400
		11,400			11,400
6 Jan	Cash (FFR 10.3)	11,068	1 Jan	Bal b/d	11,400
6 Jan	P&L a/c - exchange gain	332			
		11,400			11,400

20X5 Financial Statements

If the goods have not yet been sold then they will appear in purchases at a value of £10,000 and be part of closing stock also at a value of £10,000.

The creditor at 31 December 20X5 will appear on the balance sheet at a value of £11,400 and an exchange loss of £1,400 will be charged to the profit and loss account for the year.

20X6 Financial Statements

Provided that the goods have been sold by the end of 20X6 then they will not appear as part of closing stock. However there will be a credit to the profit and loss account of £332 being the exchange gain on the eventual settlement of the outstanding amount.

Chapter 17

CASH FLOW STATEMENTS

1   SOLUTION

Task 1

Antipodean Enterprises
Cash flow statement for the year ended 31 December 20X3

Reconciliation of operating profit to net cash inflow from operating activities

	£
Operating profit (25,200 + 3,000)	28,200
Depreciation charges	7,000
Loss on sale of tangible fixed assets (740 – 430)	310
Decrease in stocks	7,830
Decrease in debtors	2,450
Increase in creditors ((32,050 – 400) – 20,950)	10,700
Net cash inflow from operating activities	56,490

Cash flow statement

	£	£
Net cash inflow from operating activities		56,490
Returns on investments and servicing of finance		
Interest paid (3,000 – 400)		(2,600)
Capital expenditure		
Payments to acquire tangible fixed assets		
(36,400 + 19,860)	(56,260)	
Receipts from sales of tangible fixed assets		
(5,630 + 1,270)	6,900	
		(49,360)
Acquisitions and disposals		
Purchase of long-term investments		(8,000)
Drawings paid		(15,130)
Management of liquid resources		
Purchase of short-term investments		(1,200)
Financing		
Part repayment of business development loan	(3,000)	
Owners' capital withdrawals	(6,500)	
Net cash outflow from financing		(9,500)
Decrease in cash (28,200 + 1,100)		(29,300)

WORKINGS

(W1)

Equipment account - NBV

	£		£
Balance b/d	17,600	NBV disposal	5,200
Additions (bal.fig.)	36,400	Depreciation provided for year	3,000
		Balance c/d	45,800
	54,000		54,000

(W2)

Equipment disposal account

	£		£
NBV disposals	5,200	Sale proceeds (bal.fig.)	5,630
Profit on disposal	430		
	5,630		5,630

Cars account - NBV

	£		£
Balance b/d	4,080	NBV disposals	2,010
Additions (bal. fig.)	19,860	Depreciation for year	3,000
		Balance c/d	18,930
	23,940		23,940

Cars disposal account

	£		£
NBV disposals	2,010	Loss on sale	740
		Sale proceeds (bal.fig.)	1,270
	2,010		2,010

Task 2

Antipodean Enterprises has increased in profit from £15,300 to £25,200 which, on the face of it, must be an encouraging sign.

However, in the year ended 31 December 20X3 there has been a substantial increase in the overdraft, being largely explained by purchases of equipment and cars, although the proprietor has, rather surprisingly, seen fit to increase his long-term investments, which also helps to explain the increase.

In fact the increase would have been even more substantial had it not been for the large reduction in stock levels and, to a lesser degree, the fall in the debtors, and a very large increase in creditors. Divestment in working capital has been around £20,000.

Overall criticisms of business management could be:

(i)   There has been excessive withdrawal of profits at a time of expansion when funds are needed by the business.

(ii)   The owner has long and short term investments, along with a substantial overdraft. The cash position would ease considerably if he could dispose of the investments, or increase long term loans to finance the fixed asset expenditure.

2   SOLUTION

Task 1

Reconciliation of operating profit to net cash flow from operating activities

	£
Operating profit (see working)	17,000
Depreciation	9,000
Increase in debtors	(16,000)
Decrease in stock	2,000
Decrease in creditors	(7,000)
Net cash inflow from operating activities	5,000

WORKING

	£
Operating profit before interest (bal fig)	17,000
Interest charged	
$(10\% \times 20,000) + (15\% \times 40,000)$	(8,000)
Dividend	(9,000)
Retained for year	Nil

(Tutorial note: there is no set format for the statement required in Task 1. The approach adopted in the answer is to present the statement that would normally be prepared reconciling operating profit to net cashflow.

In order to arrive at operating profit a further statement/working is required as the question does not give a profit and loss account for the year.)

Task 2

Aida plc
Cash flow statement for the year ended 31 December 20X1

	£	£
Net cash inflow from operating activities		5,000
Returns on investments and servicing of finance		
Interest paid		(8,000)
		(3,000)
Capital expenditure		
Purchase of fixed assets		
Property (20 - 3 revaluation)	(17,000)	
Plant	(16,000)	
		(33,000)
Equity dividends paid		(5,000)
		(41,000)
Financing		
Issue of shares	10,000	
Issue of debentures	40,000	
Redemption of debentures	(20,000)	
		30,000
Decrease in cash		(11,000)

3   SOLUTION

Task 1

Y Ltd
Cash flow statement for the year ended 31 December 20X2

Reconciliation of operating profit to net cash inflow from operating activities

	£'000
Operating profit	210
Depreciation charge	59
Loss on disposal of fixed assets	9
Increase in stocks	(2)
Increase in trade debtors	(8)
Increase in trade creditors	3
	271

Cash flow statement

	£'000	£'000
Net cash inflow from operating activities		271
Returns on investments and servicing of finance		
Interest paid		(14)
Taxation		
Tax paid (W2)		(55)
Capital expenditure		
Payments for new fixed assets	(45)	
Receipts from sales of fixed assets (W3)	6	
		(39)
Equity dividends paid (W1)		(32)
Financing		
Issue of shares (including premium)	16	
Repayment of long-term loan	(150)	
		(134)
Decrease in cash		(3)

WORKINGS

(W1)

Dividends payable

	£'000		£'000
∴ Balance = dividends paid	32	b/d	16
c/d	20	P&L a/c	36
	52		52

(W2)

Tax payable

	£'000		£'000
∴ Balance = tax paid	55	b/d payable	39
c/d payable	46	P&L a/c	62
	101		101

(W3)

Fixed assets at cost

	£'000		£'000
b/d	780	∴ Cost of disposals	27
Additions	45	c/d	798
	825		825

Accumulated depreciation

	£'000		£'000
∴ Depreciation on disposals	12	b/d	112
c/d	159	Charge	59
	171		171

Disposal of fixed assets

	£'000		£'000
Cost	27	Acc depreciation	12
		Loss on disposal	9
		∴ Proceeds of disposal	6
	27		27

Task 2

FRS 1 (revised) defines cash as follows:

Cash is cash in hand and deposits repayable on demand with any qualifying financial institution, less overdrafts from any qualifying financial institution repayable on demand. Cash includes cash in hand and deposits denominated in foreign currencies.

Chapter 18

INTERPRETATION OF FINANCIAL STATEMENTS

1   SOLUTION

Task 1

		20X2	20X3	20X4
•	$\dfrac{\text{Gross profit}}{\text{Sales}} \times 100$	33%	33%	33%
•	$\dfrac{\text{Net profit}}{\text{Sales}} \times 100$	15%	14.6%	13.9%
•	$\dfrac{\text{Current assets - stock}}{\text{Current liabilities}}$	2.6:1	0.9:1	1.4:1

Task 2

These ratios indicate that PQR plc has been able to maintain its gross profit margin throughout the three year period, but has seen a slight decrease in its net profit percentage.

The movement in the quick ratio could suggest that there is little control of working capital, however a further analysis of the data shows that there was an increase in fixed assets in 20X3. These may have been funded through short-term finance and this would then explain the bank account moving into an overdraft. The overdraft would result in an interest charge which would affect profitability without changing the gross margin. This interest could be one of the causes of the reduction in the net profit percentage.

2   SOLUTION

Task 1

		20X1	20X0
(a)	Current ratio	30,500: 24,000 = 1.3:1	28,500: 20,000 = 1.4:1
	Quick ratio	16,500: 24,000 = .7:1	15,500: 20,000 = .8:1
	Stock turnover in days	$\dfrac{14,000}{42,000} \times 365 = 122$ days	$\dfrac{13,000}{34,000} \times 365 = 140$ days
	Debtors turnover in days	$\dfrac{16,000}{60,000} \times 365$ days $= 97$ days	$\dfrac{15,000}{50,000} \times 365 = 110$ days
	Creditors turnover in days	$\dfrac{24,000}{42,000}$	$\dfrac{20,000}{34,000}$

	(assume operating expenses are not incurred on credit terms)	$\times 365 = 209$ days	$\times 365 = 215$ days
Gross profit %		$\dfrac{18,000}{60,000} \times 100 = 30\%$	$\dfrac{16,000}{50,000} \times 100 = 32\%$
Net profit % (before tax)		$\dfrac{300}{60,000} \times 100 = 0.5\%$	$\dfrac{1,700}{50,000} \times 100 = 3.4\%$
Interest cover		$\dfrac{2,500}{2,200} = 1.1$ times	$\dfrac{3,000}{1,300} = 2.3$ times
Dividend cover		$\dfrac{(50)}{600} = (0.8)$ times (No cover)	$\dfrac{1,100}{600} = 1.8$ times
ROCE		$\dfrac{2,500}{13,000+6,000} \times 100 = 13.2\%$	$\dfrac{3,000}{14,000+5,500} \times 100 = 15.4\%$
Gearing		$\dfrac{6,000}{13,000+6,000} \times 100 = 31.6\%$	$\dfrac{5,500}{14,000+5,500} = 28.2\%$

Task 2

There has been a decline in the liquidity position of the business. The 'weak' position in 20X0 where quick assets (debtors and bank) do not cover the immediate liabilities has deteriorated even further in 20X1. If this trend were to continue the going concern ability of the business would probably be in question. In addition the cover provided by profits over interest payable has more than halved; this would be considered a poor indicator by the interest bearing creditors. Such creditors may question the decision to declare the same level of dividend for 20X1 as for 20X0, even though the business made an after tax loss.

The business's profitability shows only a small 2% drop at the gross profit level but because of the significant levels of operating expenses and interest payable the net profit percentage in 20X1 is only one seventh of its 20X0 level. Clearly improvements are required if the business is to continue to report positive profit after tax figures.

Finally, management has increased the level of fixed assets; with such poor trading results they should be asked if such expansion was necessary and when the benefits from the use of such resources can be expected to accrue.

3   SOLUTION

Profitability

(1) Net profit margin	20X5	20X6
$\dfrac{\text{Net profit before tax}}{\text{Sales}}$	$\dfrac{21,500}{202,900} \times 100$ $= 10.6\%$	$\dfrac{37,500}{490,700} \times 100$ $= 7.6\%$

(2)   Return on capital employed:

$\dfrac{\text{Net profit before taxation}}{\text{Net assets employed}}$	$\dfrac{21,500}{119,200} \times 100$	$\dfrac{37,500}{326,600} \times 100$
	$= 18.0\%$	$= 11.5\%$

Liquidity:

(3)   Current ratio:

$\dfrac{\text{Current assets}}{\text{Current liabilities}}$	$\dfrac{66,500}{52,300}$	$\dfrac{152,500}{85,900}$
	$= 1.3$	$= 1.8$

(4)   Quick ratio:

$\dfrac{\text{Current assets - Stock}}{\text{Current liabilities}}$	$\dfrac{35,300}{52,300}$	$\dfrac{57,200}{85,900}$
	$= 0.7$	$= 0.7$

Financial stability:

(5)   Gearing:

$\dfrac{\text{Long - term debt}}{\text{Net assets employed}}$	Nil	$\dfrac{100,000}{326,600} \times 100$
		$= 30.6\%$

(6) $\dfrac{\text{Liabilities}}{\text{Shareholders' funds}}$	$\dfrac{52,300}{119,200}$	$\dfrac{185,900}{226,600}$
	$= 0.4$	$= 0.8$

Task 2

Comment

(Tutorial note: comments need not be long. It is better that they are short and to the point. It is a good idea to state whether each ratio is showing a better or worse position compared to last year.)

Profitability

Profitability in relation to sales and capital employed has fallen. However, the fall has occurred in a period of sales increasing two and a half times and capital increasing due to the issue of loan stock.

It will take time to invest the additional capital efficiently.

The decline in the profitability compared to sales may also be a short-term problem. For example overheads are not being kept under control in the period of rapid expansion. Alternatively the sales volume may have been achieved by cutting gross profit margins.

Liquidity

The current ratio has increased to give a comfortable level of cover for short-term creditors. Most of the increase, however, is derived from higher stocks. The quick ratio is constant.

Whether these two ratios are good or bad depends on what is normal/efficient in the type of business that Nantred is in.

Financial stability

There has been a major injection of long-term finance during the year, producing a gearing ratio of 30%. The business is thus in a riskier position than last year but the expansion of the business may be necessary to protect the existing business (by becoming larger it may be better able to protect itself).

The liabilities to shareholders' funds show a similar position as the gearing (and for the same reasons).

4   SOLUTION

(a)   FRS 14 includes the following definition of earnings per share

'Basic earnings per share should be calculated by dividing the net profit or loss for the period attributable to ordinary shareholders by the weighted average number of ordinary shares outstanding during the period.

(para 9, FRS 14)

Note: That earnings are the net profit or loss for the period attributable to ordinary shareholders should be the net profit or loss for the period after deducting dividends and other appropriations in respect of non-equity shares.

(para 10, FRS 14)

(b)   Under FRS 14

$$\text{EPS} \quad = \quad \frac{6,888,000 - 200,000}{10,000,000} \quad \text{(preference dividends)}$$

$$= \quad 66.88 \text{ pence}$$

Chapter 19

CONSOLIDATED BALANCE SHEETS

1 SOLUTION

Hanson Ltd and its subsidiary
Group balance sheet as at 31 December 20X8

	£	£
Goodwill (10,900 × $\frac{2}{5}$)		4,360
Fixed assets		650,450
Current assets		
Stock (W5)	212,990	
Debtors	125,430	
Cash at bank	36,450	
	374,870	
Creditors: amounts falling due		
within one year	144,550	
Net current assets		230,320
Total assets less current liabilities		885,130
Capital and reserves		
Called up share capital		350,000
Profit and loss account (W3)		431,955
Minority interest (W4)		103,175
		885,130

WORKINGS

(W1) Shareholdings in Pickford Ltd

	Ordinary %	Preference %
Group	75	25
Minority	25	75
	100	100

(W2) Goodwill

	£	£
Cost of investment		109,150
Less: Share of net assets at acquisition		
Ordinary share capital	100,000	
Profit and loss account	11,000	
	111,000	
	× 75%	
		(83,250)
Preference share capital	60,000	
	× 25%	
		(15,000)
Goodwill - write off to reserves over 5 years		10,900

(W3)   Consolidated profit and loss account

	£
Hanson Ltd:	348,420
Less: Provision for unrealised profit on stock	
$(25/125 \times 1/4 \times 24,000)$	(1,200)
Pickford Ltd: 75% (132,700 – 11,000)	91,275
Less: Goodwill written off $(10,900 \times \frac{3}{5})$	(6,540)
	431,955

(W4)   Minority interest

Net assets of Pickford Ltd

	£	£
Ordinary share capital	100,000	
Profit and loss account	132,700	
	232,700	
	$\times 25\%$	
		58,175
Preference share capital	60,000	
	$\times 75\%$	
		45,000
		103,175

(W5)   Consolidated stock

	£
Hanson Ltd	143,070
Provision for unrealised profit	(1,200)
Pickford Ltd	71,120
	212,990

2   SOLUTION

Pixie Ltd and its subsidiary
Group balance sheet as at 31 December 20X9

	£	£
Goodwill $(4,500 \times \frac{8}{9})$		4,000
Fixed assets		320,600
Current assets (W2)	149,500	
Creditors: amounts falling due within one year		
Sundry	78,200	
Proposed dividends	20,000	
Minority dividends payable (W3)	1,465	
	99,665	
Net current assets		49,835
Total assets less current liabilities		374,435

Capital and reserves

Called up share capital	200,000
Profit and loss account (W6)	130,185
	330,185
Minority interests (W7)	44,250
	374,435

WORKINGS

(W1)   Shareholdings in Dixie Ltd

	Ordinary	Preference
Group	75%	40%
Minority	25%	60%
	100%	100%

(W2)   Consolidated current assets

	£
Pixie Ltd:	113,100
Dixie Ltd:	43,400
Less: Provision for unrealised profit on stock (W3)	(7,000)
	149,500

(W3)   Stock - unrealised profit

	£
Stock held by Pixie purchased from Dixie	42,000
Unrealised profit $\frac{20}{120} \times 42,000$	7,000
Group share 75%	5,250
Minority interest 25%	1,750

(*Tutorial note:* as the subsidiary recorded the original profit, the elimination must be shared between the group and the minority. This may be achieved if the unrealised profit is deducted from Dixie Ltd stock and reserves on the balance sheet working papers.)

(W4)   Treatment of proposed dividends of Dixie Ltd

	Ordinary £	Preference £	Total £
Proposed dividends	2,500	1,400	3,900
Less: Cancelled with dividends receivable by Pixie Ltd	(1,875)	(560)	(2,435)
Dividend payable to minority shareholders	625	840	1,465

(W5) **Goodwill**

		£	£
Cost of investment			73,000
Less:	Share of net assets at acquisition		
	Ordinary share capital	50,000	
	Profit and loss account	20,000	
		70,000	
		× 75%	
			(52,500)
	Preference share capital	40,000	
		× 40%	
			(16,000)
	Goodwill		4,500

(W6) **Consolidated profit and loss account**

		£	£
Pixie Ltd:	Per question	120,000	
	Add: dividends receivable (W4)	2,435	
			122,435
Dixie Ltd:	75% (38,000 – 7,000 (W3) – 20,000)		8,250
Less: Goodwill written off (4,500 × $\frac{1}{9}$)			(500)
			130,185

(W7) **Minority interest**

Net assets of Dixie Ltd

	£	£
Ordinary share capital	50,000	
Profit and loss account (38,000 – 7,000)	31,000	
	81,000	
	× 25%	
		20,250
Preference share capital	40,000	
	× 60%	
		24,000
		44,250

3 SOLUTION

Task 1

Goodwill

	£'000	£'000
AS plc:		
Cost of investment		1,500
Less: Net assets acquired:		
Share capital	1,200	
Reserves	800	
	2,000	
Group share (75%)		(1,500)
BS plc:		
Cost of investment		1,250
Less: Net assets acquired:		
Share capital	1,000	
Reserves	500	
	1,500	
Group share (80%)		(1,200)
Goodwill on acquisition		50

Consolidated reserves

	£'000	£'000
HC plc		2,650
Add: Dividend receivable from AS plc (75% × 120,000)		90
		2,740
AS plc		
Post acquisition reserves (1,000 – 800)	200	
Group share (75%)		150
BS plc		
Post-acquisition reserves (500 – 500)		–
		2,890

(Tutorial note:

The dividend from AS plc (75% × 120,000 = 90,000) is recorded as follows:

		£	£
DR	Debtors	90,000	
CR	P&L		90,000

In any group balance sheet these debtors of 'dividends receivable from subsidiaries' in the books of the parent company, will not appear, as they will be cancelled against the subsidiaries' liability to pay these dividends. This will leave the group's current liability for proposed dividends being the parent company's dividend plus the minority interest in the subsidiaries' proposed dividends.*)*

*(**Tutorial note:** there is no adjustment for goodwill to be amortised for 20X8 as BS plc was purchased on the last day of the year.)*

Minority interest

	£'000	£'000
AS plc		
Share capital	1,200	
Reserves	1,000	
	2,200	
MI share (25%)		550
BS plc		
Share capital	1,000	
Reserves	500	
	1,500	
MI share (20%)		300
		850

In addition, the balance sheet will include a creditor for the minority interest's share in the proposed dividend of AS plc (25% × 120,000).

Task 2

Consolidated balance sheet as at 31 December 20X8

	£'000
Goodwill (BS plc)	50
Sundry net assets (2,300 + 2,320 + 1,500)	6,120
Minority proposed dividend (25% × 120)	(30)
	6,140
Share capital	2,400
Consolidated reserves	2,890
	5,290
Minority interest	850
	6,140

Chapter 20

CONSOLIDATED PROFIT AND LOSS ACCOUNT

1 SOLUTION

Master schedule

	E plc	Y Ltd	Adjustments	Consolidated
Group details		60%		
		12 months		
	£	£	£	£
Sales	500,000	300,000		800,000
Cost of sales	(300,000)	(180,000)		(480,000)
Distribution and admin.				
expenses	(70,000)	(30,000)		(100,000)
Investment income:				
Dividends	5,000 (W1)	4,000		9,000
Interest	18,000	-	(9,000) (W2)	9,000
Interest payable	(40,000)	(30,000)	9,000 (W2)	(61,000)
Taxation	(42,000)	(20,000)		(62,000)
Profit after taxation	71,000	44,000	-	115,000
Minority interest		(17,600) (W3)		(17,600)
Inter-company dividends	12,000 (W1)	(12,000)		
Profit before dividend	83,000			
E dividend	(64,000)			(64,000)
Retained for year	19,000	14,400		33,400

WORKINGS

		£
(W1)	Inter-company dividends:	
	E – dividends receivable	17,000
	From Y 60% × £20,000	12,000
	Dividend income from external sources	5,000
(W2)	Inter-company interest:	
	Y – interest payable	30,000
	To E 30% × £30,000	9,000

(W3)   40% × £44,000 = £17,600.

(Note: It is important to note the differing treatments of inter-company dividends and inter-company interest. In the master schedule, under investment income, only the external dividend received by E has been included, whereas all the interest has been included in the separate column for E. The reason for this lies in the column for the subsidiary. As all Y's interest payable is a proper expense reducing the minority shareholders' interest in profits, it must be deducted in full to calculate the correct minority interest figure. The group share of interest is thus adjusted for outside the individual companies' columns.*)*

E plc and its subsidiary
Consolidated profit and loss account for year ended 31 December 20X2

	£	£
Turnover		800,000
Cost of sales		480,000
Gross profit		320,000
Distribution costs and administrative expenses		(100,000)
Income from fixed asset investments	18,000	
Interest payable	(61,000)	
		(43,000)
Profit on ordinary activities before taxation		177,000
Tax on profit on ordinary activities		(62,000)
Profit on ordinary activities after taxation		115,000
Minority interests		(17,600)
Profit attributable to members of E plc		97,400
Dividends		(64,000)
Retained profit for the year		33,400

2   SOLUTION

R plc group
Consolidated profit and loss account for the year ended 31 March 20X4

	£
Trading profit	1,310,500
Less: Net operating expenses	(331,472)
Operating profit	979,028
Less: Taxation	(265,750)
Consolidated profit after tax	713,278
Less: Minority interests	(98,394)
Consolidated profit for financial year	614,884
Less: Dividends	(200,000)
Consolidated retained profit for financial year	414,884
Add: Retained profits b/f (W7)	164,000
Retained profits c/f	578,884

Consolidation schedule

	R	S	J	Consolidation adjustments	Group
	£	£	£	£	£
Profits from trading	728,000	74,500 (W1)	510,000	(2,000)(W2)	1,310,500
Net operating expenses	(182,000)	(18,625) (W3)	(127,500)	(3,347)(W4)	(331,472)
Operating profit	546,000	55,875	382,500		979,028
Investment income	49,500			(49,500)	
Profit before tax	595,500	55,875	382,500		979,028
Tax	(162,250)	(14,500)(W5)	(89,000)		(265,750)
Profit after tax	433,250	41,375	293,500		713,278
Minority interests (W6)		(10,344)	(88,050)		(98,394)
Profit for the year	433,250	31,031	205,450		614,884
Dividends (W7)	(200,000)		(42,000)		(200,000)
	233,250		163,450		414,884

WORKINGS

(1) $\frac{6}{12} \times 149,000 = £74,500$

(2) $20\% \times 10,000 = £2,000$

(3) $\frac{6}{12} \times 37,250 = £18,625$

(4)   Amortisation of goodwill

On acquisition of S:	£	£
Price paid	210,000	
Net assets acquired		
Share capital 75% × 200,000	(150,000)	
Reserves 75% × (44,000 + ($\frac{6}{12}$ × 62,750))	(56,531)	
Goodwill purchased	3,469	
6 months amortisation = $\frac{6}{12} \times \frac{1}{5} \times 3,469$ =		347

On acquisition of J:		
Price paid	120,000	
Net assets acquired		
Share capital 70% × 120,000	(84,000)	
Reserves 70% × 30,000	(21,000)	
Goodwill purchased	15,000	
One year's amortisation = $\frac{1}{5} \times 15,000$		3,000
Total annual charge for goodwill amortisation		3,347

(5) $\frac{6}{12} \times 29,000 = £14,500$

(6)   Minority interests are calculated as

		£
S	25% × $\frac{6}{12}$ × 82,750	10,344
J	30% × 293,500	88,050
		98,394

(7)   Retained profits b/f at 1 April 20X3

	£
R	124,000
S Nil, since not acquired until October 20X3	-
J 70% × (100,000 − 30,000)	49,000
Adjustment for 3 years goodwill amortisation for J (3 × 3,000)	(9,000)
	164,000

Chapter 21

ASSOCIATED UNDERTAKINGS

1   SOLUTION

If one company has significant influence over another company then this normally means that it owns shares in that company. FRS 9 states that the exercise of significant influence means that the investor is actively involved in the direction of its investee through its participation in policy decisions covering aspects of policy relevant to the investor. Typically, these would include decisions on strategic issues such as the expansion or contraction of the business, changes in products, markets and activities and determining the balance between dividend and reinvestment.

If one company controls another then the normal accounting treatment is for group accounts to be prepared. Group accounts should take the form of consolidated financial statements where the controlled company, or subsidiary, and the controlling company, or parent, are treated as a single entity.

If the parent company exercises significant influence over another company rather than controlling it then in the parent company's group accounts this other company should be accounted for using the equity method of accounting.

2   SOLUTION

Task 1

Equity accounting is a method of including the results and position of an associated undertaking in the consolidated financial statements of a group. The purpose of equity accounting is to ensure that users are given more information about associates than they would be given using the normal accounting treatment of showing the investment at cost in the balance sheet and the dividend income from the associate in the profit and loss account.

Under the equity accounting method, in the consolidated balance sheet the associated undertaking is included under the heading of fixed assets at the total of:

	:	cost
plus	:	group share of post acquisition profits
less	:	amounts written off (eg, goodwill amortised).

In the consolidated profit and loss account there will be several entries for the associate:

- group share of the associate's operating profit (less any amortisation of goodwill in the period);
- group share of the associate's exceptional items;
- group share of the associate's interest receivable and payable; and
- group share of the associate's tax charge.

Task 2

Consolidated balance sheet - extract

	£
Fixed assets:	
Investment in associated undertaking (W1)	105,875

Consolidated profit and loss account - extract

	£
Share of operating profit of associates	
(25% × 100,000)	25,000
Tax charge:	
Group	X
Associated undertaking (25% × 30,000)	7,500

Consolidated profit and loss reserve account

	£
Y Ltd:	
Group share of post-acquisition profits	
(25% × (170,000 - 90,000))	20,000
Less: Premium on acquisition written off	
(13,500 (W2) × ¾)	10,125
	9,875

WORKINGS

(W1)

	£
Investment in associated undertaking	
Group share of net assets (25% × 410,000)	102,500
Goodwill not yet written off	
(13,500 (W2) × ¼)	3,375
	105,875

(W2)

Goodwill

	£
Cost	96,000
Net assets acquired (25% × (240,000 + 90,000))	82,500
	13,500

3   SOLUTION

(a)   Goodwill

	£
Cost	150,000
Group share of net assets acquired	
(30% × 450,000)	135,000
Goodwill arising	15,000

(b)   Investment in associated undertaking

	£
Group share of net assets	
(30% × 550,000)	165,000

Chapter 22

CONSOLIDATION PRINCIPLES

1 SOLUTION

(1) Different activities

The CA85 states that subsidiaries must be excluded from consolidation where their activities are so different from other undertakings in the consolidation that their inclusion would be incompatible with the obligation to give a true and fair view. However FRS 2 envisages that this situation will arise only in exceptional circumstances as normally no subsidiary will be viewed as being so different from the rest of the group as to allow exclusion.

(2) Severe long-term restrictions

A subsidiary should be excluded from consolidation if the parent company does not control the subsidiary because severe long-term restrictions prevent the parent from exercising its rights over the assets or management of the subsidiary.

(3) Temporary investment

A subsidiary that has not previously been consolidated and that is held exclusively with a view to being sold should not be consolidated as in practice such a subsidiary is not truly under the long term control of the parent company.

2 SOLUTION

(a) A business combination is the bringing together of separate entities into one economic entity as the result of one entity uniting with, or obtaining control over the net assets and operations of another.

(b) The two types of business combination that can be identified are an acquisition and a merger.

A merger is a business combination where generally the two groups of shareholders of the two companies remain the same but simply operate on a combined basis. This will normally mean that the merger has taken place by a share for share exchange rather than one group of shareholders being bought out by the other. In a merger both parties are of equal importance in the merged entity and no party to the merger is seen as the dominant one.

An acquisition is any type of business combination that is not a merger. In practice, an acquisition is a business combination in which one entity (the parent) obtains *control* over another entity (the subsidiary).

(c) The two types of accounting in consolidated accounts that are identified by FRS 6 are merger accounting and acquisition accounting, for mergers and acquisitions respectively. FRS 6 states that if the business combination is a merger then merger accounting must be used whereas if it is an acquisition then acquisition accounting must be used.

PRACTICE CENTRAL ASSESSMENT ACTIVITIES

ANSWERS

◈ FOULKS*lynch*

ASSESSMENT ACTIVITIES

These assessment activities have been taken from the June 1996 to December 1997 Central Assessments set by the AAT. The assessments have been split into sections as follows:

UNIT 11 – SECTION 1 – JUNE 1996

Task 1.1

		£000	£000
(1)	DR Final dividend	30	
	CR Dividends payable		30
(2)	DR Tax charge	211	
	CR Corporation tax payable		211
(3)	DR Interest charges	15	
	CR Interest payable		15
(4)	DR Distribution expenses	19	
	CR Accruals		19
(5)	DR Amounts written off investments	8	
	CR Investments		8

Task 1.2

Financial statements for publication:

Dowango Ltd
Profit and loss account for the year ended 31 March 1996

	£'000
Turnover	
Continuing operations (W1)	5,352
Cost of sales (W2)	2,910
Gross profit	2,442
Distribution costs	1,123
Administrative expenses	709
Operating profit	
Continuing operations	610
Amounts written off investments	8
Interest payable and similar charges	30
Profit on ordinary activities before taxation	572
Tax on profit on ordinary activities	211
Profit on ordinary activities after taxation	361
Dividends (W3)	50
Retained profit for the financial year	311

Dowango Ltd
Balance sheet as at 31 March 1996

	£'000	£'000
Fixed assets		
Tangible assets (W4)		1,153
Current assets		
Stocks	365	
Debtors (W5)	613	
Investments	56	
Cash at bank and in hand	3	
	1,037	
Creditors: amounts falling due within one year (W6)	804	
Net current assets (liabilities)		233
Total assets less current liabilities		1,386
Creditors: amounts falling due after more than one year		300
		1,086
Capital and reserves		
Called up share capital		500
Profit and loss account (W7)		586
		1,086

WORKINGS

All figures £000's

1   Sales 5,391 – Returns inwards 39 = 5,352

2   Calculation of cost of sales:

	£'000	£'000
Opening stock	298	
Purchases	2,988	
Plus: Carriage inwards	20	
Less: Returns outwards	31	
	3,275	
Less: Closing stock	365	
Cost of sales		2,910

3   Dividends:

	£'000
Interim dividend	20
Final dividend proposed	30
	50

4	Fixed assets	Cost	Acc. Depn.	NBV
	Land	431	–	431
	Buildings	512	184	328
	Fixtures & fittings	389	181	208
	Motor vehicles	341	204	137
	Office equipment	105	56	49
		1,778	625	1,153

5	Debtors		
	Trade debtors	619	
	less provision for doubtful debts	27	
			592
	Prepayments		21
			613

6	Creditors: amounts falling due within one year	
	Bank overdraft	157
	Trade creditors	331
	Corporation tax payable	211
	Dividends payable	30
	Accruals (41 + 19 + interest 15)	75
		804

7	Profit and loss account	
	At 1/4/95	275
	Retained profit for the year	311
	At 31/3/96	586

UNIT 11 – SECTION 1 – DECEMBER 1996

PART A

Task 1.1

		£'000	£'000
(1)	DR Final dividend	80	
	CR Dividends payable		80
(2)	DR Tax charge	1,356	
	CR Corporation tax payable		1,356
(3)	DR Interest charges	189	
	CR Interest payable		189
(4)	DR Land—valuation	720	
	CR Revaluation reserve		720
(5)	DR Stock (profit and loss account)	50	
	CR Stock (balance sheet)		50

Task 1.2

Adjustment 6: The Companies Act 1985 allows alternative accounting rules to apply to the recording of fixed assets. Fixed assets can either be shown under historical cost accounting rules or included in the accounts at a market value determined as at the date of their last valuation. If valuation is adopted then the comparable amounts determined according to the historical cost accounting rules, or the differences between those amounts and the corresponding amounts actually shown in the balance sheet shall be shown separately in the balance sheet or in a note to the accounts. Accordingly, the company has decided to follow the alternative accounting rules for its land and show it at a valuation.

Adjustment 8: SSAP 9 requires that stock be shown at the lower of cost and net realisable value. The receipt of proceeds of sales after the balance sheet date provides evidence of the net realisable value of the stocks and, according to SSAP 17, is thus an adjusting event which requires the stock to be recorded at its net realisable value of £355,000.

Task 1.3

Financial statements for publication:

Spiraes Ltd
Profit and loss account for the year ended 30 November 1996

	£'000
Turnover	
Continuing operations (W1)	18,147
Cost of sales (W2)	10,230
Gross profit	7,917
Distribution costs	2,514
Administrative expenses	1,820
Operating profit	
Continuing operations	3,583
Income from other fixed asset investments	52
Profit on ordinary activities before interest	3,635
Interest payable and similar charges	378
Profit on ordinary activities before taxation	3,257
Tax on profit on ordinary activities	1,356
Profit for the financial year	1,901
Dividends	80
Retained profit for the financial year	1,821

WORKINGS

All figures £000.

1   Sales 18,742 – Returns inwards 595 = 18,147

2   Calculation of cost of sales:

Opening stock	3,871	
Purchases	10,776	
Less: Returns outwards	314	
	14,333	
Less: Closing stock (4,153 – 50)	4,103	
Cost of sales		10,230

Task 1.4

Statement of Total Recognised Gains and Losses

	£'000
Profit for the financial year	1,901
Unrealised surplus on revaluation of properties	720
Total recognised gains and losses relating to the year	2,621

PART B

Task 1.5

Reconciliation between the cash flows from operating activities and the operating profit:

	£'000
Operating profit	2,099
Depreciation charges	1,347
Increase in stock	(335)
Increase in debtors	(219)
Increase in creditors	341
Net cash inflow from operating activities	3,233

UNIT 11 – SECTION 1 – JUNE 1997

PART A

Task 1.1
Corrected Version

Primavera Fashions Ltd
Balance Sheet as at 31 March 1997

	£'000	£'000
Fixed assets		
Intangible assets		128
Tangible assets (W1)		3,273
Investments		2,924
		———
		6,325
Current assets		
Stocks	1,178	
Debtors (W2)	833	
Cash at bank	152	
	———	
	2,163	
Creditors: amounts falling due within one year (W3)	(1,209)	
	———	
Net current assets		954
		———
Total assets less current liabilities		7,279
Creditors: amounts falling due after more than one year (W4)		(1,500)
		———
		5,779
		———
Capital and reserves		
Called up share capital		1,000
Share premium		800
Revaluation reserve		550
Profit and loss account (W5)		3,429
		———
		5,779
		———

WORKINGS

1   Fixed Assets:

	Cost £'000	Acc. Depn. £'000	NBV £'000
Land	525	-	525
Buildings	1,000	220	780
Fixtures & fittings	1,170	346	824
Motor vehicles	1,520	583	937
Office equipment	350	143	207
	4,565	1,292	3,273

2   Debtors:

	£'000	£'000
Trade debtors	857	
Less: Provision for doubtful debts	(61)	
		796
Prepayments		37
		833

3   Creditors: Amounts falling due within one year:

	£'000
Trade creditors	483
Corporation tax payable	382
Dividends payable	240
Accruals	104
	1,209

4   Creditors: amounts falling due after more than one year:

	£'000
10% Debentures	1,500

5   Profit and Loss account

	£'000
At 1 April 1996	2,819
Retained profit per ETB	1,232
Less: Final dividend	(240)
Less: Corporation tax charge	(382)
At 31 March 1997	3,429

PART B

Task 1.2

1   (a)   The share premium account arose because shares were issued at a premium, that is, at an amount in excess of their nominal value. When this occurs, the share capital account is credited with the nominal value of the shares issued and the share premium account is credited with the difference between the issue price and the nominal value of the share capital.

    (b)   Dividends cannot be paid out of share premium. Under the Companies Act, share premium is a non-distributable reserve.

    (c)   The Companies Act states that the share premium account may be used for the following purposes:

          -   bonus share issues;
          -   writing off preliminary expenses;
          -   writing off the expenses of, or the commission paid or discount allowed on, any issue of shares or debentures;
          -   providing for the premium payable on redemption of debentures.

2.   The balance on the debtor's account must be written off as a bad debt, even though the liquidation took place after the year end, and profits for the year ended 31 March 1997 are reduced by £24,000. This is because the liquidation of the debtor is an adjusting post balance sheet event as defined by SSAP 17. An adjusting event provides additional evidence of conditions existing at the balance sheet date. In this case, the liquidation provides evidence that the balance due from the debtor is unlikely to be received and therefore the accounts must be adjusted.

3   (a)   Investment in Spring Ltd is shown in the group balance sheet as follows:

	£
Investment in associated undertaking	410,000

    (b)   The note to the accounts will disclose the following:

	£
Group share of net assets of Spring Ltd (35% × 1,000,000)	350,000
Goodwill (see workings)	60,000
	410,000

WORKINGS

	£
Cost of investment	400,000
Group share of net assets of Spring Ltd at acquisition (35% × £800,000)	280,000
Goodwill	120,000
Less: Amortisation (120,000 × 2/4)	(60,000)
	60,000

UNIT 11 – SECTION 1 – DECEMBER 1997

Task 1.1

Financial statements for publication:

McTaggart Ltd
Profit and Loss Account for the year ended 30 September 1997

	£'000
Turnover	
Continuing operations (W1)	15,278
Cost of sales (W2)	8,312
Gross profit	6,966
Distribution costs	2,033
Administrative expenses	1,562
Operating profit	
Continuing operations	3,371
Interest payable and similar charges	192
Profit on ordinary activities before taxation	3,179
Tax on profit on ordinary activities	1,113
Profit on ordinary activities after taxation	2,066
Dividends (W3)	600
Retained profit for the financial year	1,466

McTaggart Ltd
Balance Sheet as at 30 September 1997

	£'000	£'000
Fixed assets		
Tangible assets (W4)		4,950
Current assets		
Stocks	4,731	
Debtors (W5)	2,143	
Cash at bank and in hand	1,086	
	7,960	
Creditors: amounts falling due within one year	3,535	
Net current assets		4,425
Total assets *less* current liabilities		9,375
Creditors: amounts falling due after more than one year (W6)		2,750
		6,625
Capital and reserves		
Called up share capital		3,000
Profit and loss account (W7)		3,625
		6,625

WORKINGS

1   Sales £15,373,000 – Returns inwards £95,000 = £15,278,000

2   Calculation of cost of sales:

	£'000	£'000
Opening stock	2,034	
Purchases	11,166	
Less: Returns outwards	157	
	13,043	
Less: Closing stock	4,731	
Cost of sales		8,312

3   Dividends:

	£'000
Interim dividend	240
Final dividend proposed	360
	600

4   Fixed Assets:

	Cost £'000	Acc. Dep £'000	NBV £'000
Land	1,820	—	1,820
Buildings	2,144	872	1,272
Fixtures & fittings	1,704	898	806
Motor vehicles	1,931	1,027	904
Office equipment	236	88	148
	7,835	2,885	4,950

5   Debtors:

	£'000	£'000
Trade debtors	2,191	
Less: Provision for doubtful debts	85	
		2,106
Prepayments		37
		2,143

6   Creditors: amounts falling due within one year:

	£'000
Trade creditors	1,891
Corporation tax payable	1,113
Dividends payable	360
Accruals (145 + interest 26)	171
	3,535

7   Profit and Loss account

	£'000
At 1 October 1996	2,159
Retained profit for the year	1,466
At 30 September 1997	3,625

UNIT 11 – SECTION 1 – DECEMBER 1998

PART A

Task 1.1

(a)   The organisations and their users are as follows:

Profit-making organisations:

Type of organisation	*Example of user*
Companies	Shareholders
Partnerships	Bank
Sole traders	Creditors

Public sector/not-for-profit organisations:

Type of organisation	*Example of user*
Local authorities	Council taxpayers
National Health Service Trusts	Department of Health
Charities	People making donations
Clubs	Members

Other reasonable types of organisation and users are also acceptable.

(b)   The types of decisions may be as follows:

Profit-making organisations:

User	*Example of decisions*
Shareholders	To sell or buy more shares
	To assess stewardship of managers
Bank	To decide whether to grant a loan
Creditors	To decide whether to supply goods or services

Public sector/not-for-profit organisations:

User	*Example of decisions*
Council taxpayers	To decide whether the local authority has given value for money
Department of Health	To decide whether the trust has been efficiently run by the managers
People making donations	To decide whether donations have been effectively used
Members	To decide if the officers have run the club efficiently

Other reasonable examples of decisions are acceptable.

Task 1.2

(a)   'Assets' are rights or other access to future economic benefits controlled by an entity as a result of past transactions or events.

'Liabilities' are obligations of an entity to transfer economic benefits as a result of past transactions or events.

'Ownership interest' is the residual amount found by deducting all of the entity's liabilities from all of the entity's assets.

(b)   In the ownership interest section of the balance sheet of a profit-making organisation capital balances would appear. These can include amounts paid in by owners (such as share capital in the case of companies) plus reserves which are owed to owners (such as the balances in the profit and loss account). In a public sector or not-for-profit organisation fund balances would appear in the ownership interest section of the balance sheet. These are amounts which have been allocated to certain purposes of the organisation.

PART B

Task 1.3

REPORT

To: **_Managers of Bimbridge Hospitals Trust_**
From: **AAT Student**
Date: **3 December 1998**
Re: **Analysis of Patch Ltd's financial statements**

Introduction

The purpose of this report is to analyse the financial statements of Patch Ltd for 1998 and 1997 to determine whether to use the company as a supplier.

Calculation of Ratios

The following ratios for the company have been computed:

	1998	Industry Average 1998	1997	Industry Average 1997
Return on capital employed	$\frac{552}{5,334} = 10.3\%$	9.6%	$\frac{462}{5,790} = 8.0\%$	9.4%
Net profit percentage	$\frac{552}{2,300} = 24\%$	21.4%	$\frac{462}{2,100} = 22\%$	21.3%
Quick ratio/acid test	$\frac{523}{475} = 1.1{:}1$	1.0:1	$\frac{418}{465} = 0.9{:}1$	0.9:1
Gearing:				
Debt/Capital employed	$\frac{1,654}{5,334} = 31\%$	36%	$\frac{2,490}{5,790} = 43\%$	37%
or				
Debt/Equity	$\frac{1,654}{3,680} = 45\%$		$\frac{2,490}{3,300} = 75\%$	

Comment and Analysis

The overall profitability of the company has improved from 1997 to 1998. The return on capital employed has increased from 8% in 1997 to 10.3% in 1998. This means that the company is generating more profit from the available capital employed in 1998 as compared with 1997. The company was below average for the industry in 1997, but has performed better than the average in 1998. The net profit percentage has also improved. It increased from 22% in 1997 to 24% in 1998. This means that the company is generating more profit from sales in 1998 than in the previous year. In both years the company had a higher than average net profit percentage when compared against the industry average. From these ratios it would seem that the company is relatively more profitable in 1998 as compared with 1997 and that it now performs better than the average of the industry. This suggests that its long-term prospects for success are higher than the average of the industry.

The liquidity of the company has also improved in the year. The quick ratio shows how many current assets, excluding stock, there are to meet the current liabilities and is often thought of as a better indicator of liquidity than the current ratio. The quick ratio in Patch Ltd has improved from 1997 to 1998. It has gone up from 0.9:1 to 1.1:1. This means that in 1998 there were more than enough quick assets to meet current liabilities. Again the quick ratio of Patch Ltd is better than the industry average in 1998, and matched it in 1997. We can conclude that Patch Ltd is more liquid than the average of the industry in 1998.

There has been a considerable decline in the gearing of the company in 1998 as compared with 1997. In 1997 the gearing ratio was 43% and this has fallen to 31% in 1998. This means that the percentage of debt funding to equity funding has declined between the two years. High gearing ratios are often thought of as increasing the risk of the company in that, in times of profit decline, it becomes increasingly difficult for highly geared companies to meet interest payments on debt, and in extreme cases the company could be forced into liquidation. The gearing ratio of Patch Ltd was above the industry average in 1997, making it relatively more risky, in this respect, than the average of companies in the industry. However, the ratio in 1998 is considerably less than the industry average and hence may now be considered less risky than the average. There is thus less of a risk from gearing in doing business with the company than the average of companies in the sector.

Conclusions

Overall, based solely on the information provided in the financial statements of the company, it is recommended that you use Patch Ltd as a supplier. The company has increasing profitability and liquidity and a lower level of gearing in 1998 than in 1997. It also compares favourably with other companies in the same industry and seems to present a lower risk than the average of the sector.

UNIT 11 – SECTION 2 – JUNE 1996

Task 2.1

(a)   (i)   The Companies Act 1985 states that historical cost principles constitute the normal basis for preparing financial statements. However, alternative bases are allowed for revaluation of assets.

(ii)   If the alternative basis was used the land and buildings would be shown in the balance sheet at their valuation of land £641,000 and buildings £558,000. The difference between NRV and valuation (land: £641,000 - £431,000 = £210,000; buildings: £558,000 - £328,000 = £230,000 giving a total revaluation of £440,000) would be credited to a 'revaluation reserve' which would form part of the capital and reserves of the company.

(iii)   Gearing before and after revaluation would be as follows:

	Before £'000	*After* £'000
Gearing ratio	$\dfrac{300}{1,386} = 22\%$	$\dfrac{300}{1,826} = 16\%$

The lower gearing would make the company look less risky from the point of view of the bank and thus they may be more willing to lend the company the money to finance the acquisition. However, the fact that the gearing is already fairly low, it may not make too much difference to the bank's attitude.

(iv)   Future results would be affected because depreciation on the buildings would be calculated on the revalued amount and not on the basis of the original cost.

(b)   The investment is a current asset, as it was purchased for resale, and, in accordance with the concept of prudence, should be shown at the lower of purchase price and net realisable value. The prudence concept says that profits should not be anticipated but foreseeable losses provided for. As we can foresee a loss on the sale of the investment it should be shown at its realisable value of £56,000.

(c)   SSAP 9 states that stocks should be shown at the lower of cost and net realisable value (NRV). NRV is the expected selling price less any costs of getting them into a saleable condition and selling costs. If NRV is less than cost then, given the prudence concept that requires losses to be provided for as soon as they become probable, the stock should be reduced to NRV. The comparison of cost and NRV should be done for separate items of stock or groups of similar items and not on the total of all stocks. Applying this policy would lead us to value the undervalued items at cost of £340,000 and the overvalued items at the sales price of £15,000. The effect of this is to reduce the value of stock overall from the £365,000 in the accounts to £355,000.

Task 2.2

	Company A	*Company B*
Return on capital employed	$\dfrac{200}{1,000} = 20\%$	$\dfrac{420}{2,800} = 15\%$
Net profit margin	$\dfrac{200}{800} = 25\%$	$\dfrac{420}{2,100} = 20\%$
Asset turnover	$\dfrac{800}{1,000} = 0.8$	$\dfrac{2,100}{2,800} = 0.75$

Other possible ratios:

Gross profit margin	$\dfrac{360}{800} = 45\%$	$\dfrac{1,050}{2,100} = 50\%$
Expenses: Sales	$\dfrac{160}{800} = 20\%$	$\dfrac{630}{2,100} = 30\%$

From the calculations we can see that Company A has both the highest return on capital employed and also the highest profit margin and asset turnover. It would, therefore, be the better company to target for takeover. However, the gross profit margin for Company B is, in fact, higher suggesting that the underlying business is more profitable. It is only because of the expenses of Company B in relation to sales that it has a lower net profit margin. If Company B could be made more efficient in terms of expenses and utilisation of assets by the introduction of a new management team on takeover, then, given the more profitable underlying business, it might be worth considering as a target for takeover.

Task 2.3

As a result of the takeover, Dowango Ltd would become a parent undertaking, given that it would own more than 50% of the voting rights in the subsidiary undertaking. Under FRS 2 consolidated accounts would be required in addition to the accounts required for the individual companies.

UNIT 11 – SECTION 2 – DECEMBER 1996

Task 2.1

Thomas Ltd
Consolidated balance sheet as at 30 September 1996

	£'000	£'000
Fixed assets		
Intangible assets		480
Tangible assets		16,932
Current assets		
Stocks	8,702	
Debtors	6,378	
Cash	331	
	15,411	
Current liabilities		
Trade creditors	4,494	
Taxation	1,007	
	5,501	
Net current assets		9,910
Total assets *less* current liabilities		27,322
Long-term loan		9,500
		17,822
Capital and reserves		
Called up share capital		5,000
Share premium		2,500
Profit and loss account		9,390
		16,890
Minority interest		932
		17,822

WORKINGS

(i)   Thomas Ltd holding in James Ltd: $\dfrac{800,000}{1,000,000} = 80\%$

Minority interest $\dfrac{200,000}{1,000,000} = 20\%$

(ii)   Revaluation of assets in James Ltd to fair value at date of acquisition:

DR Fixed assets   £500,000
CR Revaluation reserve   £500,000

(*Note:* the assumption made here is that the book value of James Ltd fixed assets at 30 September 1995 was not significantly different from that at 30 September 1996 (that is, there were no significant additions or disposals). Full credit is given for alternative assumptions.)

(iii)   Calculation of goodwill arising on consolidation and minority interest:

| | | (Attributable to Thomas Ltd) | | |
	Total *Equity* £'000	*At* *Acquisition* £'000	*Since* *Acquisition* £'000	*Minority* *Interest* £'000
Share capital	1,000	800		200
Share premium	400	320		80
Revaluation reserve	500	400		100
P & L:				
at acquisition	2,000	1,600		400
since acquisition	760		608	152
	4,660	3,120	608	932
Consideration		3,760		
Goodwill arising on consolidation		640		
P & L account Thomas Ltd			8,942	
Less: Goodwill amortised (640 × ¼)		(160)	(160)	
		480	9,390	

UNIT 11 – SECTION 2 – JUNE 1997

Task 2.1

Report

To: Shareholders of Botticelli Ltd
From: AAT Student
Date: June 1997
Re: Profitability and liquidity of Botticelli Ltd

As requested, I set out my comments on the profitability and liquidity of Botticelli Ltd for 1995 and 1996. My comments are based on the ratios calculated below:

The relevant ratios are as follows:

	1996	1995
Return on capital employed	$\dfrac{509}{2,941} = 17.3\%$	$\dfrac{342}{1,596} = 21.4\%$
Gross profit percentage	$\dfrac{1,329}{2,963} = 44.9\%$	$\dfrac{779}{1,736} = 44.9\%$
Net profit percentage	$\dfrac{509}{2,963} = 17.2\%$	$\dfrac{342}{1,736} = 19.7\%$
Current ratio	$\dfrac{863}{722} = 1.2:1$	$\dfrac{924}{341} = 2.7:1$
Quick ratio (acid test)	$\dfrac{444}{722} = 0.6:1$	$\dfrac{583}{341} = 1.7:1$

Return on capital employed (ROCE) has fallen during 1996. This shows that the capital employed by the company has generated less profit in 1996 than in 1995. This may be connected with the substantial capital investment which took place during 1996 and if so, probably indicates that this investment took place near the end of the year and is therefore not yet producing additional profit. Alternatively, the attempt to expand the company's operations may have been a failure.

Gross profit percentage has remained at 45% throughout the period, which indicates that although sales have been increased, profit margins have been maintained.

Net profit percentage has fallen during 1996. This is partly due to the increased depreciation charges resulting from the fixed asset purchases mentioned above and may be offset by increased profits in future.

Liquidity appears to be deteriorating. The current ratio and the quick ratio show that during 1995 the company could easily meet its short term liabilities as they fell due. During 1996 cash has been used to pay for fixed asset purchases with the result that the company now has an overdraft. It would have been better to finance the capital investment by means of either a share issue or long term debt.

In conclusion, it is difficult to predict the future performance of the company. The capital investment may have its full impact on results in 1997, and ROCE and net profit margin may return to their former levels. Alternatively, the deterioration in performance may continue. The company may face a liquidity crisis unless it can either raise additional finance or the profits from the expansion can generate more cash.

I hope that this is satisfactory for your purposes.

Task 2.2

Reconciliation between the cash flows from operating activities and the operating profit:

	£'000
Operating profit	509
Depreciation charges	247
Profit on sale of tangible fixed assets	(15)
Increase in stock	(78)
Increase in debtors	(63)
Increase in creditors	125
Net cash flow from operating activities	725

UNIT 11 – SECTION 2 – DECEMBER 1997

Task 2.1

Reconciliation of operating profit to net cash inflow from operating activities

	£'000
Operating profit	1,254
Depreciation charges	971
Profit on sale of tangible fixed assets	(20)
Increase in stock	(48)
Increase in debtors	(105)
Decrease in creditors	(84)
Net cash flow from operating activities	1,968

Task 2.2

Cash flow statement of Hegel Ltd for the year ended 30 September 1997

	£'000	£'000
Net cash inflow from operating activities		1,968
Returns on investments and servicing of finance		
Interest paid		(302)
Taxation		(276)
Capital expenditure		
Payments to acquire tangible fixed assets	(5,441)	
Sale of asset	93	
		(5,348)
Equity dividends paid		(120)
		(4,078)
Financing		
Loan	3,000	
Issue of ordinary share capital	600	
		3,600
Decrease in cash		(478)

(*Tutorial note:* It would be acceptable to include analysis of items in notes rather than on the face of the cash flow statement.)

WORKINGS

Fixed asset additions

Fixed assets (NBV)

	£'000		£'000
Balance b/d	2,075	Depreciation	971
		Disposals (156 – 83)	73
Additions (bal fig)	5,441	Balance c/d	6,472
	7,516		7,516

Task 2.3

Goodwill on acquisition:

	Total Equity £'000	Group Share (80%) £'000
Consideration		3,300
Share capital	1,200	
Share premium	400	
Revaluation reserve	200	
Profit and loss account	1,850	
Group share (80%)	3,650	2,920
Goodwill on acquisition		380

Task 2.4

REPORT

To: Directors of McTaggart Ltd
From: AAT Student
Re: Questions about the takeover of Hegel Ltd
Date: 4 December 1997

Following your recent enquiry requesting answers to various questions concerning the takeover of Hegel Ltd by McTaggart I set out my comments below:

(a)   The current and quick ratios show that the liquidity position of Hegel Ltd has deteriorated:

	1997	*1996*
Current ratio	$\dfrac{1,303}{975} = 1.3$	$\dfrac{1,470}{820} = 1.8$
Quick ratio	$\dfrac{574}{975} = 0.6$	$\dfrac{789}{820} = 1.0$

Both ratios have fallen in 1997. In 1996 the company's position appeared healthy, but in 1997 the figures suggest that it may have difficulty in realising cash from its current assets quickly enough to meet its current liabilities as they fall due. In the event of a takeover it may be necessary to inject cash into the company to meet the shortfall.

The cash flow statement highlights the reasons for this. There were substantial purchases of fixed assets for £5,441,000. The company financed the purchases by issuing shares for £600,000 and by raising a loan of £3,000,000. However, there was still a deficit, which was financed from operating activities and existing cash balances. As a result, there has been a total decrease in cash of £478,000 and the company now has an overdraft of £158,000.

(b)

	1997	*1996*
Gearing ratio	$\dfrac{3,350}{3,350 + 3,450} = 49\%$	$\dfrac{350}{350 + 2,375} = 13\%$

In 1996 Hegel Ltd had a low level of gearing, but in 1997 it increased its borrowing and is now very highly geared, with debt making up almost half its total finance. As a result, a greater proportion of the profits of the company will have to be used to pay interest on its borrowings. If profits fall, the company may not be able to meet the interest payments. The increased borrowings mean that the company is a more risky investment and may need cash support in the event of a takeover.

On consolidation, the borrowings of Hegel Ltd will be added to the borrowings of McTaggart Ltd in the group balance sheet. This means that the long term loan to Hegel Ltd will increase the gearing ratio of the group as a whole and therefore the group will appear to be a riskier investment.

(c)   FRS 10 requires that goodwill is capitalised and amortised over its useful economic life. In almost all cases the useful economic life of purchased goodwill is 20 years or less, but goodwill can be amortised over a longer period or carried in the balance sheet indefinitely provided that the following conditions are met:

- the durability of the purchased goodwill can be demonstrated; and
- the goodwill is capable of continued measurement.

If the goodwill is amortised over a period exceeding 20 years or is not amortised it should be reviewed for impairment at the end of each accounting period and written down if necessary.

I hope that this is satisfactory for your purposes.

Regards

AAT Student

UNIT 11 – SECTION 2 – DECEMBER 1998

PART A

Task 2.1

		£'000	£'000
(1)	DR Final dividend	800	
	CR Dividends payable		800
(2)	Dr Tax charge	972	
	CR Corporation tax payable		972
(3)	DR Interest charges	24	
	CR Interest payable		24

Task 2.2

Fun Ltd
Profit and Loss Account for the year ended 30 September 1998

	£'000
Turnover	
Continuing operations (W1)	14,363
Cost of sales (W2)	6,464
Gross profit	7,899
Distribution costs	2,669
Administrative expenses	2,042
Operating profit	
Continuing operations	3,188
Interest payable and similar charges	324
Profit on ordinary activities before taxation	2,864
Tax on profit on ordinary activities	972
Profit for the financial year	1,892
Dividends (W3)	1,280
Retained profit for the financial year	612

WORKINGS

All figures £'000

1   Sales 14,595 – Returns inwards 232 = 14,363

2   Calculation of cost of sales:

	£'000	£'000
Opening stock:	1,893	
Purchases	6,671	
Plus Carriage inwards	87	
Less Returns outwards	146	
	8,505	
less Closing stock	2,041	
Cost of sales		6,464

3.   Dividends:
Interim dividend   480
Final dividend proposed   800
                                                  ─────
                                                  1,280
                                                  ─────

Task 2.3

NOTES

(a)   The balance on the share premium arose when shares were issued at more than their nominal value. For example, if a share with a nominal value of £1.00 was issued for £1.50 then the accounting would be:

	£	£
DR Cash	1.50	
CR Share capital		1.00
CR Share premium		0.50

The revaluation reserve represents the excess of the valuation of an asset over its net book value. If the fixed assets had a net book value of £500,000 and their market value was established by a valuation as £700,000 then the (simplified) entry would be:

	£	£
DR Fixed assets	200,000	
CR Revaluation reserve		200,000

(b)   The accounting for the leased asset would depend upon whether the lease was a finance lease or an operating lease. SSAP 21 defines a finance lease as a lease which transfers substantially all the risks and rewards of ownership of an asset to the lessee. An operating lease is a lease other than a finance lease. A finance lease should be recorded in the balance sheet of Fun Ltd as an asset and as an obligation to pay future rentals. The amount recorded should be the present value of the minimum lease payments derived by discounting them at the interest rate implicit in the lease. If the asset was leased on an operating lease it would not be shown on the balance sheet of the lessee, but on the balance sheet of the lessor. The obligation to pay future rentals would not be shown as a liability on the balance sheet of the lessee.

PART B

Task 2.4

Reconciliation between the cash flows from operating activities and the operating profit:

	£'000
Operating profit	302
Depreciation charges	277
Increase in stock	(45)
Increase in debtors	(144)
Increase in creditors	71
Net cash inflow from operating activities	461

WORKINGS

	£'000
Profit on ordinary activities before taxation	246
Plus Interest charges	56
Operating profit	302

Task 2.5

NOTES

(a)   Calculation of minority interest:

	Total Equity £'000	Minority Interest £'000
Share capital	1,000	250
Share premium	100	25
Revaluation reserve (W1)	200	50
P&L at acquisition	1,180	295
	2,480	620

Workings (W1):

Revaluation of assets in Games Ltd to fair value at date of acquisition:

DR Fixed assets	£200,000
CR Revaluation reserve	£200,000

(b)   The minority interest should be shown as a separate item in the capital and reserves part of the balance sheet following the capital and reserves balances attributable to the group.

(c)   A minority interest is defined by FRS 2 as the interest in a subsidiary undertaking included in the consolidation that is attributable to the shares held by persons other than the parent undertaking and its subsidiary undertakings.

UNIT 11 – SECTION 3 – JUNE 1996

Task 3.1

1   Under the matching principle, costs should be matched against revenue to which they apply. It has been estimated that half of the revenue generated by the advertising will be received in 1995 and half in 1996. Applying the matching concept, the business should match half of the cost of the advertising against revenue in 1995 and half of the cost against revenue in 1996. This would mean that £1,400 would be treated as deferred expenditure in the financial statements for the year ended 31 December 1995. However, the prudence concept says that provision should be made for all known liabilities, including expenses. As it is not certain that the revenue will be increased by the amount stated, it would be prudent to write-off all of the advertising expenditure as an expense in 1995.

2   The removal of stock from the business came within the period for which the business is reporting. It should be treated as drawings and should be deducted from the capital of the owner in the financial statements for the year ended 31 December 1995.

3   The receipt of compensation from the insurance company is contingent upon the outcome of the court case. As such, it would be classified as a contingent gain. As the gain is not certain the prudence principle, which states that profits should not be anticipated, dictates that it should not be accrued for in the financial statements for the year ended 31 December 1995. It is unclear whether the solicitor's claim of 'reasonable' success renders the gain probable or only possible. If the gain is probable it should be disclosed in a note to the accounts, whereas, if it is only possible it should not be disclosed at all.

4   Putting his house up as security for a loan is a personal transaction between Jonathan Brown and the bank. The house does not belong to the business and so, on the business entity concept, there is no need to disclose this fact in the financial statements of the business.

UNIT 11 – SECTION 3 – DECEMBER 1996

Task 3.1

Pride & Co
Appropriation Account for the year ended
31 October 1996

	£	£
Net profit		90,000
Less: Interest on loan		1,000
		89,000
Adjusted net profit		89,000
Less: Partners' salaries		
Jane	15,000	
Elizabeth	10,000	
Lydia	5,000	
		30,000
Less: Interest on capital		
Jane (8% × 25,000)	2,000	
Elizabeth (8% × 22,000)	1,760	
Lydia (8% × 3,000)	240	
		4,000
		55,000
Balance of profits shared		
Jane 5/10	27,500	
Elizabeth 3/10	16,500	
Lydia 2/10	11,000	
		55,000

Task 3.2

Report

To: Partners of Pride & Co

From: AAT Student

Date: 5 December 1996

Re: Admission of Asmah to the partnership

In answer to your queries as set out in your memorandum of 31 October 1996 I set out my reply as follows:

(a)   Pride & Co has the following profitability ratios (all figures in £000):

Gross profit % $\dfrac{240}{600} = 40\%$

Net profit % $\dfrac{90}{600} = 15\%$

Expenses/sales $\dfrac{150}{600} = 25\%$

Asmah has the following profitability ratios (all figures in £000):

Gross profit % $\dfrac{90}{200} = 45\%$

Net profit % $\dfrac{20}{200} = 10\%$

Expenses/sales $\dfrac{70}{200} = 35\%$

It is clear that although Asmah has a more profitable underlying business as is shown by the higher gross profit figure, because her expenses use up a greater proportion of the income than in Pride & Co, as shown by the expenses/sales ratio, she has a lower net profit ratio and hence, overall, a less profitable business. The combined business would have the following ratios:

Gross profit % $\dfrac{240 + 90}{600 + 200} = \dfrac{330}{800} = 41\%$

Net profit % $\dfrac{90 + 20}{600 + 200} = \dfrac{110}{800} = 14\%$

Expenses/sales $\dfrac{150 + 70}{600 + 200} = \dfrac{220}{800} = 28\%$

Although the gross profit percentage in the combined business would increase, the overall net profit percentage would fall because of the higher percentage of expenses to sales. On this basis one might advise caution about admitting Asmah into the partnership. However, if economies of scale could be achieved by combining the two businesses, or the expenses of Asmah's operation could be reduced then, given the greater profitability of Asmah's underlying operation, the combination may well prove a good thing for the existing partnership.

(b)   As the admission of a new partner effectively dissolves the old partnership and creates a new partnership a new partnership agreement is required. It should include details of the capital contributed by each partner, the profit sharing ratios, the rate of interest on capital and the salaries to be paid to the partners. All of these have already been agreed except for the salaries to be paid to the partners which have now to be determined.

(c)   Adjustments required on entry of Asmah to the partnership:

Partners' Capital Accounts

	J £'000	*E* £'000	*L* £'000	*A* £'000		*J* £'000	*E* £'000	*L* £'000	*A* £'000
Goodwill	25	15	10	10	Balance b/d	25	22	3	
					Reval.	20	12	8	
Balance					Goodwill	30	18	12	
c/d	50	37	13	25	Net assets				35
	75	52	23	35		75	52	23	35

I hope that this is satisfactory for your purposes.

Regards

AAT Student

UNIT 11 – SECTION 3 – JUNE 1997

Task 3.1

		£	£
(1)	DR Increase in provision for doubtful debts	937	
	CR Provision for doubtful debts		937
(2)	DR Drawings	500	
	CR Purchases		500
(3)	DR Motor vehicles - accumulated depreciation	2,400	
	DR Sundry debtors	3,500	
	CR Motors vehicles - cost		5,500
	CR Profit on sale of motor vehicle		400

Task 3.2

Sandro Venus
Profit and loss account for the year ended 31 March 1997

		£	£
Sales		187,325	
Less:	Returns inwards	1,437	
			185,888
Less:	Cost of Sales		
	Opening Stock	27,931	
	Purchases	103,242	
	Carriage inwards	923	
Less:	Returns outwards	1,014	
		131,082	
Less:	Closing stock	30,229	
			100,853
Gross profit			85,035
Plus:	Profit on the sale of motor vehicle		400
	Interest on bank deposit		972
Less:	Expenses		
	Wages and NIC	29,344	
	Rent, rates & insurance	7,721	
	Depreciation - Motor vehicles	6,094	
	- Office equipment	1,375	
	- Fixtures and fittings	2,780	
	Bad debts	830	
	Increase in provision for doubtful debts	937	
	Motor expenses	4,762	
	Bank charges	693	
	Lighting & heating	3,755	
	Postage and stationery	524	
	Telephone	4,307	
	Carriage outwards	657	
	Discounts allowed	373	
			64,152
Net profit			22,255

Task 3.3

NOTES

(i)   A sole trader is liable for all the debts of the business and his personal possessions can be used to meet them. A company normally has limited liability and the shareholders of the company are only liable for the full value of their shares. They cannot be forced to contribute more money to meet the debts of the company.

(ii)   Legally, a sole trader is not distinct from his business. A company is a separate legal personality apart from its owners and can therefore sue and be sued in its own right.

(iii)   Although sole traders may be required to prepare accounts for taxation and other purposes, the production of their accounts is not regulated by law. A company is legally obliged to prepare annual financial statements, circulate them to members and file them with the Registrar of Companies, thereby making them available to all interested parties. The financial statements of a company must comply with the requirements of the Companies Acts.

UNIT 11 – SECTION 3 – DECEMBER 1997

Task 3.1

	£	£
DR Current account–Bob	1,500	
CR Purchases		1,500
DR Bad Debts	5,595	
CR Debtors		5,595
DR Increase in provision for doubtful debts	2,600	
CR Provision for doubtful debts		2,600
DR Electricity	1,758	
CR Accruals		1,758

Task 3.2

AAT Student
Address

4 December 1997

Dear Partners,

I set out the following answers in respect of your questions about the adjustments to the draft accounts.

1.   Under the business entity concept the business is treated as being distinct from its owners and therefore business transactions must be kept separate from personal transactions. The books costing £1,500 that Bob removed for his own personal use have been deducted from purchases and treated as drawings from the partnership. Only the purchases for the business are included in the profit and loss account.

2.   Under the prudence concept, all losses must be recognised as soon as they are known. The partnership will experience a loss because the customer owing £5,595 has gone into liquidation during the year and the debtor balance will not be collected. Therefore the debt must be treated as bad and written off.

The partnership is anticipating further losses because it is unlikely that the partnership will collect all the amounts owed by debtors. The prudence concept requires that these losses are recognised immediately. It is impossible to predict which debtor balances will go bad and therefore it is necessary to set up a provision for doubtful debts, which has been estimated at £4,350. As there is already a provision of £1,750 from last year this is increased by £2,600 to make it up to the required level.

3.   Under the matching concept all expenses must be matched with the income to which they relate. Although the electricity bill was not received until after the year end the electricity expense relates to the year ended 30 June 1997 and must therefore be matched with the income for that year. The electricity expense is increased by £1,758 and an accrual is set up for the same amount.

I hope that this answers your questions about the adjustments to the draft accounts. If you have any further queries do not hesitate to contact me.

Yours sincerely,

AAT Student

Task 3.3

		£	£
Net profit per draft accounts			145,453
Adjustments:			
Add:	Drawings	1,500	
Deduct	Bad debts	(5,595)	
	Increase in provision for doubtful debts	(2,600)	
	Electricity accrual	(1,758)	
			(8,453)
Adjusted net profit			137,000

Task 3.4

Partners Capital Accounts

	Georgina £	Bob £		Georgina £	Bob £
Goodwill	60,000	45,000	Balance b/d	34,000	22,000
Balance c/d	46,000	31,000	Goodwill	72,000	54,000
	106,000	76,000		106,000	76,000

	Jeremy £	Louise £		Jeremy £	Louise £
Goodwill	45,000	30,000	Balance b/d	14,000	
			Cash		35,000
Balance c/d	23,000	5,000	Goodwill	54,000	
	68,000	35,000		68,000	35,000

Task 3.5

Apostles & Co
Appropriation Account for the year ended
30 June 1997

	£	£
Adjusted net profit		137,000
Less: Partners' salaries		
Georgina	13,000	
Bob	11,000	
Jeremy	10,500	
Louise	8,000	
		42,500
Less: Interest on capital		
Georgina (10% × 46,000)	4,600	
Bob (10% × 31,000)	3,100	
Jeremy (10% × 23,000)	2,300	
Louise (10% × 5,000)	500	
		10,500
		84,000
Balance of profits shared		
Georgina 4/12	28,000	
Bob 3/12	21,000	
Jeremy 3/12	21,000	
Louise 2/12	14,000	
		84,000

Task 3.6

Partners' Current Accounts

	Georgina £	Bob £			Georgina £	Bob £
Drawings	13,000	12,500	Balance b/d		6,000	4,000
			Interest on capital		4,600	3,100
			Salaries		13,000	11,000
Balance c/d	38,600	26,600	Profit		28,000	21,000
	51,600	39,100			51,600	39,100

	Jeremy £	Louise £			Jeremy £	Louise £
Drawings	12,000	9,000	Balance b/d		1,000	-
			Interest on capital		2,300	500
			Salaries		10,500	8,000
Balance c/d	22,800	13,500	Profit		21,000	14,000
	34,800	22,500			34,800	22,500

UNIT 11 – SECTION 3 – DECEMBER 1998

Task 3.1

	£
Profit per Jack	164,100
Bad debt written off	(12,500)
Accrual for delivery costs	(4,200)
Adjusted profit for appropriation	147,400

Task 3.2

(a) The liquidation of the debtor during the year and the lack of funds to pay off the debt to the partnership means that the business has sustained a loss. The prudence concept says that all losses must be provided for as soon as they are known. As the business is aware that a loss has been sustained it must be provided for immediately and the bad debt of £12,500 be written off in the year to 30 September 1998.

(b) The invoice for £4,200 representing delivery costs for sales made during the year to 30 September 1998 must be included in this year's accounts even though the invoice was not received until after the year end. The accrual or matching concept states that all costs must be matched against the income which they helped to generate. As the income was recorded in the year the costs of delivery must be matched against this income and recorded in the year to 30 September 1998.

Task 3.3

Partners' Capital Accounts

	Jack	Jane		Jack	Jane
	£	£		£	£
Goodwill 1/10/97	60,000	48,000	Balance 1/10/97	37,000	31,000
Balance c/d 30/9/98	52,000	43,000	Goodwill 1/10/97	75,000	60,000
	112,000	91,000		112,000	91,000

	Sreela	Bhatti		Sreela	Bhatti
	£	£		£	£
Goodwill 1/10/97	36,000	36,000	Balance 1/10/97	26,000	
Balance c/d 30/9/98	35,000	14,000	Cash 1/10/97		50,000
			Goodwill 1/10/97	45,000	
	71,000	50,000		71,000	50,000

Task 3.4

Jack, Jane, Sreela & Bhatti
Appropriation Account for the year ended
30 September 1998

		£	£
Net profit			147,400
less Partners' salaries			
Jack		15,000	
Jane		12,000	
Sreela		8,000	
Bhatti		8,000	
			43,000
less Interest on capital			
Jack		5,200	
Jane		4,300	
Sreela		3,500	
Bhatti		1,400	
			14,400
			90,000
Balance of profits shared			
Jack	5/15	30,000	
Jane	4/15	24,000	
Sreela	3/15	18,000	
Bhatti	3/15	18,000	
			90,000

Workings–interest on capital

Jack $10\% \times £52,000 = £5,200$
Jane $10\% \times £43,000 = £4,300$
Sreela $10\% \times £35,000 = £3,500$
Bhatti $10\% \times £14,000 = £1,400$

Task 3.5

Partners' Current Accounts

	Jack	Jane		Jack	Jane
	£	£		£	£
Drawings 30/9/98	48,200	39,300	Balance 1/10/97	5,300	4,200
Balance c/d 30/9/98	7,300	5,200	Interest on capital 30/9/98	5,200	4,300
			Salaries 30/9/98	15,000	12,000
			Profit 30/9/98	30,000	24,000
	55,500	44,500		55,500	44,500

	Sreela	Bhatti		Sreela	Bhatti
	£	£		£	£
Drawings 30/9/98	29,800	25,400	Balance 1/10/97	3,100	–
Balance c/d 30/9/98	2,800	2,000	Interest on capital 30/9/98	3,500	1,400
			Salaries 30/9/98	8,000	8,000
			Profit 30/9/98	18,000	18,000
	32,600	27,400		32,600	27,400

◆ FOULKS*lynch*

UNIT 11 – SECTION 4 – JUNE 1996

Task 4.1

		£	£
Balance of net profit per extended trial balance			80,000
Less: Interest on capital:			
Curly		4,600	
Larry		2,600	
Mo		2,800	
			10,000
Balance of profits			70,000
Profit share			
Curly		35,000	
Larry		21,000	
Mo		14,000	
			70,000

Task 4.2

Partners' capital accounts

	C £	L £	M £		C £	L £	M £
Goodwill	30,000	18,000	12,000	Balance per ETB	40,000	20,000	40,000
Balance	46,000	26,000	28,000	Goodwill	36,000	24,000	
	76,000	44,000	40,000		76,000	44,000	40,000

Partners' current accounts

	C £	L £	M £		C £	L £	M £
Balance b/d		4,000		Balance b/d	6,000		
Drawings	30,000	24,000	32,000	Interest on capital	4,600	2,600	2,800
Balance c/d	45,600	15,600	4,800	Salary	30,000	20,000	20,000
				Profit share	35,000	21,000	14,000
	75,600	43,600	36,800		75,600	43,600	36,800

UNIT 11 – SECTION 4 – JUNE 1997

Task 4.1

Partners' Capital Accounts

	Alice £	Ethel £		Alice £	Ethel £
			Balance b/d	55,000	45,000
			New values	31,000	24,800
Balance c/d	146,000	117,800	Goodwill	60,000	48,000
	146,000	117,800		146,000	117,800

	Isabella £	Flora £		Isabella £	Flora £
			Balance b/d	40,000	
			Cash		30,000
			New values	18,600	
Balance c/d	94,600	30,000	Goodwill	36,000	
	94,600	30,000		94,600	30,000

WORKINGS

New valuations		£
Land and buildings – Cost		120,000
– Accumulated depreciation		25,000
– Net book value		95,000
– Valuation		179,000
– Credited to old partners		84,000
Motor vehicles – Cost		24,000
– Accumulated depreciation		8,400
– Net book value		15,600
– Valuation		6,000
– Debited to old partners		9,600

Total credited to old partners: £84,000 - £9,600 = £74,400

		£
Alice	5/12	31,000
Ethel	3/12	24,800
Isabella	3/12	18,600
		74,400

FOULKS*lynch*

Task 4.2

The net increase in the value of the partnership assets has given rise to an unrealised profit. If the partners' capital accounts are not adjusted, the new partner will benefit from the increase in the value of the assets when they are eventually sold, despite the fact that the increase occurred before she became a partner. This would clearly be unfair. Therefore it is necessary to credit the old partners' capital accounts with their share of the unrealised profit before the new partner is admitted.

PRACTICE CENTRAL ASSESSMENTS

ANSWERS

FOULKS*lynch*

TECHNICIAN STAGE

NVQ/SVQ LEVEL 4 IN ACCOUNTING

PRACTICE CENTRAL ASSESSMENT 1

DRAFTING FINANCIAL STATEMENTS
(ACCOUNTING PRACTICE, INDUSTRY AND COMMERCE)

(UNIT 11)

DRAFTING FINANCIAL STATEMENTS

(ACCOUNTING PRACTICE, INDUSTRY AND COMMERCE)

SUGGESTED ANSWERS

SECTION 1

PART A

Task 1.1

(a) The purpose of a set of financial statements for a company is to provide information to the shareholders of the company about the performance and the stewardship of the management of the company, for example how profitable and stable the company is. The shareholders will then use this information in order to decide whether to continue to hold the shares, acquire more shares or whether to dispose of some or all of their holding.

The financial statements of a public sector body are not designed to concentrate on profit as making a profit is not the purpose of such bodies. The purpose of the financial statements however is to illustrate to users how the costs, assets and liabilities of the body have been controlled. The financial statements should also show how economically, efficiently and effectively the body has provided the service that it was set up to provide.

(b) There will tend to be a wide variety of different users of a set of financial statements for a company each having different needs and requirements from them.

The **management** of the company will be interested in the costs, revenues and profit of the company and the control of the assets and liabilities. However such information will be provided to management on a regular daily, weekly or monthly basis in order for them to plan and control the business. Therefore the annual financial statements will be of limited practical use as they do not appear on a timely basis.

The **shareholders** and potential shareholders of a company will use the financial statements in order to assess the management's stewardship of that company. Their requirement of the financial statements is to provide historical information about the way in which the company has been managed over the past accounting period and to use that information in order to act as a guide to any future decisions about their investment in that company.

Providers of credit to the company, for example banks, other lenders and trade creditors, will use a company's financial statements. Their requirements for information will be to do with the security of their loans. They will therefore be interested in the company's ability to meet any interest payments and eventual capital repayments on the due dates.

The **employees** of a company may also be users of its financial statements. Their concern will tend to be for information regarding the potential performance and profitability of the company. Their needs will be to assess the safety of their long term employment with the company and to assess the profitability of the company for the purposes of wage increase claims, improved conditions etc.

A variety of **government agencies** will use the financial statements of a company. Some will require general information for statistical evidence of economic trends whilst others such as the Inland Revenue will require detailed information regarding income and expenses in order to assess the company's tax liability.

Task 1.2

The ownership interest in a company is known as the capital of the company. This is made up of the share capital contributed by the original purchasers of the company's shares and all of the accumulated profits of the company to date.

The ownership interest in a public sector or not-for-profit organisation is however of a different nature. In a public body the funds that body requires will be provided by the government. The funds for a not-for-profit organisation will be provided normally by its members. In either case case the ownership interest is normally known as a fund balance. This fund is a separate pool of monetary and other resources established in order to support specified activities or services.

PART B

Task 1.3

REPORT

To: Directors of Metre Ltd
From: AAT Student
Date: 2 August 1998
Re: Analysis of Metre Ltd's financial statements

Introduction

The purpose of this report is to analyse the financial statements of Metre Ltd for 1996 and 1997 in order to assess the performance and financial position of the company. The report will consider the profitability, liquidity and level of gearing of the company, how this has changed over the last two years and how it compares to industry average figures.

Profitability

Metre Ltd has achieved a 17.5% increase in turnover between 1996 and 1997 although this appears to have been at the cost of the profitability of the company. The gross profit margin has decreased from 19% to 16% and the net profit margin from 8% to 5%. This indicates not only a substantial decrease in the profitability of Metre Ltd's trading but this also is contrary to the movement in the industry as a whole. In 1996 both Metre Ltd's gross profit margin and its net profit margin were above the industry average figures. By 1997 the industry average profit margins have increased but Metre Ltd's have decreased.

This movement is also mirrored in the return on capital employed for Metre Ltd which has fallen from 7% in 1996 to only 3% in 1997 compared to an industry average increase from 4% to 5%. The cause of this fall in overall return is purely to do with the decrease in profitability of the company as the asset turnover has remained constant at approximately 1, although again this is somewhat below the industry average of 1.2.

Liquidity

The liquidity of the company however does appear to be strengthening. In 1996 the current liabilities of the company were covered only 1.7 times by the current assets whereas by 1997 the current liabilities were covered 2.0 times. In comparison the industry average figures show reduced cover from 2.5 in 1996 to 2.0 in 1997.

Gearing level

The level of gearing as a percentage of the balance sheet total of Metre Ltd has increased from 23% in 1996 to 32% in 1997 as Metre Ltd has taken on an extra £120,000 of bank loans during the year. This is again contrary to the industry trend which has seen a decrease in gearing levels from 38% in 1996 to 26% in 1997. From the profit and loss account aspect, gearing can also be measured by looking at the number of times that the interest payable figure is covered by the profit before interest. For Metre Ltd this has reduced from interest cover of 6.4 times in 1996 to only 2.5 times in 1997, in marked contrast to the industry increase from 5.0 times to 8.0 times.

Conclusion

Metre Ltd appears to have significant problems with the profitability of its activities. This has shown a marked decrease when the industry as a whole appears to be increasing its profitability. Metre Ltd has quite clearly invested heavily in fixed assets during the period and this has been financed by additional bank loans and an issue of shares. However despite the new fixed assets there appears to be no increase in productivity as the asset turnover has remained constant over the two year period and below the industry average.

As far as the bank are concerned if approached for an additional bank loan, it is likely that they would turn the company down unless good reasons can be given for this decrease in profitability. The company is already more highly geared than others in the industry and is indeed increasing its gearing levels whilst the industry trend is a decrease.

SECTION 2

PART A

Task 2.1

JOURNAL

	Debit £'000	Credit £'000
Dividends payable (P&L)	240	
Proposed dividend creditor		240
(4,000,000 shares × 6 pence)		

Being the final proposed dividend for the year.

	Debit £'000	Credit £'000
Interest payable (P&L)	36	
Interest payable creditor		36
(£800,000 × 6% × 9/12)		

Being the amount of debenture interest due for the year.

	Debit £'000	Credit £'000
Corporation tax (P&L)	380	
Corporation tax creditor		380

Being the corporation tax charge for the year.

	Debit £'000	Credit £'000
Land and buildings at cost	104	
Revaluation reserve		104

Being the upwards revaluation of the land.

	Debit £'000	Credit £'000
Cash (600,000 shares × 80 pence)	480	
Ordinary share capital		300
Share premium (600,000 shares × 30 pence)		180

Being the issue of new ordinary shares.

	Debit £'000	Credit £'000
Corporation tax (P&L)	98	
Provision for deferred tax		98

Being the setting up of a provision for deferred tax.

Task 2.2

Profit and loss account for the year ended 31 December 1997

	£'000
Turnover	
- Continuing operations	10,320
Cost of sales (W1)	5,440
Gross profit	4,880
Distribution costs	(1,516)
Administrative expenses	(1,188)
Operating profit	
- Continuing operations	2,176
Interest payable and similar charges (Task 2.1)	(36)
Profit on ordinary activities before taxation	2,140
Tax on profit on ordinary activities (W2)	(478)
Profit on ordinary activities after taxation	1,662
Dividends (W3)	(440)
Retained profit for the financial year	1,222

WORKINGS

1	£'000
Opening stock	2,749
Purchases	6,112
	8,861
Less: Closing stock	3,421
Cost of sales	5,440

2	£'000
Corporation tax charge	380
Deferred tax provision	98
	478

3	£'000
Interim dividend paid	200
Proposed final dividend	240
Total dividend	440

Task 2.3

Statement of total recognised gains and losses for the year ended 31 December 1997

	£'000
Profit for the financial year	1,662
Unrealised surplus on revaluation of land	104
Total gains and losses for the year	1,766

Task 2.4

	£'000	£'000
Cost of investment in Orange Ltd		2,007
Net assets acquired:		
Net assets at 31 December 1997	1,718	
Revaluation reserve (2,121 – 1,964)	157	
	1,875	
	× 80%	1,500
Goodwill on acquisition		507

The treatment of positive goodwill under FRS 10 is that it should be capitalised and therefore appear on the balance sheet. Therefore this goodwill on consolidation will be categorised as a fixed asset and will appear on the consolidated balance sheet as such. FRS 10 has a rebuttable presumption that purchased goodwill has a limited useful economic life that will not exceed 20 years. If the useful economic life of this goodwill is believed to be less than 20 years then it should be amortised, usually on a straight line basis, over this estimated useful economic life.

If the useful economic life is believed to be more than 20 years but the value of the goodwill is not significant or not capable of future measurement then it should be amortised over a period of 20 years. If the useful economic life is believed to be more than 20 years and the value is significant and is capable of future measurement then if the useful economic life can be estimated it should be amortised over that period. If the useful economic life is indefinite then the goodwill should not be amortised. In both cases the goodwill should be reviewed for impairment in value each accounting period.

Task 2.5

	£'000
Net asset value of Orange Ltd at 31 December 1997	1,718
Revaluation reserve	157
	1,875
Minority interest at 31 December 1997	
20% × 1,875	375

This is a credit balance and can appear in the capital section of the consolidated balance sheet beneath the group reserves.

SECTION 3

Task 1

When a government grant is received the accounting principle set out in SSAP 4 is that the grant should be spread over the useful life of the asset to which it relates. The deferred credit method of effecting this is that initially the grant is debited to the bank account and credited to a deferred credit - government grant account. The balance on this deferred credit account is then credited to the profit and loss account on a straight line basis each year of the related asset's useful economic life.

Task 2

Bad and doubtful debts - a bad debt of £220 is to be written off. This will be done by reducing debtors and charging the amount to office expenses. The doubtful debt provision required is then 3% of the remaining debtors, £17,200 = £516. This requires an increase over last year's provision of (£516 – 213) £303. This amount is also charged to office expenses.

Government grant - the £3,100 is debited to the suspense account and credited to a deferred credit account. As the asset has a useful economic life of 5 years then in this first year £620 (£3,100/5) will be credited to the profit and loss account leaving a balance on the deferred credit account of £2,480 (£3,100 – 620).

Sales of fixtures
and fittings - the fixtures and fittings at cost account must be reduced by £1,240 and the accumulated depreciation account reduced by £600 (£1,240 – 640). The proceeds of £830 must be debited to the suspense account and the profit of £190 (£830 – 640) must be credited to the profit and loss account.

Cash drawings - the remaining balance on the suspense account (£24,912 + 3,100 + 830) £28,842 are the owner's cash drawings and as such will be debited against profits in the balance sheet.

Bank interest due - the bank interest must be charged to the profit and loss account and treated as a further accrual in the balance sheet.

Drawings of goods - the accounting treatment for drawings of goods by the owner is that purchases should be decreased (credited) and drawings increased (debited).

Stock value - all items of stock should be valued at the lower of cost and net realisable value. Therefore the closing stock value should be reduced by £710 (£1,580 – 870) in both the profit and loss account and the balance sheet.

Task 3

Trading and profit and loss account for the year ended 31 March 1998

	£	£
Sales		193,277
Less: Returns inwards		(1,441)
		191,836
Opening stock	8,996	
Purchases (115,967 – 440)	115,527	
Less: returns outwards	(970)	
	123,553	
Less: closing stock (9,487 – 710)	(8,777)	
Cost of sales		114,776
Gross profit		77,060
Office expenses (12,321 + 220 + 303)	12,844	
Sundry expenses	5,348	
Wages	20,389	
Bank interest	560	
Profit on sale of fixtures and fittings	(190)	
Government grant	(620)	
		38,331
Net profit		38,729

Balance sheet as at 31 March 1998

	Cost £	Acc Depr'n £	NBV £
Fixed assets:			
Machinery	48,200	25,565	22,635
Fixtures and fittings			
(4,320 – 1,240)	3,080		
(2,592 – 600)		1,992	1,088
Motor vehicles	47,300	27,345	19,955
	98,580	54,902	43,678
Current assets:			
Stock (9,487 – 710)		8,777	
Debtors (17,420 – 220)	17,200		
Less: provision	516		
		16,684	
Prepayments		1,569	
Bank		1,263	
		28,293	
Creditors: amounts falling due within one year			
Trade creditors	9,532		
Accruals (1,740 + 560)	2,300		
		11,832	
			16,461
			60,139
Creditors: amounts falling due after more than one year			
Bank loan		5,000	
Deferred credit (3,100 - 620)		2,480	
			7,480
			52,659
Opening capital			43,212
Profit for the year		38,729	
Less: drawings (28,842 + 440)		29,282	
			9,447
			52,659

TECHNICIAN STAGE

NVQ/SVQ LEVEL 4 IN ACCOUNTING

PRACTICE CENTRAL ASSESSMENT 2

DRAFTING FINANCIAL STATEMENTS
(ACCOUNTING PRACTICE, INDUSTRY AND COMMERCE)

(UNIT 11)

DRAFTING FINANCIAL STATEMENTS

(ACCOUNTING PRACTICE, INDUSTRY AND COMMERCE)

SUGGESTED ANSWERS

SECTION 1

PART A

Task 1.1

(a)   The financial position of an enterprise is represented by the economic resources that it controls, its financial structure and its liquidity and solvency. Such information is primarily presented in the balance sheet.

The financial performance of an enterprise consists of the return obtained by it on the resources that it controls, including the cost of its financing. This information is provided in the profit and loss account and the statement of total recognised gains and losses.

The financial adaptability of an enterprise consists of its ability to take effective action to alter the amount and the timing of its cash flows so that it can respond to unexpected events and opportunities. This information is provided by all of the primary financial statements.

The stewardship of management is the accountability of management for the resources entrusted to it. The overall assessment of the performance of management in this context will be evidenced by all of the primary financial statements.

(b)   Information is said to be relevant when it influences the economic decisions of users by helping them to evaluate past, present or future events or by confirming, or correcting, their past evaluations.

Information is reliable when it is free from material error and bias and can be depended upon by users to represent faithfully in terms of valid description that which it either purports to represent or could reasonably be expected to represent.

Comparability of information can be achieved by consistency of treatment and presentation and by disclosure of accounting policies and prior year figures.

Understandability of information can be achieved by aggregating and then classifying the information and by a full understanding of the users' abilities. The Draft Statement of Principles expects users to have a general understanding and awareness of business and economic matters.

Task 1.2

Many accounting transactions are relatively simple in nature and their commercial substance is fully represented by their legal form. Therefore there is no conflict in terms of their respresentation as they simply appear in the financial statements according to both substance and form.

However there are some types of financial transactions that are more complex and for which there is a difference between their actual legal nature and their true commercial effect. Where there is this conflict between substance and form FRS 5 has now made it clear that it is the commercial or economic substance of the transaction that should be reflected in the financial statements, rather than simply the legal form.

To illustrate the concept SSAP 21 deals with the accounting treatment of finance leases and operating leases in totally different manners. A finance lease is one where the lessee is effectively the owner of the asset concerned. This is deemed to be the case if the lessee has the benefit of substantially all of the rewards of the asset and also bears the significant risks of the asset. In such cases the asset is treated as if it is owned outright by the lessee and as such is included on the balance sheet of the lessee as a fixed asset together with a related liability for the capital repayments for the asset. As the asset is treated according to the commercial substance of being owned it must also be depreciated over its useful economic life. A further charge is made to the profit and loss account each period for the element of the total lease rental that is the finance cost of having the use of this asset without actually having to purchase it.

In contrast an operating lease is one where the lessee does not have the majority of the risks and benefits of the asset. An operating lease is also treated according to its economic substance which is simply that of a hire agreeement for the asset. Therefore the asset does not appear on the balance sheet of the lessee and the only accounting entry for the asset is to charge the profit and loss account with the full amount of the lease rental payable in each period.

PART B

Task 1.3

REPORT

To: Directors
From: AAT Student
Date: April 1998
Re: Analysis of A Ltd's and B Ltd's financial statements

Introduction

The purpose of this report is to consider the financial position and performance of A Ltd and B Ltd who are both potential acquirers of this company. The report will comment upon the profitability, liquidity and level of gearing of each company.

Calculation of ratios

The following ratios for the companies have been computed:

	A Ltd	*B Ltd*
Gross profit percentage	330/1,000 = 33%	96/240 = 40%
Net profit percentage	110/1,000 = 11%	26/240 = 11%
Return on capital employed	110/1,222 = 9%	26/433 = 6%
Asset turnover	1,000/1,222 = 0.82	240/433 = 0.55
Current ratio	470/280 = 1.7	100/20 = 5.0
Gearing	500/1,222 = 41%	20/433 = 5%

Comment and analysis

A Ltd is clearly a much larger company than B Ltd with approximately four times the turnover and asset base of B Ltd. However B Ltd appears to be the more inherently profitable with a gross profit percentage of 40% compared to that of A Ltd of 33%. This could be due to the smaller company paying lower wage rates to its production staff or having more skilled or efficient employees. However both companies have the same net profit percentage indicating that B Ltd perhaps has less control of its total costs and expenses than A Ltd.

The concern of the level of control over costs and resources in B Ltd might also be evidenced by its asset turnover and current ratio. B Ltd's asset turnover is 0.55 compared to 0.82 for A Ltd. This means that for every £1 of net assets B Ltd is only producing 55 pence of sales compared to 82 pence of sales for A Ltd. It may well be therefore that B Ltd is not using its assets as efficiently as it might despite its higher profit margin. B Ltd's current ratio is also perhaps of some concern at a level of 5.0, meaning that its current liabilities are covered 5 times by its current assets. This is a high figure for the current ratio and might indicate either excessive levels of stocks, debtors or cash or that suppliers are being paid too early and not enough trade credit is being taken.

In terms of overall profitability and return to the providers of capital in the companies, A Ltd has a higher return on capital employed at 9% compared to that of B Ltd of just 6%. As the net profit percentages of the two companies are the same then this higher return on capital employed is due solely to the more efficient use of A Ltd's assets as indicated by the asset turnover figures.

A Ltd is also much more highly geared than B Ltd. A Ltd's gearing level does not appear to be excessive at 41% (although no industry comparatives are available) but it would appear by A Ltd's better overall profitability that the use of such long term loans has been of benefit to A Ltd.

Conclusion

From the limited information that is available about A Ltd and B Ltd it would appear that B Ltd is capable of being a more profitable company than it currently is. Its higher gross profit margin is a good starting point but there appear to be weaknesses in control of expenses, efficient use of its assets and control of its current assets. B Ltd might also benefit from some additional gearing when finance is next required.

On the whole A Ltd would appear to be the stronger company with reasonable overall profit levels and returns and no obvious problems in management of assets and resources. If our company is to be purchased by either A Ltd or B Ltd then probably a purchase by A Ltd would be the most satisfactory.

Task 2.1

Craig Ltd
Profit and loss account for the year ended 31 March 1998

	£'000
Turnover	
- Continuing operations (W1)	25,443
Cost of sales (W2)	14,893
Gross profit	10,550
Distribution costs (4,716 + 146)	(4,862)
Administrative expenses	(3,264)
Operating profit	
- Continuing activities	2,424
Interest payable and similar charges	
$(123 + 4,100 \times 6\% \times 6/12)$	(246)
Profit on ordinary activities before tax	2,178
Tax on profit on ordinary activities	927
Profit on ordinary activities after taxation	1,251
Dividends (W3)	(500)
Retained profit for the financial year	751

Craig Ltd
Balance sheet as at 31 March 1998

	£'000	£'000
Fixed assets		
Tangible assets (W4)		6,865
Investments		2,410
Current assets		
Stocks	5,941	
Debtors (W5)	4,098	
Cash at bank and in hand (395 + 1,200)	1,595	
	11,634	
Creditors: amounts falling due within one year (W6)	(3,966)	
Net current assets		7,668
Total assets less current liabilities		16,943
Creditors: amounts falling due after more than one year		4,100
		12,843
Capital and reserves		
Called up share capital (5,000 + 1,000)		6,000
Share premium (2,250 + 200)		2,450
Revaluation reserve		240
Profit and loss account (3,402 + 751)		4,153
		12,843

WORKINGS

1	£'000
Sales	25,625
Less: returns inwards	182
	25,443

2	
Opening stock	5,625
Purchases	15,217
Less: Returns outwards	(126)
Add: Carriage inwards	118
Less: Closing stock	(5,941)
Cost of sales	14,893

3	
Interim dividend paid	300
Final dividend proposed (10m shares × 2 pence)	200
	500

◈ FOULKS*lynch*

4

Cost -	Land and buildings (4,670 + 240)	4,910
	Fixtures and fittings	1,750
	Motor vehicles	2,625
		9,285
Less: Accumulated depreciation		
	- Buildings	(576)
	Fixtures and fittings	(700)
	Motor vehicles	(1,144)
		6,865

5

Debtors	4,232
Less: Provision	(212)
Add: prepayments	78
	4,098

6

Trade creditors	2,576
Corporation tax payable	927
Final proposed dividend	200
Interest payable (4,100 × 6% × 6/12)	123
Accruals	140
	3,966

Task 2.2

The concept of control over another company is that one company controls another if that company either owns the majority of the shares in that company or controls the economic and financial decisions of the company in some way. If one company (the parent) controls another then this controlled company is known as a subsidiary.

FRS 2 gives five separate possible definitions of a subsidiary undertaking and therefore of a situation where one company controls the other. These are:

(a)   the parent holds the majority of the rights to vote at general meetings of the undertaking on all or substantially all matters;

(b)   the parent is a member and has a right to appoint or remove directors having a majority of the rights to vote at board meetings on all or substantially all matters;

(c)   the parent is a member and has the right to control alone a majority of the rights to vote at general meetings of the undertaking pursuant to an agreement with other shareholders;

(d)   the parent has the right to exercise dominant influence over the undertaking;

(e)   the parent has a participating interest and actually exercises dominant influence or the parent and the subsidiary are managed on a unified basis.

If one company controls another company then CA85 and FRS 2 together require that the parent company should produce group accounts in the form of consolidated accounts.

It is entirely possible for a parent to own shares in another company without meeting the FRS 2 criteria of control of that company. The parent may not control the other company but it may exercise significant influence over that other company. This means that the parent is actively involved and is influential in the direction of the company through its participation in policy decisions covering decisions such as strategic issues of expansion/contraction of the business, participation in other entities, changes in products, markets and activities and determining the balance between dividends and reinvestment.

If a parent company which produces group accounts for its subsidiary undertakings has significant influence over a company then that company should be treated as an associated undertaking according to FRS 9 and equity accounted in the consolidated financial statements.

Task 2.3

(a)   According to FRS 9 an associated undertaking is an entity (other than a subsidiary) in which another entity (the investor) has a participating interest and over whose operating and financial policies the investor exercises a significant influence. A participating interest is defined in FRS 9 as an interest held in shares on a long term basis for the purpose of securing a contribution to the investor's activities by the exercise of control or influence. The CA85 definition of a participating interest includes a presumption that this will exist where the investor holds 20% or more of the shares. However the FRS 9 definition of an associated undertaking is more concerned with evidence of significant influence than with the actual number of shares held.

(b)   Equity accounting is a method of accounting that initially brings the investment into the consolidated financial statements at cost, identifying any goodwill arising. Then in each subsequent accounting period the carrying value is adjusted to reflect the investor's share of the post acquisition profits of the associate.

Therefore in the consolidated balance sheet the interest in associated undertaking is valued at cost plus group share of post acquisition profits less any amounts written off (eg, goodwill amortised). In the consolidated profit and loss account the figures to be included under equity accounting are the group's share of the associate's operating profit and interest receivable or payable, and the group's share of the tax charge of the associate.

Task 2.4

(a)   Investment in associated undertaking to appear in the balance sheet:

$£6,300,000 \times 40\%$ =   £2,520,000

(b)   Premium on acquisition (goodwill)

		£
Cost of investment		2,410,000
Net assets acquired		
$(£4,500,000 + £800,000) \times 40\%$		2,120,000
		290,000

(c)   Figures to appear in the consolidated profit and loss account:

Share of operating profit of associate

$40\% \times £160,000$ =   £64,000

Taxation - associate

$40\% \times £60,000$ =   £24,000

Task 2.5

If the directors of Craig Ltd do acquire the shares in Freesia Ltd then in order for the acquisition to be treated as a merger both the CA criteria and FRS 6 criteria for a merger must be satisfied.

The CA89 criteria are:

(a)   the subsidiary was acquired by an arrangement providing for the issue of equity shares;

(b)   the group obtains at least 90% of the shares;

(c)   the fair value of any consideration other than equity shares does not exceed 10% of the nominal value of the shares issued;

(d)   the adoption of merger accounting complies with generally accepted accounting principles ie, FRS 6.

The FRS 6 criteria are:

(a)   no party to the combination is portrayed as either acquirer or acquired;

(b)   all parties participate in establishing the management structure for the combined entity;

(c)   the relative sizes of the combining entities are not so disparate that one party dominates the combined activity by virtue of its relative size;

(d)   the consideration received is primarily equity shares in the combined entity; any non-equity consideration must represent only an immaterial proportion of the consideration;

(e)   no equity shareholders of the combined entities retain any material interest in the future performance of only part of the combined entity.

If a combination satisfies all five of the criteria, it is a merger and FRS 6 requires that merger accounting must be used for the combination.

Task 3.1

Appropriation account for the year ended 31 March 1998

	£	£
Net profit		235,572
Less: Partners' salaries		
Peter	10,000	
Daphne	12,000	
Ken	14,000	
Francis	8,000	
		(44,000)
Less: Interest on capital		
Peter (41,000 × 8%)	3,280	
Daphne (35,800 × 8%)	2,864	
Ken (31,200 × 8%)	2,496	
Francis (26,600 × 8%)	2,128	
		(10,768)
		180,804
Balance of profits shared		
Peter 2/6	60,268	
Daphne 2/6	60,268	
Ken 1/6	30,134	
Francis 1/6	30,134	
		180,804

Task 3.2

Partners' Capital Accounts

	Peter £	Daphne £	Ken £	Francis £		Peter £	Daphne £	Ken £	Francis £
Goodwill	43,200	-	32,400	32,400	Bal b/d	41,000	35,800	31,200	26,600
					Goodwill	36,000	36,000	18,000	18,000
Cash		20,000			Transfer from				
Loan a/c		59,332			current account		7,532		
Bal c/d	33,800		16,800	12,200					
	77,000	79,332	49,200	44,600		77,000	79,332	49,200	44,600
					Bal b/d	33,800	-	16,800	12,200

Partners' Current Accounts

	Peter £	Daphne £	Ken £	Francis £		Peter £	Daphne £	Ken £	Francis £
Drawings	64,000	71,000	39,000	31,000	Bal b/d	2,100	3,400	1,100	1,000
					Salaries	10,000	12,000	14,000	8,000
Transfer to					Interest on				
capital a/c		7,532			capital	3,280	2,864	2,496	2,128
Bal c/d	11,648		8,730	10,262	Profit share	60,268	60,268	30,134	30,134
	75,648	78,532	47,730	41,262		75,648	78,532	47,730	41,262
					Bal b/d	11,648	-	8,730	10,262

CLASS ACTIVITIES

QUESTIONS

Chapters 1, 2

FRAMEWORK, GAAPS AND CONCEPTS

1 ACTIVITY

Your managing director has approached you saying that he is 'confused at all the different accounting bodies that have replaced the old Accounting Standards Committee'.

Task

Draft a memorandum to your managing director explaining the purpose, a description of the type of work and, where applicable, examples of the work to date of the following:

(a) Financial Reporting Council
(b) Accounting Standards Board
(c) Financial Reporting Review Panel
(d) Urgent Issues Task Force.

2 ACTIVITY

You have recently been appointed as assistant accountant of PQR Ltd. You have assisted in preparing a forecast set of final accounts for the company whose year end is 31 December 20X3. The forecast shows that the company is expected to make a loss during the year to 31 December 20X3. This would be the first time that the company has made a loss since it was incorporated twenty years ago.

The managing director is concerned that the company's shareholders would be unhappy to hear that the company had made a loss. He is determined to avoid making a loss if at all possible. He has made the following suggestions in order to remedy the situation:

(a) Make no further provision for obsolete stock and consider crediting the profit and loss account with the provision made in previous years.

(b) Do not provide for depreciation for the year to 31 December 20X3.

(c) Capitalise all research expenditure.

(d) Do not make any further provision for doubtful debts and credit the profit and loss account with the full amount of provisions made in previous years.

Task

Consider the managing director's suggestions and draft a report to him stating whether you agree or disagree with them. Make reference to accounting concepts as appropriate.

Chapters 3–7

SOLE TRADERS AND PARTNERSHIPS

1   ACTIVITY

Alpha and Beta are in partnership. They share profits equally after Alpha has been allowed a salary of £4,000 pa. No interest is charged on drawings or allowed on current accounts or capital accounts. The trial balance of the partnership at 31 December 20X9 before adjusting for any of the items below, is as follows:

			Dr £'000	*Cr* £'000
Capital	-	Alpha		30
	-	Beta		25
Current	-	Alpha		3
	-	Beta		4
Drawings	-	Alpha	4	
	-	Beta	5	
Sales				200
Stock 1 Jan 20X9			30	
Purchases			103	
Operating expenses			64	
Loan	-	Beta (10%)		10
	-	Gamma (10%)		20
Land and buildings			60	
Plant and machinery	-	cost	70	
	-	depreciation to 31 December 20X9		40
Debtors and creditors			40	33
Bank				11
			376	376

(i)   Closing stock on hand at 31 December 20X9 was £24,000.

(ii)   On 31 December Alpha and Beta agree to take their manager, Gamma, into partnership. Gamma's loan account balance is to be transferred to a capital account as at 31 December. It is agreed that in future Alpha, Beta and Gamma will all share profits equally. Alpha will be allowed a salary of £4,000 as before, and Gamma will be allowed a salary of £5,000 pa (half of what he received in 20X9 as manager, included in operating expenses).

The three partners agree that the goodwill of the business at 31 December should be valued at £12,000, but is not to be recorded in the books. It is also agreed that land and buildings are to be revalued to a figure of £84,000 and that this revalued figure is to be retained and recorded in the accounts.

(iii)   Interest on the loan has not been paid.

(iv)   Included in sales are two items sold on 'sale or return' for £3,000 each. Each item had cost the business £1,000. One of these items was in fact returned on 4 January 20Y0 and the other one was formally accepted by the customer on 6 January 20Y0.

Task 1

Submit with appropriately labelled headings and subheadings:

(a)   partners' capital accounts in columnar form;
(b)   partners' current accounts in columnar form;
(c)   trading, profit and loss and appropriation account for 20X9;
(d)   balance sheet as at 31 December 20X9.

Task 2

Write a brief note to Gamma, who cannot understand why his capital account balance seems so much less than those of Alpha and Beta.

Explain to him the adjustments you have made.

2   ACTIVITY

Timmy and Lucy have been in partnership for some years, sharing profits equally. After the preparation of accounts for the year ended 31 December 20X2 their trial balance is as shown below (all figures £s).

		Dr	Cr
Timmy	- capital account		30,000
	- current account		3,000
Lucy	- capital account		40,000
	- current account	4,000	
Land		12,000	
Buildings	- cost	25,000	
	- depreciation		2,000
Machinery	- cost	30,000	
	- depreciation		16,000
Goodwill		10,000	
Net current assets		10,000	
		91,000	91,000

With effect from 1 January 20X3, Charlie is admitted into the partnership, and on that day he pays in £20,000 which is entered in his capital account. From that date the partners are to share profits Timmy 40%, Lucy 40%, Charlie 20%.

It is agreed that at 1 January 20X3 the land is worth £20,000, the buildings are worth £30,000 and the goodwill is worth £16,000. The necessary adjustments are not to be recorded in the asset accounts, but should be made in the capital accounts.

The operating profit for the year 20X3 is £40,000, after charging depreciation of 1% on cost of the buildings and of 10% on cost of the machinery. There have been no sales or purchases of fixed assets in the year.

The partners are allowed 10% per annum interest on capital account balances on a *pro rata* basis. No interest is allowed or charged on current account balances. On 31 December 20X3 the partners are advised that the buildings are now worth only £20,000 (though the value of the land is not affected). It is agreed that this revised valuation should be incorporated in the accounts as at 31 December 20X3.

Each partner has taken drawings of £4,000 in the year to 31 December 20X3.

Task 1

Prepare the partners' capital accounts in columnar form for the year 20X3.

Task 2

Prepare the appropriation account for the year 20X3.

Task 3

Prepare the partners' current accounts in columnar form for the year 20X3.

Task 4

Draw up a summary balance sheet as at 31 December 20X3, taking net current assets as the balancing figure.

Task 5

Prepare a reconciliation of net current assets at 1 January 20X3 with net current assets at 31 December 20X3.

3   ACTIVITY

A and B are in partnership, sharing profits equally after taking account of interest on opening balances on capital accounts at 10% pa, and allowing A a management salary of £5,000 pa. No interest is allowed or charged on current accounts or on drawings.

You are presented with the following trial balance as at 31 December 20X1.

		£'000	£'000
Capital account	A		50
Capital account	B		30
Current account	A		12
Current account	B		3
Drawings	A	7	
Drawings	B	6	
Property		90	
Fixtures and fittings, cost and depreciation		40	14
Motor vehicles, cost and depreciation		40	24
Sales			250
Cost of sales		120	
Stocks		20	
Debtors and creditors		40	30
Operating expenses		40	
Goodwill		40	
Bank overdraft			10
Loan from A at 12% pa			15
Loan from D at 12% pa			5
		443	443

The following information is to be taken into account.

(i)   Depreciation on motor vehicles has already been provided for the year 20X1 at 20% pa by the reducing balance method. It is now decided to change this for the year 20X1 to 25% pa by the reducing balance method.

(ii)   It is agreed that a desk included in fixtures and fittings above, at a cost of £3,000, depreciation to date £1,000, is to be transferred to A personally at a valuation of £2,500.

(iii)   Interest on the loans from A and D has neither been paid nor provided.

(iv)   From the bank statement for December you discover that:

(a)   Bank charges of £500 have not been taken account of.

(b)   A standing order receipt for £1,000 from a customer has been omitted.

(c)   A cheque for £2,000 from a customer deposited on 29 December has been returned by the bank marked 'refer to drawer'.

(d)   A cheque for £3,000 sent to a supplier on 25 November is still outstanding.

(v)   C is to join the partnership with effect from the close of business on 31 December 20X1. It is agreed that for the purposes of this admission the property of the partnership is revalued at £120,000, and goodwill at £50,000. However, the property is to remain recorded in the books at the original figure, and goodwill is to be eliminated entirely from the balance sheet. A, B and C are in future to share profits in the ratio of 2:2:1, after taking account of interest on capital accounts at 10%, and allowing both A and C management salaries of £5,000 each. On 31 December C paid £20,000 into a special bank account in the name of the partnership as a capital contribution. This transaction was not accounted for on that date.

Task 1

Prepare journal entries to take account of item (i) to item (iv) above.

Task 2

Prepare capital and current accounts for A, B and C in columnar form.

Task 3

Prepare profit and loss account, appropriation account, and balance sheet for the partnership in relation to the year 20X1.

Chapters 8, 9

LIMITED COMPANIES

1   ACTIVITY

D plc has been involved in three lines of business: the operation of a chain of retail pharmacies; the manufacture and sale of cosmetics; and the manufacture and sale of a skin-care ointment. The following summarised trial balance has been extracted from the books of D plc:

Trial balance at 31 March 20X6

	£'000	£'000
Retail sales		4,700
Cost of retail sales	1,645	
Cosmetic sales		7,300
Cost of cosmetic sales	3,285	
Ointment sales		1,600
Cost of ointment sales	880	
Administration expenses	1,900	
Distribution costs	1,600	
Closure costs	920	
Taxation	100	
Dividends	1,200	
Fixed assets - cost	7,700	
Fixed assets - depreciation		1,600
Stock at 31 March 20X6	911	
Trade debtors	240	
Bank	27	
Trade creditors		310
Deferred taxation		600
Share capital		4,000
Retained profits		298
	20,408	20,408

(i)   The company closed down its ointment factory during the year. This involved expenses totalling £920,000.

(ii)   Administration costs should be split between retailing, cosmetics and ointment in the ratio 5: 3: 2. Distribution costs should be split in the ratio 3: 1: 1.

(iii)   The balance on the taxation account comprises £100,000 left after the final settlement of the corporation tax liability for the year ended 31 March 20X5.

(iv)   The company expects to receive tax relief of £240,000 on the costs incurred in closing the ointment factory. Corporation tax on the operating profits for the year has been estimated at £1,020,000.

(v)   The provision for deferred taxation is to be increased by £90,000.

(vi)   The directors have proposed a final dividend of £800,000.

(vii)   Four users of the company's skin-care ointment claim to have been injured by it. D plc's lawyers are contesting this claim, but they are uncertain whether any damages will have to be paid. The plaintiffs' lawyers are claiming damages totalling £750,000.

Task 1

Prepare a profit and loss account and balance sheet for D plc. These should be in a form suitable for publication (insofar as is possible given the information provided).

Task 2

Prepare the note to the financial statements required in respect of item (vii) above.

2   ACTIVITY

L plc operates several large shopping centres across the country. These centres are located on the outskirts of major towns and cities; each centre has at least three major retail stores which belong to L plc. The company advertises heavily, both on national television and on regional radio stations.

The company rents out smaller shops in each of its centres. The tenants pay rent and are also required to contribute to the costs of advertising. Both rents and contributions to advertising are paid in advance.

L plc has recently commissioned an advertising campaign. This will be broadcast over a two-year period commencing in June 20X7. The company has paid the consultants who designed the campaign, and has purchased most of the television and radio advertising time in advance. L plc's marketing experts expect that the advertising campaign will help to build customer loyalty and will continue to attract income for anything up to three years after the end of the campaign.

L plc's accountant is unsure whether the expenditure on the advertising campaign should be written off immediately or carried forward and written off over either two years (the length of the advertising campaign) or five years (the length of the period which is expected to benefit).

L plc has invoiced its tenants for 40% of the cost of the campaign. The invoices were sent out just prior to the end of the current financial year. Given that L plc has effectively "sold" this advertising, the company's managing director is in favour of treating the £800,000 invoiced as turnover for the year ended 31 March 20X7.

The following summarised trial balance has been extracted from the books of L plc:

Trial balance at 31 March 20X7	£'000	£'000
Retail sales		25,000
Cost of retail sales	16,250	
Administration expenses	250	
Distribution costs (excluding advertising campaign)	500	
Advertising campaign	2,000	
Rental income		1,500
Advertising charges to tenants		800
Balances recoverable from tenants for advertising	800	
Interest paid	350	
Corporation tax over provided for year to 31 March 20X6		50
Fixed assets - cost or valuation	27,000	
Fixed assets - depreciation		4,200
Revaluation reserve		8,000
Stock at 31 March 20X7	850	
Bank	780	
Trade creditors		1,800
Long-term loans		2,300
Share capital		4,000
Retained profits		1,130
	48,780	48,780

The following additional information is also available:

(i)   The company revalued its land during the year. This was the first time that such a revaluation had taken place. The land had cost £9 million and had not been depreciated. The valuation was conducted by Valier and Co, a firm of Chartered Surveyors.

(ii)   During the year the company spent £11 million on new fixed assets. These replaced assets which had originally cost £4 million. Those assets were sold for £1.8 million, including a gain on disposal of £300,000. The gain has been included under the appropriate cost headings on the trial balance.

(iii)   Depreciation of £3.7 million has been charged during the year and is included under the appropriate cost headings on the trial balance.

(iv)   The only dividend paid during the year was the final dividend for the year ended 31 March 20X6. The directors have proposed a final dividend of £600,000 for the year ended 31 March 20X7.

(v)   Corporation tax for the year has been estimated at £2.1 million.

Task 1

Prepare L plc's profit and loss account for the year ended 31 March 20X7, and balance sheet at that date.

These should be in a form suitable for publication AND should include the notes to the financial statements (insofar as is possible given the information provided).

You are NOT required to provide a statement of accounting policies OR to calculate the company's earnings per share.

Task 2

Explain an appropriate accounting treatment for the amount spent by L plc on the advertising campaign. State any assumptions made.

Note: There are no SPECIFIC Accounting Standards or Companies Act requirements governing the accounting treatment of this item.

Task 3

Explain whether or not you agree with the managing director's argument that the proportion of advertising billed to tenants has been sold and can, therefore, be included in turnover for the year ended 31 March 20X7. State any assumptions made.

Chapters 10–16

ACCOUNTING STANDARDS

1 ACTIVITY

The managing director of a company has recently returned from a conference on the techniques of business valuation.

She has now realised that the accounts prepared by the company for publication probably understate the value of the company by

(i)   the exclusion of goodwill,
(ii) the valuation of fixed assets at cost, and
(iii) the treatment of the costs of research.

She has asked you to draft a report stating why the accounting treatment of these items understates the value of the company.

Task

Draft an appropriate report, making reference to accounting concepts where applicable.

2 ACTIVITY

D plc is a large paper manufacturing company. The company's finance director is working on the published accounts for the year ended 31 March 20X3. The chief accountant has prepared the following list of problems which will have to be resolved before the statements can be finalised.

(a)   *Post balance sheet events*

A fire broke out at the company's Westown factory on 4 April 20X3. This has destroyed the factory's administration block. Many of the costs incurred as a result of this fire are uninsured.

A major customer went into liquidation on 27 April 20X3. The customer's balance at 31 March 20X3 remains unpaid. The receiver has intimated that unsecured creditors will receive very little compensation, if any.

(b)   *Possible investment property*

The company decided to take advantage of depressed property prices and purchased a new office building in the centre of Westville. This was purchased with the intention of the building being resold at a profit within five years. In the meantime, the company is using the property to house the administrative staff from the Westown factory until such time as their own offices can be repaired. It is anticipated that this will take at least nine months. The managing director has suggested that the building should not be depreciated.

(c)   *Possible development expenditure*

The company paid the engineering department at Northtown University a large sum of money to design a new pulping process which will enable the use of cheaper raw materials. This process has been successfully tested in the University's laboratories and is almost certain to be introduced at D plc's pulping plant within the next few months.

The company paid a substantial amount to the University's biology department to develop a new species of tree which could grow more quickly and therefore enable the company's forests to generate more wood for paper manufacturing. The project met with some success in that a new tree was developed. Unfortunately, it was prone to disease and the cost of the chemical sprays needed to keep the wood healthy rendered the tree uneconomic.

(d)   *Possible contingent liabilities*

One of the company's employees was injured during the year. He had been operating a piece of machinery which had been known to have a faulty guard. The company's lawyers have advised that the employee has a very strong case, but will be unable to estimate likely financial damages until further medical evidence becomes available.

One of the company's customers is claiming compensation for losses sustained as a result of a delayed delivery. The customer had ordered a batch of cut sheets with the intention of producing leaflets to promote a special offer. There was a delay in supplying the paper and the leaflets could not be prepared in time. The company's lawyers have advised that there was no specific agreement to supply the goods in time for this promotion and, furthermore, that it would be almost impossible to attribute the failure of the special offer to the delay in the supply of the paper.

Task

Explain how **each** of these matters should be dealt with in the published accounts for the year ended 31 March 20X3. You should assume that the amounts involved are material in every case.

Chapter 17

CASH FLOW STATEMENTS

1 ACTIVITY

You are presented with the following information relating to SH Limited:

Profit and loss account for the year ended 30 June 20X6

	£'000
Gross profit	980
Trading expenses	475
Depreciation	255
Net profit	250
Dividends	80
Retained profit for the year	170

	20X5	20X6
Balance sheets at 30 June	£'000	£'000
FIXED ASSETS at cost	3,000	3,500
Less: Accumulated depreciation	2,100	2,300
Net book value	900	1,200
CURRENT ASSETS		
Stocks	825	1,175
Debtors	5,200	5,065
Bank and cash	2,350	2,160
	8,375	8,400
Less: CURRENT LIABILITIES		
Creditors	5,000	4,350
Dividends	75	80
	5,075	4,430
NET CURRENT ASSETS	3,300	3,970
TOTAL NET ASSETS	4,200	5,170
FINANCED BY:		
Ordinary shares of £1 each	2,800	3,200
Share premium	-	400
Profit and loss account	1,400	1,570
	4,200	5,170

During the year ended 30 June 20X6, fixed assets which had cost £230,000 were sold for £145,000. The loss on this disposal has been included in trading expenses in the profit and loss account.

Task 1

Produce a cash flow statement for the year ended 30 June 20X6, which reconciles the profit with the change in cash balances.

Task 2

Discuss the liquidity of SH Limited, using TWO ratios to assist you.

2   ACTIVITY

The following information has been extracted from the draft financial information of V Ltd.

Profit and loss account for the year ended 31 December 20X3

	£'000	£'000
Sales		490
Raw materials consumed	(49)	
Staff costs	(37)	
Depreciation	(74)	
Loss on disposal	(4)	
		(164)
Operating profit		326
Interest payable		(23)
Profit before tax		303
Taxation		(87)
		216
Dividend		(52)
Profit retained for year		164
Balance brought forward		389
		553

Balance sheets

	31 December 20X3		31 December 20X2	
	£'000	£'000	£'000	£'000
Fixed assets (see below)		1,145		957
Current assets:				
Stock	19		16	
Trade debtors	40		30	
Bank	24		36	
	——		——	
	83		82	
	——		——	
Current liabilities:				
Trade creditors	(12)		(17)	
Taxation	(79)		(66)	
Proposed dividend	(21)		(15)	
	——		——	
	(112)		(98)	
	——		——	
Working capital		(29)		(16)
		——		——
		1,116		941
Long term liabilities:				
Long-term loans		(70)		(320)
		——		——
		1,046		621
		——		——
Share capital		182		152
Share premium		141		80
Revaluation reserve		170		
Profit and loss		553		389
		——		——
		1,046		621
		——		——

	Land & buildings £'000	Machinery £'000	Fixtures & fittings £'000	Total £'000
Fixed assets:				
Cost or valuation				
At 31 December 20X2	830	470	197	1,497
Additions	-	43	55	98
Disposals	-	(18)	-	(18)
Adjustment on revaluation	70	-	-	70
	——	——	——	——
At 31 December 20X3	900	495	252	1,647
	——	——	——	——

Depreciation

At 31 December 20X2	(90)	(270)	(180)	(540)
Charge for year	(10)	(56)	(8)	(74)
Disposals	-	12	-	12
Adjustment on revaluation	100	-	-	100
At 31 December 20X3	0	(314)	(188)	(502)

Net book value

At 31 December 20X3	900	181	64	1,145
At 31 December 20X2	740	200	17	957

Task 1

Prepare a cash flow statement for V Ltd for the year ended 31 December 20X3 in accordance with the requirements of the revised Financial Reporting Standard 1 (FRS 1 (Revised)).   This should include a reconciliation of operating profit to net cash flow from operating activities. No other notes to the cash flow statement are required.

Task 2

It has been suggested that the management of long-term profitability is more important than short-term cash flow.

Explain why this might be so.

Chapter 18

INTERPRETATION OF FINANCIAL STATEMENTS

1 ACTIVITY

You are the management accountant of SR plc. PQ plc is a competitor in the same industry and it has been operating for twenty years.

Summaries of PQ plc's profit and loss accounts and balance sheets for the previous three years are given below:

Summarised profit and loss accounts for year ended 31 December

	20X7 £m	20X8 £m	20X9 £m
Turnover	840	981	913
Cost of sales	554	645	590
Gross profit	286	336	323
Selling, distribution and administration expenses	186	214	219
Profit before interest	100	122	104
Interest	6	15	19
Profit on ordinary activities before taxation	94	107	85
Taxation	45	52	45
Profit on ordinary activities after taxation	49	55	40
Dividends	24	24	24
Retained profit for year	25	31	16

Summarised balance sheets at 31 December

	20X7 £m	20X8 £m	20X9 £m
Fixed assets:			
Intangible assets	36	40	48
Tangible assets at net book value	176	206	216
	212	246	264
Current assets:			
Stocks	237	303	294
Debtors	105	141	160
Bank	52	58	52
	606	748	770
Creditors – Amounts falling due within one year:			
Trade creditors	53	75	75
Other creditors	80	105	111
	133	180	186

Creditors – Amounts falling due after more than one year:

Long-term loans	74	138	138
	207	318	324
Shareholders' interests:			
Ordinary share capital	100	100	100
Retained profits	299	330	346
	606	748	770

Task

Write a report to the finance director of SR plc analysing the performance of PQ plc and showing any calculations in an appendix to this report.

2   ACTIVITY

The directors of Lusty Ltd appointed a new sales manager towards the end of 20X2. This manager devised a plan to increase sales and profit by means of a reduction in selling price and extended credit terms to customers. This involved considerable investment in new machinery early in 20X3 in order to meet the demand which the change in sales policy had created.

The financial statements for the year ended 31 December 20X2 and 20X3 are shown below. The sales manager has argued that the new policy has been a resounding success because sales and, more importantly, profits have increased dramatically.

Profit and loss accounts

	20X2 £'000	20X3 £'000
Sales	900	2,800
Cost of sales	(360)	(1,680)
Gross profit	540	1,120
Selling expenses	(150)	(270)
Bad debts	(18)	(140)
Depreciation	(58)	(208)
Interest	(12)	(192)
Net profit	302	310
Balance b/f	327	629
	629	939

FOULKS*lynch*

Balance sheets

	20X2		20X3	
	£'000	£'000	£'000	£'000
Fixed assets:				
Factory		450		441
Machinery		490		1,791
		940		2,232
Current assets:				
Stock	30		238	
Debtors	83		583	
Bank	12			
	125		821	
Current liabilities:				
Creditors	(36)		(175)	
Bank			(11)	
	(36)		(186)	
Current assets less current liabilities		89		635
		1,029		2,867
Borrowings		(100)		(1,600)
		929		1,267
		£'000		£'000
Share capital		300		328
Profit and loss		629		939
		929		1,267

Task 1

Explain whether you believe that the performance for the year ended 31 December 20X3 and the financial position at that date have improved as a result of the new policies adopted by the company. You should support your answer with appropriate ratios.

Task 2

All of Lusty Ltd's sales are on credit. The finance director has asked you to calculate the immediate financial impact of reducing the credit period offered to customers. Calculate the amount of cash which would be released if the company could impose a collection period of 45 days.

Chapters 19–22

CONSOLIDATED FINANCIAL STATEMENTS

1 ACTIVITY

Bath Ltd acquired 80% of the ordinary share capital of Jankin Ltd on 1 January 20X1 for the sum of £153,000 and 60% of the ordinary share capital of Arthur Ltd on 1 July 20X1 for the sum of £504,000.

(1)   The balance sheets of the three companies at 31 December 20X1 are set out below:

	Bath Ltd £	Jankin Ltd £	Arthur Ltd £
Share capital - Ordinary shares of 25p each	750,000	100,000	400,000
Share premium	15,000	-	-
Profit and loss account, 1 January 20X1	191,000	19,400	132,000
Retained profits for 20X1	37,000	3,000	54,000
Taxation	78,000	24,000	56,000
Creditors	162,000	74,400	149,000
Bank overdraft - Bank A	74,000	-	-
Depreciation - Freehold property	9,000	-	40,000
- Plant and machinery	87,000	39,000	124,600
Dividends proposed	30,000	15,000	24,000
Current account	-	9,800	-
	1,433,000	284,600	979,600

	Bath Ltd £	Jankin Ltd £	Arthur Ltd £
Freehold property, at cost	116,000	-	200,000
Plant and machinery, at cost	216,000	104,000	326,400
Investments in subsidiaries			
Jankin Ltd	153,000	-	-
Arthur Ltd	504,000	-	-
Trade investment	52,000	-	-
Stocks and work in progress	206,000	99,000	294,200
Debtors	172,200	73,000	95,000
Bank balance: Bank B	-	7,900	62,800
Cash	1,100	700	1,200
Current account	12,700	-	-
	1,433,000	284,600	979,600

(2)   No interim dividends were declared or paid in 20X1 out of 20X1 profits. Bath Ltd has not yet accounted for dividends receivable from its subsidiary companies.

(3)   A remittance of £1,700 from Jankin Ltd in December 20X1 was not received by Bath Ltd until January 20X2.

(4)   An invoice for £1,200 for stock material (including £240 profit) had been included in sales in 20X1 by Bath Ltd but the invoice and the stocks were not received by Jankin Ltd until 20X2.

(5)   In Jankin Ltd's stock at 31 December 20X1, were goods to the value of £8,000 ex Bath Ltd on which the latter had taken profit of £1,600.

(6)   Profits of Arthur Ltd are deemed to have accrued equally throughout the year.

(7)   Any goodwill arising on consolidation is to be amortised over four years on a strict monthly basis.

Task

Prepare the consolidated balance sheet of Bath Ltd at 31 December 20X1.

2   ACTIVITY

N plc acquired 60% of the ordinary shares of S Ltd several years ago when the reserves of S Ltd were £80,000. N plc also acquired 20% of the preference shares of S Ltd on the same date.

The summarised profit and loss accounts of the two companies for the year ended 30 September 20X7 are as follows:

		N plc		S Ltd
	£'000	£'000	£'000	£'000
Sales		4,500		1,100
Cost of sales		2,320		620
Gross profit		2,180		480
Expenses		1,400		220
Trading profit		780		260
Investment income		52		
Profit before taxation		832		
Taxation		200		80
Profit after taxation		632		180
Dividends paid:				
Ordinary	140		20	
Preference	15		10	
Dividends proposed:				
Ordinary	280		60	
Preference	15		10	
	—	450	—	100
Profit retained		182		80
Reserves brought forward		600		250
Reserves carried forward		782		330

N plc sold goods to S Ltd during the year at an invoice price of £250,000. The goods were invoiced at cost + 25%. Of these goods, one half were still in S Ltd's stock at the end of the year.

Task

Prepare the consolidated profit and loss account for the year ended 30 September 20X7. Ignore goodwill.

◆ FOULKS*lynch*

AAT

FOULKS LYNCH
4 The Griffin Centre
Staines Road
Feltham
Middlesex, TW14 0Hs
United Kingdom

HOTLINES: Telephone: +44 (0) 20 8831 9990
Fax: +44 (0) 20 8831 9991
E-mail: info@foulkslynch.com

For information and online ordering, please visit our website at:
www. foulkslynch.com

PRODUCT RANGE

Our publications cover all assessments for the AAT standards competence.

Our AAT product range consists of:

Textbooks	£10.50	Workbooks	£10.50
Combined Textbooks/Workbooks	£10.50	Lynchpin	£6.25

OTHER PUBLICATIONS FROM FOULKS LYNCH

We publish a wide range of study material in the accountancy field and specialize in texts for the following professional qualifications:

- **Chartered Institute of Management Accountants (CIMA)**
- **Association of Chartered Certified Accountants (ACCA)**
- **Certified Accounting Technicians (CAT)**

FOR FURTHER INFORMATION ON OUR PUBLICATIONS:

I would like information on publications for: ACCA ❑   AAT ❑
CAT ❑   CIMA ❑

Please keep me updated on new publications: ❑   By E-mail ❑   By Post ❑

Your Name……………………………………..   Your email address……………………………….
Your address:……………………………………………..
…………………………………………………………………
…………………………………………………………………
…………………………………………………………………

Prices are correct at time of going to press and are subject to change